THE WOVEN UNIVERSE
Selected Writings of Rev. Māori Marsden

Edited by
Te Ahukaramū
Charles Royal

Illumination is from above,
a revelation gift from God.
When it occurs,
it acts as a catalyst
integrating knowledge
to produce Wisdom.

© The estate of Rev. Māori Marsden 2003

ISBN: 0-473-07916-X

Published in 2003 by The Estate of Rev. Māori Marsden.

Design and Production Services: Mauriora-ki-te-Ao/Living Universe Ltd.
Printer: Printcraft '81 Ltd., Masterton
Cover concept by Ross Gregory. Cover art by Derek Rēnata
Manuscript edited and prepared by Te Ahukaramū Charles Royal. 'Educating. Māori ',
edited by Dame Joan Metge and Hiraina Marsden. Preparation of the manuscript was
assisted by Maewa Kaihau, Arapine Walker and Murray Hemi.

Te Wānanga-o-Raukawa

E kore au e ngaro, he kākano i ruia mai i Rangiātea

Publication of *The Woven Universe* was assisted by a generous contribution from Dr. Mīria
Simpson of Ngāti Awa and a grant from Te Wānanga-o-Raukawa, Ōtaki.

Contents

──────────────── He Mihi ────────────────

Takapau tūranga maomao
Kei hea te tō e rangona nei?
Ko te hiki o te wae, ko te hiki whakamua,
Ko te hiki o te wae, ko te hoki whakamuri.
Kia mau, kia ū, tū mai te uru!
I ngā tai mimihi o Hokianga
I ngā wai marama i runga o Hūnoke.

E tū ana ahau i runga i te taumata kōrero e kiia nei ko ngā wehi ki tō tātou Matuanui-i-te-rangi, kia hora tōna marino ki runga i te mata o te whenua, he whakaaro pai ki a tātou katoa. Kia tau mai te mauri o te tokotoru tapu, tapu nui, tapu roa, tapu whakahirahira! Ko te tokomauri tapu tēnei i poua, te tokomauri o te ripeka o Kawari, ki a Papatuanuku e takoto ake nei, taiāwhiowhio te ao whānui. Uhi, wero, tau mai te mauri, haumī e, hui e, tāiki e!

Ka mihi te ngākau ki te hunga kua takahia Te Ara Whānui-a-Tāne, i tae ai rātou ki te kuititanga o te motu, i ngaro ai hoki rātou ki Te Reinga. Kei ngā tūpuna katoa e noho mai ana i Te Pō, i te kāinga tuturu o te tangata, i te urunga-tē-taka, i te moenga-tē-whakaarahia, moe mai rā koutou. Heoi anō rā, e Māori, tēnei ōu mokopuna e karanga atu nei kia maranga wairua mai koe me he whetū e ara ana i te pae. Tiakina mātou katoa, tō whānau e noho atu nei, ā, whakatinanatia mai hoki ngā kaupapa o Ārai-te-uru, o Te Waipuna-ariki, ērā kaupapa katoa i kōrerotia, i haria i a koe e hikoi ana i te mata o te whenua. Me waiho mā tāku mōteateatanga hei whakaahua i te aroha:

Te kairuirui o ngā purapura
o te whakapono, o te whare wānanga
Nāu te mahi nui, kua oti e.
Tērā te tatau o te rangi kua huakina
Rā runga o Te Kōpuru, te kāinga o te maunga-ā-rongo
E piki atu, e kara, waihotia mai tō tinana hei tangihanga māku.

Nō reira, e Māori kia kaua mātou e whakarerea, engari, tukuna mai he māramatanga e pai ai tā mātou noho i Te Ao Mārama. Heoi, kāti te wāhi ki a koutou.

Ka tahuri anō ki a tātou o te pito ora, ka mihi te ngākau ki ngā maunga whakahī, ki ngā wai karekare, ki ngā whare katoa o ō tātou tūpuna. Kia tau tonu rā ngā manaakitanga ki a tātou katoa.

E te iwi, e tukuna ana ngā tuhituhi, ngā whakaaro a te tupuna nei kia whitingia e te rā, kia puhipuhia e te hau. Kei konei, kei tēnei pukapuka te wānanga a Māori Marsden i ngā tini āhuatanga o tō tātou 'Māoritanga'. Nāna tonu te whakaaro kia tāia ai ēnei tuhituhi, kia kitea hoki e te iwi whānui. Nō reira, tirohia mai, tangohia tā koutou e pai ai. Heoi, kia mahara hoki tātou, kihai ēnei taonga i waihotia hei taumahatanga, kāore hoki i waihotia i runga i te whakaaro kua ngaro katoa te wānanga a ngā tūpuna. Kao. Kei ēnei tuhituhi e takoto ana tētahi momo wānanga e tika ana hei pupuri, hei whai mā tātou i ēnei rā. I tukuna ai hoki e Māori hei āwhina i te wānanga a tēnā iwi, a tēnā iwi i ngā āhuatanga e pā ana ki a tātou katoa.

Kāti, ka tukuna ngā mihi ki te hunga nā rātou tēnei kaupapa i āwhina, i whakawhānui. I te tuatahi, e tika ana kia mihia te whānau a te koroua nei, arā, tana pouwaru me ā rāua tamariki, aku mātua. Mei kore rātou i takatū ki te poipoi i ngā taonga nei, kua ngaro noa atu i waenganui i a tātou. Me mihi rā hoki ki ngā tuākana, ki ngā tēina, ki ngā tuāhine hoki o Māori nā rātou hoki te kaupapa i kite. Otirā, ki ngā mātua, ki ngā whaea katoa, o Te Hiku-o-te-ika, ki ngā iwi o te kaumātua nei, tēnei ka rere atu ngā mihi ki a koutou katoa. Ko te tūmanako ka eke rā tēnei pukapuka ki te taumata e wawatatia ana. Me mutu ake ēnei kupu whakamihi ki tēnei kōrero e whai ake nei. He kōrero tēnei i ngākaunuitia e Māori, ā, i tuhituhia hoki ki tētahi o ana pepa. Tēnā koutou katoa.

E kore, kore rawa taku mate, e ea i te moni.
Mā ngā toto anake rā o taku Ariki,
E hoko kia ea.
Ngā mate o te iwi, o te ao,
Waiho atu ki ngā ara tawhito i poua ai,
Te ara mai o te mana –
Mana Atua, Mana Tupuna, Mana Whenua

Editor's Introduction

It has been a pleasure and an honour to compile and edit the writings of Rev. Māori Marsden, an elder who has been tremendously important to myself and to many of my generation. As a healer, an Anglican Minister, a *tohunga* and as a scholar, Māori touched a lot of people and it is appropriate that a publication of his writings should appear both as a memorial to Māori and as a guide to his thinking, his passions and his concerns.

I would like to introduce this collection by telling a personal story that captures something of the mystique of Māori Marsden, and *tohunga* of his ilk, and illustrates the contemporary Māori relationship with 'Māoritanga'. In the brief five years that I knew Māori, I looked upon him as a representative of our Māori past for he was raised with 19th century Māori philosophy and *rangatiratanga* still influential and tangibly present. In our time together, I saw glimpses of that earlier way of knowing and seeing the world and also felt the sense of *mana* that he and his peers possessed.

'Looking through a Window', A Personal Story
In 1988, I invited Māori to attend an immersion hui that was taking place at Raukawa Marae in Ōtaki. Māori had attended a previous hui at Takapūwāhia Marae in Porirua and was happy to return and to share his knowledge with us. I was one of the students who were part of the immersion and we had a tremendous week together. During the first four days of the hui, I silently congratulated myself and my growing knowledge of the language. I was chuffed that I could keep up with Māori. I attended all his lectures and at night we

stayed up late talking about all sorts of things. I felt that my fluency in the language was rising and growing and I felt good. Whilst I did not consider myself an expert in the language, I wasn't a novitiate either in the world of Māori language learning.

On the Thursday of the hui, Māori received an invitation to tea with the Ngāti Maniapoto and *Kīngitanga* tohunga, Dr. Henare Tūwhāngai who was staying in Ōtaki at the time. During his later years, Henare often spent time in Ōtaki seeking reprieve from his many responsibilities in Waikato and Ngāti Maniapoto. Māori asked me to take him to see Henare which I agreed to immediately. For a young learner, the prospect of spending time with two tohunga was too good an opportunity to miss and I eagerly anticipated the meeting.

The time arrived and we left for the home where Henare was staying. I recall my excitement rising as we drove through Ōtaki. Upon arrival, we walked to the porch and Māori spotted Henare's hat lying on a seat outside. He yelled out, "I recognise that hat!". At this, a door opened to reveal Henare sitting at a table in a small kitchen. He beckoned us in and so we entered and sat down. Māori said hello and introduced me to Henare. After our introductions, which were good humoured and not at all formal, a curious thing happened. Māori and Henare slipped into a style of language and conversing (in Māori of course) which I had great difficulty understanding. I tried very hard to catch what they were saying but no matter how hard I tried I couldn't understand them. Our visit lasted four hours and for most of the time I paid close attention to them, attempting to decipher the direction of the *kōrero.* But, for the life of me, I couldn't. There was only one point in the entire four hours when I did understand them and that was when Māori turned to ask me a question. When I answered, he returned to Henare and that was that!

I found this very puzzling indeed. When Māori met with Henare, it was as if an invisible veil had been drawn between us for they spoke a Māori language that I could only assume was the language of the tohunga, understood and used by the initiated only. The experience demonstrated to me the depth and sophistication present in the Māori language and in Māori knowledge. It illustrated something of the distance between what I knew at that point and what Māori must have known.

Later, I looked back at this event and I likened myself to a boy standing on the porch of a *wharenui,* looking through the window into a meeting of the *tohunga* of the *whare wānanga.* I see myself trying very hard to enter. I stretch my neck out so my ears can capture some of the kōrero, but no matter how hard I try, I am never able to catch it all. Only snippets and fragments are heard and even then there is this sense that I am only allowed to hear what they want me to hear. The door remains closed to me and I can not enter the wānanga fully as Māori had done in his youth.

This image of 'looking in through the window' captures a good deal of the way we Māori today feel about our Māoritanga. There is this sense that the version of Māoritanga that we possess and exhibit today is not quite the real thing, that it is somehow inferior. I remember feeling this way after Māori's death in 1993 as I felt that we had lost something fundamental, something authentic and of great value, something we would never be able to possess again.

This feeling remained with me for a while and eased a little as I got caught up with other projects and responsibilities. But every time I thought of our uncle, I could not shake that feeling of loss, that sense of disconnection and alienation from a 'source'. This remained for quite some time until I turned to reading Māori's papers.

Following Māori's tangi, I was given the task of arranging Māori's numerous papers and to establish his manuscript collection at Auckland City Library. His collection of papers is extensive and was held at his home in Te Kōpuru. Arranging the collection meant firstly gathering the material together and then taking it all to Auckland. Following that, I made several trips to Auckland City Library to prepare an inventory of all of the papers. This is now available at the Library.

During the course of preparing the inventory, I read a great deal of Māori's writings and came to understand that in a very real and practical way, Māori prescribed and described a tremendous amount concerning the Māori worldview or 'Māoritanga'. In fact, I came to be astounded by the amount of material that he wrote and the depth and profundity of his thinking and interpretations. I now believe that he has bequeathed to us a complex and sophisticated model of a Māoritanga that is appropriate for us today. It's as if the tohunga inside that meeting house elected Māori as their representative and charged him with the task of sharing a range of their taonga with the outside world.

The Woven Universe contains a broad sketch of this taonga and a considerable number of his ideas concerning aspects of his model of a modern Māoritanga appear on these pages. His statements on *mana, tapu, mauri,* the 'centre', the educated person, the 'route to Māoritanga' and much more, for example, are outstanding. Some of these statements have been extracted from the essays and appear in Appendix Two.

The value of Māori Marsden's writing is found not so much in the quantity of traditional *kōrero,* but rather in the quality of *wānanga* or analysis he brings to bear to the study of the Māori worldview. For those who wish to see, there is a rich vein of thinking and experience in his writings that can be perceived by carefully considering the models and interpretations contained within them. We need not, therefore, feel a sense of insecurity about our Māoritanga but rather feel assured that a tohunga of his ilk has provided us with a model of *wānanga* appropriate for the modern Māori person, and any one else who wishes to partake of this way of seeing and experiencing the world.

Māori's model for the *wānanga* is thoroughly modern in that it employs both English and Māori, makes use of the written word and relishes comparison with other wisdom traditions (see, for example, his use of Greek words and concepts and his study of the New Physicists). It also contains a set of enduring traditional ideas in that it demands discipline and commitment from its exponents, it urges students to embrace scholarship and tells them that they need not fear to create and to expand the traditions and knowledge of their ancestors. If there is one overall theme in Māori's writing it is his urging us to be *free* and to admit no oppression in our lives, whether from our own internal limitations which deny us knowledge and experience of our 'authentic being' or from external forces which conspire to deny us 'social justice'.

Biographical Sketch

Rev. Māori Marsden was born on the 10th of August 1924 in the small settlement of Awanui near Kaitaia. His father was Hoani Mātenga Te Paerata, a local Anglican Minister and member of all the northern most iwi of Muriwhenua. His particular *karangatanga,* however, were Te Patukōraha of Karepōnia and Ngāi Takoto of Awanui proper. Māori's mother was Hana Toi of the Ngāti Korokoro and Ngāti Whārara people of the southern side of the mouth of the Hokianga Harbour. Hana's family are particularly associated with marae at Pākanae, Kōkōhuia and Waiwhatawhata.

Māori was raised in Awanui and while young he was selected by his elders to enter the *whare wānanga,* or tribal centre of higher and esoteric learning. Māori was baptised in various ceremonies and then became a student of the traditions of his peoples. These early experiences under the guidance of many *tohunga* prior to and after the Second World War were to maintain a powerful influence over his life and his subsequent career. He attended Wesley College in Auckland as Marsh Scholar (see 'Educating Māori') from 1938 to 1941. Māori also attended the Second World War as a member of the Māori Battalion and following the war he entered St. John's Theological College in Auckland. He graduated with a Bachelor of Theology in 1957 and was ordained a Deacon in the Anglican Church in 1957 and was priested in 1958. He also attended Auckland University from 1952 to 1954 taking papers in Education, Anthropology and Māori Studies. As an Anglican Minister, Māori was posted to a number of pastorates, particularly in Taranaki and in Hamilton, Waikato. There his ministry matured and he became active in the affairs of the local tribes.

In 1963 Māori joined the New Zealand Navy and acted as Navy Chaplain at Devonport Naval Base in Auckland, a position he maintained until 1974. It was during this time that Māori became involved in a range of issues of national significance that grew during the 1970s and 1980s. Māori became involved in the Protest Movement of the North and in a range of other intiatives such as rearrangements in the Anglican Church. From the late 1970s through to his death in 1993, Māori became an important figure in Te Tai Tokerau and in national Māori issues. He was often a spokesperson on behalf of Te Tai Tokerau and he wrote numerous submissions, essays and contributions to a wide variety of activities and Government affairs. Rev. Māori Marsden passed away at his home in Te Kōpuru in 1993. He was mourned at Ōtūrei Marae, Dargaville and upon his home marae of Maimaru and Te Patukōraha at Awanui, near Kaitaia. He was buried in the family urupā upon Karepōnia Hill where his father was Minister many decades earlier.

The Woven Universe

'The Woven Universe' was suggested as a title for this book by my brother Haunui Royal. It arose from his understanding of a story that Māori told us on a number of occasions. Māori had returned home from the Second World War and attended a gathering of the *whare wānanga.* He was shocked to see that the number of *tohunga* (experts, teachers, priests) had fallen from some 77 to approximately 17 in the space of a few years. Despite this great fall in number, the whare wānanga did continue to meet until it went into recess in 1958. Māori explained that students of this whare wānanga were graduates of smaller, local whare wānanga of which he too was a graduate. His father was a tohunga of the whare wānanga of the Awanui area near Kaitaia. The larger *Tai Tokerau* whare wānanga traveled throughout the north, convening at various localities with the assistance of tohunga of the local area.

Following the Second World War, the whare wānanga convened in Hokianga. One of the prominent *tohunga* and *kaumātua* of the Hokianga area was Toki Pāngari and it was Toki who precipitated the following exchange that Māori mentions briefly in his essay entitled 'Kaitiakitanga: A Definitive Introduction to the Holistic World View of the Māori'. Upon arrival, Māori was questioned as to his experiences of the Second World War. He was asked about the causes of the war, the protagonists, key events and more. Finally, Māori was asked about the reasons that brought the war to a close. Here he spoke on a number of matters but made particular mention of the dropping of the atom bombs upon Hiroshima and Nagasaki in Japan. He was asked to speak further on the workings of nuclear weapons and so Māori found himself speaking on the construction of the atom and the splitting of the atom by Ernest Rutherford. He explained that when an atom is split, a tremendous amount of energy is released. Māori used the term *hihiri* for energy.

It was at this point that Toki Pāngari again entered the discussion. Māori related this story to us in the Māori language and his words were as follows:

> Ka tū mai a Toki, ka kī, "E mea ana koe, kua oti i ngā tohunga Pākehā te hahae i te kahu o te Ao?"
> Ka kī atu au, "Ki taku mohio, ae."
> Ka kī mai a Toki, "E taea e rātou te tuitui?"
> Ka kī atu au, "Ki taku mohio, kao."
> Ka kī mai anō a Toki, "Nā, koia tēnā te mate o te whāngai i ngā mātauranga tapu ki ngā tūtūā, ka tūkinotia i a rātou."

Māori provides an English language version of this same story in his essay (written with Te Aroha Henare) on *kaitiakitanga*:

> After the war, when I returned to the Wānanga I was questioned by the elders of the Wānanga about my war experiences. In the course of my sharing our experiences I mentioned the atom bomb. One of the elders who had of course heard of the atom bomb asked me to explain the difference between an atom bomb and an explosive bomb. I took the word 'hihiri' which in Māoridom means 'pure energy'. Here I recalled Einstein's concept of the real world behind the natural world as being comprised of 'rhythmical patterns of pure energy' and said to him that this was essentially the same concept. He then exclaimed "Do you mean to tell me that the Pākehā scientists (tohunga Pākehā) have managed to rend the fabric (kahu) of the universe?" I said "Yes" "I suppose they shared their knowledge with the tūtūā (politicians)?" "Yes" "But do they know how to sew (tuitui) it back together again?" "No!" "That's the trouble with sharing such 'tapu' knowledge. Tūtūā will always abuse it."

It was this fascinating exchange and particularly the phrase, *te kahu o te ao* ('the fabric of the universe') that inspired the name of this collection. *The Woven Universe* is a title that briefly summarises the traditional whare wānanga view of reality. The whare wānanga sees and interprets the world as a *kahu*, a fabric comprising of a fabulous mélange of energies. Accordingly, it was the preoccupation of the whare wānanga to view the world as a music, a singing, as 'rhythmical patterns of pure energy' that are woven and move with cosmological purpose and design. Our concern, therefore, should be to pay attention to how this fabric is woven and the nature of our place within it.

The Woven Universe is also reflected in the Io 'creation' tradition as related by Māori in 'God, Man and Universe: A Māori View':

>The universe itself is a process or event within the cosmic process by which Io orders creation.

Io is the grand weaver, sewing the universe together into a magnificent fabric. This is not some kind of 'mechanistic' weaving or construction, however. Io is not an external 'god' who 'constructs' the world as in the Old Testament concept. Rather the immanent Io presence in the world takes the form of *reo,* a 'voice', as Māori explains elsewhere. Haunui drew this analogy further when he explained that *The Woven Universe* also reflects the work of the *tohunga whakapapa,* the expert genealogist. This person, through their *reo,* is able to weave people and all things together into a fabric of *whanaungatanga* or relationships. The tohunga whakapapa knows and understands the power of relationships as the essential nature of all reality. The *ethical* act, therefore, of the tohunga is the fostering of relationships for, as Toki Pāngari points out, humanity severs the fabric of the universe at our peril.

Preparing the Manuscript

The volume is divided into two themes; namely, 'The Achievement of Authentic Being' and 'The Quest for Social Justice'. These themes are taken from a sentence that Māori includes in his essay entitled 'Māori Health - A Case for Reform'. The two themes neatly capture the broad thrust of Māori's thinking and concerns. He writes:

>...I have deliberately chosen a conflict, rather than a pluralist/consensus model (now termed multicultural/bicultural model) - models generally offered as best suited to an analysis of the relationship between the indigenous people and the colonial power. From the historical/economic/political perspective, this model offers a context to accommodate the past experience of the tangata whenua... and as illustrating the contemporary methods by which the Pākehā in the New Zealand situation utilises new apparatus and mechanisms of social control to ensure his continued dominance, and abort Māori aspirations in his struggles for social justice and the achievement of authentic being.

'The Achievement of Authentic Being' is concerned with how one nurtures one's being through living an authentic life. It urges one to consider carefully one's passage through life – our values and actions – and how this impacts upon the state of our being, and *vice versa.* This part of the collection commences with the well-known essay, 'God, Man and Universe: A Māori View' which captures Māori's vision for 'Māoritanga' It commences with a discussion of states of being (*ihi, wehi, mana, tapu),* analyses various roles and behaviours (*tikanga*) designed to perpetuate those states of being and concludes with a rendition of the Io 'creation' story. 'Creation' traditions throughout the world contain complex, mythological image statements about the nature of reality. They are 'part of the corpus of fundamental knowledge', as Māori explains. Importantly, they do not contain *data* detailing the *historical creation of the world,* but rather they act as an ongoing oral rendition of reality as we experience it here and now. By retelling these stories, particularly through oral delivery in ritual, one participates in the reality that the traditions are attempting to symbolise and represent. Hence, by retelling the Io 'creation' story, one comes to experience the states of 'authentic being' that Māori explains at the beginning of his essay.

'The Quest for Social Justice' outlines Māori's political philosophy. This section commences with a composition entitled 'He Pepeha mō ēnei rā'. It also includes a number of items including two pieces that were written as submissions to the Royal Commission on Social Policy in 1987. Here he presents a highly critical analysis of colonisation and Government policy. In response, Māori sets forth his ideas on structural arrangements for the Māori world *viz a viz* the nation. 'The Quest for Social Justice' also includes a series of prescriptions regarding rearrangements in the Department of Māori Affairs. The essays that appear here also include material repeated from Section One. The book concludes with two small papers entitled 'Hui Protocols' and 'Fisheries Commission Hui'. In this second section, one can see how Māori is attempting to apply his thesis concerning 'Authentic Being' to his socio-political concerns. Section Two, therefore, is not a departure from Section One but rather it is a 'working out' of his theological and spiritual philosophy in the context of real world scenarios. The reader will also note that the material in Section Two might have been edited a little further (removing repeated material, for example), however, I chose not to do so in order to allow us to trace something of Māori's thinking pathway. (One might also note that some of the material is reflective of concerns and issues prevalent in the late 1980s.)

The thrust of the second half of *The Woven Universe* is best summarised by the following extracts from 'He Pepeha mō ēnei rā'. Māori directs his people to the 'ancient pathways' and urges them to remain committed.

E tū e te Tari Māori, ki te wehenga o ngā ora,
Tirohia atu ngā ara tawhito o namata.
Uia ki te wāhi ngaro, "Kei hea tō wāhi pai?"
Haere rā reira ka kitea rā e koe,
Te tānga manawa mō te iwi – mō te rahi, mō te iti
Hoea tō waka kia mārō te haere
Wāhia te moana waiwai o te Ao Pākehā

Arise Māori house and seek out life.
Study the ancient pathways of long ago
Ask of the hidden reality, "Where should I go?"
Go there, and you shall see
The beating heart of your people, of the great and the small.
Row your canoe and be committed to your journey
Cross the open sea of the European.

He encourages Māori by reminding them that they have prowess and ability and can reach the goals they set for themselves.

Kia mai e tauiwi kāhore ōu toa.
Kao! He toa anō tōu!
He uru mataku te uru o te hoe
He kakau whakawhana.

Foreigners say that you have no ability.
No! You have ability and prowess!
The oar strikes the water with awesome power,
The handle that leads out.

Finally, Māori reminds us of the intimate connection between 'social justice' and 'authentic being'. Social justice will only be finally achieved when a renewal of authentic being, of *mana*, takes place.

He aha tēnei kupu e wawara mai nei,
"Te tuku rangatiratanga" a Te Kāwanatanga?
E kore, kore rawa taku mate, e ea i te moni.
Mā ngā toto anake rā o taku Ariki,
E hoko kia ea.
Ngā mate o te iwi, o te ao,
Waiho atu ki ngā ara tawhito i poua ai,
Te ara mai o te mana
Mana Atua, Mana Tupuna, Mana Whenua
What is this word that comes hither,
The 'devolution' of the Government?
My pain will never be eased by money.
Only by the blood of my ariki,
Will my pain be eased.
Leave it to the ancient pathways
By which mana was established

Divine Mana, Ancestral Mana, the Mana of the Land

The entire collection is appended with a sermon delivered by Rev. Takiwairua Marsden, Māori's younger brother, at his *tangihanga* (funeral). Taki discusses a number of things in his sermon including his brother's character. It was delivered with a mixture of humour and pathos and was received very warmly. Appendix Two contains a range of definitions of statements developed by Māori. He took time to define and describe a range of cultural concepts and some of these are presented in Appendix Two for easy reference. Finally, Appendix Three contains an abridged *whakapapa* (genealogy) for the 'creation' of the world. It appears here because Māori refers to it often and it acts as a backdrop to his thinking and ideas.

The selection of the material has been based primarily on two principles. Firstly, the essays are those that Māori himself intended for a wider audience. These include submissions to commissions of inquiry - such as 'Te Ara Hou' - to papers for public lectures - such as 'Mental Health: A Case for Reform' - to contributions to publications - such as 'God, Man and Universe: A Māori View'. Concerning 'Mātauranga Māori, Mātauranga Pākehā', this is an extract from his last seminar conducted at Te Wānanga-o-Raukawa in Ōtaki in 1993. During the introduction to the seminar, Māori explained that in time he wished the material discussed be made available to a wider audience when appropriate. *The Woven Universe* is such an opportunity to share this material.

Secondly, the papers that appear in this volume are his substantial writings that he wrote to their completion. Māori wrote a lot of other material, but many of these papers, which are held in the Auckland City Library and elsewhere, remain incomplete. They represent fragments of thinking rather than thoroughly written papers. Additionally, Māori also passed on amount of *kōrero* or traditional knowledge which has not been included here so that *The Woven Universe* can not be said to be a complete rendition of the thinking and concerns of Rev. Māori Marsden. Rather it is a collection of his writings that he intended for a wider audience. Other material that was written or was passed orally was done so for specific purposes and for specific audiences, such as a *hapū* (subtribe) or his own family.

We have tried to provide a collection of material that captures the broader themes within Māori Marsden's thinking and concerns. *The Woven Universe* briefly presents a series of ideas that Māori was passionate about and that he asks his people to be concerned with. In this way, whilst *The Woven Universe* does not contain everything to be said about the topics discussed, it nevertheless sketches broadly important avenues of thinking and inquiry within 'Māoritanga'.

Editing the texts

The texts have been edited according to the following policy:

a. where required, mark vowel length on Māori words by use of the macron
b. add endnotes for further information and the sourcing of key statements
c. preserve unusual formatting that Māori himself employed, including compounding adjectives and the use of English suffixes on Māori words (e.g. Māoridom)
d. check spelling and punctuation

On the whole, the papers required little editing. Except for the absence of the macron, the papers were well presented in their initial form. Editing, therefore, has not been heavily influential upon the final presentation of material. In acting as editor, it has not been my role to make judgements about the material but rather to assist in bringing Māori's vision to the written page and in published form. My judgements have been reserved to smaller details such as vowel length and the selection of material.

Sources
The sources for the various texts found in this volume are as follows:

Educating Māori, is an extract from an interview with Rev. Māori Marsden and conducted by Dame Joan Metge. We thank Dame Joan for allowing us to reprint this extract here. Hiraina Marsden completed substantial editing of this text.

God, Man and Universe, A Māori View was first published in *Te Ao Hurihuri: The World Moves on,* a collection of essays on aspects of Māoritanga edited by Michael King. This book was initially published by Hicks, Smith and Sons Ltd. in 1979 and a new edition was published by Reed Books in 1992. Our thanks to Michael King and to Peter Janssen of Reed Books for allowing us to reprint this important essay.

The Natural World and Natural Resources: Māori Value Systems and Perspectives, is a previously unpublished paper which was written for the Resource Management Law Reform, a project conducted under the auspices of the Ministry for the Environment in the late 1980s and early 1990s. We would like to thank Denise Church, Chief Executive of the Ministry for the Environment, for allowing us to reprint this essay here.

Kaitiakitanga: A Definitive Introduction to the Holistic World View of the Māori is a paper written with Te Aroha Henare for Maruwhenua, Ministry for the Environment. It is dated November 1992. We would like to again thank Denise Church, Chief Executive of the Ministry for the Environment for allowing us to reprint this essay here.

Mātauranga Māori, Māori Pākehā is an extract from a seminar delivered by Rev. Māori Marsden at Te Wānanga-o-Raukawa in 1993. This was Māori's last seminar and it was convened by Professor Whatarangi Winiata, *Tumuaki* of Te Wānanga-o-Raukawa. It was one of a series of seminars whose purpose was to discuss theories of knowledge by inviting a number of Māori scholars to present ideas on a range of matters. Other scholars who participated included Pāteriki Te Rei, first *Ahorangi* of Te Wānanga-o-Raukawa and elder of Ngāti Toarangatira, and Dr. Huirangi Waikerepuru of Taranaki. These seminars were conducted in the late 1980s and early 1990s and catalysed the development of graduate studies at Te Wānanga-o-Raukawa. (The translation is mine.)

The version of *He Pepeha mō ēnei rā* that appears here was taken from *Te Ao Mārama: Contemporary Māori Writing,* Volume 5, edited by Witi Ihimaera. This was published by Reed Books in 1996. We thank Peter Janssen of Reed Books for allowing us to reprint it here. A different version of the same composition can be found in 'Te Ara Hou Formula' on page 144.

Mental Health - A Case for Reform is a paper that was prepared for the Legal Research Foundation and is dated 5 September 1986.

Rangatiratanga me Te Kāwanatanga is a previously unpublished paper and is also undated.

Prognosis for the Socio-Economic future of Māoridom is Part One of a submission to the Royal Commission on Social Policy. It is dated November 1987. The Royal Commission on Social Policy was established by the then Labour Government as a body to inquire into the nature of social policy in New Zealand. The Commission convened meetings throughout New Zealand and invited submissions on a range of topics.

'Te Ara Hou Formula': The Principle of Evolution not Devolution for the Department of Māori Affairs is Part Two of the same submission to the Royal Commission on Social Policy. It too is dated November 1987.

Ngā Tikanga Whakahaere-Hui Protocols is again unpublished and undated.

Fisheries Commission Hui is a submission to a meeting held at the Beehive, Parliament Buildings, Wellington, in 1993.

Appendix One contains an extract from a sermon delivered by Rev. Takiwairua Marsden at the *tangihanga* for Rev. Māori Marsden. This took place at Te Patukōraha Marae, Kareponia, near Kaitaia, in 1993. Our thanks to Rev. Takiwairua Marsden for allowing us to reprint his sermon here.

Acknowledgements
Firstly, our thanks are due to Rev. Māori Marsden whose vision is contained in these pages. We thank him for being the bridge between the old and the new *whare wānanga.*

Great thanks and mihi are also due to members of his family; to Jane

Marsden, Māori's widow, and to their children, Rangi, Hiraina, Kahu, Raiha, Raphael and Michael. I must also acknowledge the great support I have received from Māori's brothers, namely Hone Toi Marsden and Rev. Takiwairua Marsden.

We also thank Peter Janssen of Reed Books, Dr. Michael King and Professor Ranginui Walker; Maewa Kaihau, Murray Hēmi and Arapine Walker for typing various parts of the manuscript. We would like to acknowledge Denise Church of the Ministry for the Environment. Thanks are also due to Ross Gregory and Derek Rēnata for assisting with the cover art and to Te Wānanga-o-Raukawa for helping with much needed resources. Finally, to Dr. Miria Simpson of Ngāti Awa for making a generous contribution toward costs.

To all those who assisted this project and allowed Māori Marsden's *taonga* to emerge, many thanks. Kia tau tonu rā ngā manaakitanga o tō tātou Matuanui-i-te-rangi ki a koutou katoa.

Nāku noa, nā
Te Ahukaramū
Charles Royal
Paremata, Wellington 2003

'EDUCATING MĀORI'
An Interview with Rev. Māori Marsden
Dame Joan Metge, 9 November 1982

He iti marangai, e tū ana te pāhukahuka,
he iti pioke nō Rangaunu, he au tōna.

The first and strongest impressions I've retained over the years are those I had as a child. I was brought up in Maimaru, ten kilometres east of Awanui. Our community revolved round the Ngāi Takoto and Patukōraha people. Ngāi Takoto had 2 main papakāinga; Maimaru and Waimanoni.

Waimanoni, situated on the southern end of the Rangaunu Harbour was regarded as the heart of our people. The Rangaunu was the main source of food for us. Inside the harbour we gathered mainly small fish and shellfish and outside the harbour we had large fishing grounds generally known and fished by the majority of the hapū. Our lands were fertile, largely silt - built up over the centuries by the flooding of the Awanui River.

At the time I came into the world my father Rev. Hoani Matenga-Paerata was a priest of the Mihinare Church. By this time he was semi-retired, attending to preaching to the people on weekends, and developing the farm during the week. The reason he retired was he soon realised that his church stipend couldn't hope to educate us as a family. The only hope that he had to meet our educational needs was to go dairy farming.

My parents returned to Awanui from Waimate North where he was priest of the Waimate North Pastorate, to develop the family farm. In all that he did, he was very meticulous and one of the first things I ever learned as a child was how to fence - by holding a can of staples for my father.

Father was an expert with the adze and the axe - along with many other tools and bevelled all the *pūriri* strainer posts we used for fencing. If from strainer post, to strainer post, there was but one post out of alignment, he then dug it up and reset it so that if you looked from one end of the fence line to the other you could naturally see only one post. This was the nature of my father and the example he always set. Father was a perfectionist in this regard.

I was raised in a community where from our earliest memories we knew that we were all related. We learnt right from the outset that we were all one large whānau - and later during the Depression, because of these kinship bonds, we helped each other out.

As a people we did a lot of community gardening and fishing together and going to the beaches to get *mātaitai*. On these occasions my father was generally the leader. From my earliest memories we were taught to be independent; and at eight it wasn't unusual to take out the punt, with my haversack, and stay out sometimes 2 or 3 days, by myself, fishing. Nobody worried. In fact we were encouraged by our father to do so. In hindsight I'd have probably absorbed from other whānau members fears about *kēhua*. Still there was no time for such matters when busy out exploring my place. Summer nights, I'd take a loaf of bread and water with me, build a fire then throw in my line and go to sleep. A fish tugging on the line woke me up and I'd haul them in and literally struggle home with my catch. It was always a welcome addition to our larder. It was an uncomplicated life where we were encouraged to explore our environment and as a consequence we were confidently independent at an early age. The rest of my siblings were not as keen on fishing as I, but give me a fishing line and I was happy. My childhood memories are happy ones.

Looking back I was a bit of a loner leaving home in the early hours of the morning, taking off to the harbour and finding me a camping spot. From one year old my father and other fathers would take us as babies out camping to the fishing grounds. As we got older he taught us the names of all the bends in the rivers, and the reasons for these names, as well as the best fishing grounds for each particular species.

Before leaving early Saturday mornings I'd consult with Dad about where the best fishing grounds were for the day. He'd look at the weather, the wind, the natural elements and say. "You go to *Kautahi* or *Ahuaraiti*." Whatever place he recommended he was always pretty accurate. I realised later, that he was passing on the fishing tikanga of the hapū learnt over many centuries of occupation.

By observing the natural surroundings, he was able to accurately pinpoint the optimum places for food gathering. Sometimes father would tell me that I was wasting my time going out that day, however, I'd persist and still go. He never tried to stop me and I soon learnt from experience that the majority of his predictions were right. I began to comprehend that there was a huge wealth of knowledge known generally by most of the elders, about fishing.

From early the elders recognised my passion for this pursuit, and took special attention to teach me the fishing tikanga of our people.

Our Home Environment

In our home we were not allowed to speak English - not in the home itself. However, before going to Primary School most of us learnt English and Croatian through our associations with non-Māori children in our community. Te Reo Māori was my first language which was the standard for children in our hapū. Our mother could not speak English so father was strict in this regard. I later discovered that Mother was the founder of Mothers' Union in Northland so I suspect she could speak English but wouldn't.

Father always maintained that if we learnt one language thoroughly first, then we could apply these same principles to learning other languages. Having fluency in 8 languages, I suspect now, Father was right.

My father was better educated than most in the wider community with an extensive library of Bibles, the Classics and many other authors, his favourite being Shakespeare. He delighted in reading these to us and that was the only time English was spoken in our home. As children we liked Dickens a lot although we didn't understand some English words or phrases at that stage. For our benefit and mothers', he'd read a page in English then translate it into Māori and so on, so that we could follow the story.

In the evenings, especially in the winter, we would sit around the fireplace and father with a book on his knees would read to us. The whole whānau including other extended whānau members who often stayed, enjoyed sitting around the fire listening to him read. As a result my siblings and I learnt to value books at an early age. As a family we valued books more than most people in our community.

Generally speaking life was very pleasant. We related and communicated well with our parents and had close relationships with my father's cousins who were regarded as our extended parents along with their children who we regarded as our extended siblings. If we were too far away from home around meal times, we went to the nearest house and this was considered the right of all children in our hapū. It wasn't uncommon in the weekends to find about 20 of us at one time playing together at one of our homes.

More often than not when it came to meal times, whose ever place we were at, took the responsibility for feeding the lot of us. While we all had our own homes we often stayed nights at each other's places. The attitude we maintained in our community was "Your home is my home and my home is your home."

Schooling

At five years old I started at Awanui School. Fathers' diligent readings of the Bible and Classics before we went to school helped us easily comprehend reading, writing and arithmetic, and before long I was heading the class.

Then I fell foul of one of the Pākehā teachers, I suspect now that it was because I constantly headed the class. She had favourites - Pākehā's - cocktailed with a serious superiority complex. It puzzled her continually that I and my siblings spoke and wrote good grammatical English and she resented that we headed our classes. As a result I began to switch off.

My parents realising this, switched me to Paparore School which was about 20 kilometres north of Maimaru. Dad said to me "Well son if you don't like Awanui School then you'll have to walk to Paparore." So at seven, I was making a b-line to school, cutting through paddocks swimming the Awanui River plus a few smaller tributaries, going through obstacles rather than around just to get to school on time.

Initially, to make it easier, my father took me to my cousins' place to stay during the week. Waimanoni was a little closer for me to school from there and up to this point my cousin's son, who I was staying with, was head of the class.

Healthy competition between families was enjoyed and when school reports came out, the whole community compared notes. My cousin however resented the fact that I soon became head of the class and her son took second place. She indicated in subtle ways her displeasure so I decided to move back home.

Respecting my decision; father decided to get me a horse. My big brother, Toko, was married with a family - and crazy about horses and had a number of them on his farm. He said, "If you want a horse bro, come see me on Saturday." Saturday came, we went to the paddock. Toko lassoed this horse, knocked it down and said, "If you want this horse you'll have to break it in yourself." At that he tied me, all of eight, to the horse and let it go. Naturally I was afraid at first but grinned and bared it. Eventually I got over my fear and got into the stride of the horse. In due course I mastered the technique of riding. So with a combination of riding, swimming and walking I got to school. As

Kapowairua, Spirit's Bay

winter came along I began staying nights again at Waimanoni but this time with other cousins who were happy to put me up for the night during the week. As I mentioned this was no big deal for us to stay at each others homes and soon I became regarded as part of the Waimanoni whānau because I stayed there so often. On Friday evenings though, I took the fastest route home to Mum and Dad.

Primary School

The Headmaster Mr. Robert Shutt, his wife and two of my cousins were our teachers. About 80% of the students were Māori and 20% Pākehā. Our Headmaster was a Christian and a Theologian and every morning he opened our day with prayers - and for him this was something meaningful and not just a formality. I believe that as a result of a comprehensive understanding of the history, customs and traditions of his peoples, that he had no difficulty in understanding ours.

Quite a number of the students lived further north at Kauri Flat up on the gum fields, gum being a reliable source of extra income for the majority of our families. However, those that lived and worked fulltime on the gum fields suffered very poor conditions. They tended to be covered with scabies and one of the jobs I had was to stoke the school boiler on Friday afternoons, put the boys through hot baths and then apply an evil-looking and smelling brown ointment. Mrs. Shutt supervised the girls.

To me I thought this was tremendous that this Pākehā couple took a personal interest in the health and well-being of us children just like family members. Later on when becoming an educationalist, I learned how accelerated he was in his methods of teaching. The Shutts had a remarkable relationship with the Māori Community and whenever job vacancies came up at the school the parents always got first option.

My uncle, Rev. Henare Paraone, was Chairman of the School Board and the school committee, bar one, was Māori. We all responded well in this learning environment and Mr. & Mrs. Shutt were very much part of our community.

Secondary School

The community was big on sending us to secondary school and I gained a Native School Scholarship. On winning the scholarship Mr. Shutt said, "Ask your father which college he intends sending you".

The oldest of us kids, Meri, before going to nursing school went to Queen Victoria Girls, and I had two older brothers at St Stephens and one at Te Aute. I remember asking my big brother Herepete, who was Head Prefect of St Stephens and what his school was like. and he said, "For you bro, avoid it like the plague". I said, "You know already what Dad will say to that answer c'mon bro' is there an alternative?"

"Go to Wesley", he said.

I knew father would insist I go to secondary school, like it or not, so I accepted the inevitable, Nevertheless I decided this time, I was going to have a bit of a say.

When I got home that evening, I said to father,

"Mr Shutt wants to know what school you intend sending me to so that he can fill out the papers".

"You go to St Stephens" he said.

So when I went back to school Mr. Shutt asked,

"Well, what did your father say?" And I said,

"Wesley College."

My cousin Dave Rivers, also looking at his schooling prospects, asked,

"What school have you decided on?" and I said,

"Wesley" and he said,

"That must be us then, I'll come to Wesley too."

Then the time came to buy my school uniform so off to the store we went. My father asked the storekeeper to pull down navy blue shorts and navy blue shirts. After the storekeeper got ready the rows of boxes, I said,

"Dad, those are no good to me. These are not the colours of our uniform."

He said, "When did St Stephens change its colours?" and that's when I told him, "I'm not going to St Stephens I've enrolled at Wesley".

"Well aren't you the smart-Alec" he said.

"You'll have to go down to Auckland and outfit yourself."

At that stage I hadn't even been out of Awanui, but I did leave the store with a pair of brand new boots.

I was so proud of my new boots that the following Sunday I wore them to church. After Church we came outside where the usual *whaikōrero* took place and I remember sitting with my legs stiffly projected before me, so everybody could see my new boots.

Fortunately for me my siblings were boarding at schools around or passing through Auckland so they helped me get to Auckland and from there, I was on my own. There weren't many Māori staying in Auckland those days so my father made arrangements for me to stay in a hotel overnight at the bottom of Queen Street. The next day I walked up Queen Street - this Māori kid raw out of Awanui who hadn't even seen a tram until the previous day!

If I needed any help my father told me to ask a policeman. The police were hard knockers in those days and were easily recognisable. In spite of this, I got to Smith and Caugheys safely and didn't need to call on their services. As it happened Mr. Caughey was Chairman of the Wesley School Board of Governors and he had me outfitted – and personally took me out there. Wesley College was predominantly 70% Māori/ Islander and 30% Pākehā.

In my third year I got my UE and my Higher Learning Certificate in Honours. In spite of this, I was still too young to attend University. My father was closely involved in the Young Māori Party from his student days at Te Rau Kahikatea Theological College, Gisbourne. As a result he had ambitions of ensuring that as many of us as possible had tertiary education.

I returned home and enrolled at Kaitaia College just to mark time till I was old enough to attend university. It came to pass that Dad died before I was of age, so that was my opportunity to enlist in the Battalion and go overseas. I matured physically quite early due to what I believe - the rigors of attending school in my earlier years and a little later from representative sport - nevertheless, because of our builds it was easy for me and my cousins to bluff the authorities that we were old enough. So enlisted we were - and shortly afterwards we found ourselves in the Middle East. In the main that's my early childhood education and as far as that was concerned it was predominantly in a Māori environment.

Collective Hapū Activities

As youngsters we were encouraged, within reason, to do our own thing. Apart from this fishing craze, I had a genuine bond with the elders of my people. A passion for me was learning about Fathers' Far North - Te Hiku o Te Ika affiliations and Mothers' prominent Ngā Puhi connections.

Father, during the Depression had a reputation of Gardener Extraordinaire preparing acres and acres of land for planting - mainly kūmara. He had a passion for Standard Roses and Delias too.

When planting time came, we boys did most of the heavy work disking and ploughing and when it was ready, Dad would call in the hapū. As a rule, it was full-moon when Dad would call in the hapū because immediately following the full-moon were the best days for planting. He would delegate ones to go fishing and bring back loads of fish and others to go to the Ninety-Mile Beach to load up with toheroa and tuatua and some to kill a beef - and all to feed upwards to a hundred people that gathered to help during planting times.

A huge fire was lit in these fresh early October evenings — and after the evening meal together, we offered thanks to God for a good day and his blessings for a bumper crop. At Evensong (generally my father presiding) he would often give one of the lay-readers an opportunity to share a word from the scripture. Afterward the elders departed and had whaikōrero that was richly interlaced with scriptural quotations.

Church

Church was the place the whole community regularly met. Customarily, communion was had twice a month at Awanui Church or alternately at Kareponia Church. My father himself had a wide area to cover - Lake Ōhia, Ōturu and all the families further north, they gathered at Sweetwaters for their Sunday service.

Dad suffered from a hernia which prevented him from riding a horse, so he walked. He would set out early in the morning, with me as his companion. I carried a light bag with prayer books and Bible, and Dad would carry the vestments. We set out early in the morning about 3.00am and we'd go to Ōturu and there he'd take early morning Communion. From there we'd come back to Awanui Church, take service, followed by the long hike up to Sweetwaters to take communion there. At Sweetwaters we'd have service then lunch and then move on to Paparore for the last service about 3.00pm. So that was our day, then we'd return home. That was just one of the rounds he did and all on foot to boot!

Church was an important part of the hapū life. Lots of other community activities also revolved around church. Historically, Rev. Joseph Matthews, after arriving in Kaitaia, became closely associated with the peoples in the Pārengarenga, Ahipara and Peria areas and one of the first schools set up was in Awanui. Here a lot of the people were taught by the early missionaries and so as time went on Church became a feature of the way of life. Very few people stayed home – 95% of the people present at the services - were from every community and village.

Evening services particularly during planting - was always a favourite time to discuss the lesson in the readings relative to our tikanga. Most of the Māori adults in our hapū were really knowledgeable regarding the Bible. Many of the elders had phenomenal computer-like memories and many could easily quote the total Bible from Genesis to Revelations. They took delight in trying to test each others knowledge of the Bible with some obscure text, challenging others about where it was to be found. Many preachers in those days were often fond of doing this, quoting obscure texts saying to the congregation, "I'm not going to tell you where the text is. You can look it up for yourselves"

As far and the Canticles were concerned everybody knew them by heart. And every morning at about 7 o'clock you'd find them at their prayers. For the elders, they had their prayers before sunrise.

At first light, the head of the family would sit up, you'd hear a banging in the house and everybody was expected to get up. They didn't wait, just started off and one by one each crept out of their beds and came in. Some turned a deaf ear – the kids - however, Dad, in the mornings before we went to school, sat us down as a family to have morning prayers. In smaller more basic homes - where there was a kitchen and dining-room combined with one bedroom - these families needed only to sit up in their beds to have their prayers. For rich and for poor alike, this was the custom.

After Evensong there would be fair discussion about the *kauwhau* and time to critique the preacher's delivery. Then someone would pop a question, "Now, who was so and so's father again?" That was the usual signal to move into recalling the past. This is where I heard genealogical experts of our people recall the genealogical history of the families, their relationships and their traditions and achievements. I was one of those kids, who listened captivated at their feet.

The elders were indeed Storytellers Supreme. We enjoyed every moment of it. Amongst them were raconteurs with their own techniques – and I was mesmerized as they retold famous tales of the past in their own particular way.

Others were so extremely hilarious – you had to be very careful not to *mimi* yourself for the laughing. With these various methods of storytelling you had an enthralling evening, a learning experience and exciting entertainment.

Evening story time was our TV and this was one of the main ways I and several others learnt the tikanga and the history of our people. We heard about the maidens. We heard about the warriors. We heard about the battles and detailed accounts of their successes and not so detailed accounts of the defeats. Whatever the storyline chosen for that night, the boasting was hard to beat.

It was within this framework that the health and wellbeing of our community was established, maintained and sustained.

Daily Duties

As farmers we milked quite a number of cows, however, the older children did the milking and we were allowed to sleep in until we got a bit older. For most of the children in our community our daily duties were milk the cows, come home, have breakfast and then rush off to school. Going to Paparore School I was excused from milking a lot and I had breakfast earlier than the rest and was off to school before the milking was finished. In the evenings we had various duties but these were seasonal.

We had an extensive orchard with a 101 different varieties of peaches and during harvest as soon as we arrived home, we had a bite to eat and the knife was put in your hand and we were expected to peel the peaches. Mum was a renowned homemaker and preserved hundreds and hundreds of bottles of preserves and a lot of these were put aside for the maraes.

When we planted kūmara father put aside about 50 lines between 50 and 100 metres long - and special pits were made for these and they were earmarked 'Marae only.' When there was a tangi or communal function we used the kūmara from these pits and the same thing applied for Mum who put aside so many hundred bottles of preserves each season for the same purpose.

Weekends were regarded as a holiday for us younger ones. During haymaking it was the custom for us to pitch in, but on Saturdays we were fairly free.

Saturday mornings, I'd be off to Rangaunu Harbour fishing. Sundays twice a month we had communion at either Awanui or Kareponia Church. On alternate Sundays we went to Maimaru Marae or Waimanoni Marae for Morning Prayers. Here it was mostly lay people who took the services as the clergy were out on their rounds in different parts of the pastorate. At 11 o'clock everybody turned up at the marae, then we'd have morning prayers followed with a shared lunch. We all contributed to lunch each home bringing a pot of food to share together as one people at the marae.

It changed over the years. People began to go home and have their lunch at home as a family.

It was the accepted custom - when we went to Kareponia Church - that afterwards we came down to lunch at Kareponia Marae. On their way to church everybody dropped in a plate as their contribution. When we came down to the marae there would be the usual whaikōrero as lunch was prepared. Then we'd all sit down to a meal.

If there was any issue that concerned the community, after lunch was the time it was discussed and resolved and about milking time, people would begin to disperse.

In those days every marae had their tennis and basketball teams and were very sports orientated and all marae had tennis courts.

We had football teams as well, however, these were more territorial. Te Pātū had their team, Rarawa and so on. Most of the inter-hapū matches were blood matches.

Te Wānanga o Te Tai Tokerau

Now to the more formal side of my education, the Whare Wānanga. I want recorded my own impressions of the way in which it was conducted, some of the personalities involved, the format used and the general management and origins of the wānanga in Tai Tokerau.

As far as I can gather, the whare wānanga as it became known in the Tai Tokerau, originated in the early 1850s. It was born out of a concern for the continued wellbeing of Māori Tikanga due to, principally, the impact of the missionary teachings. This social and political upheaval resulted in radical changes taking place in my mothers' area of the Bay of Islands and Hokianga and my fathers' area of Te Hiku-o-te-ika in the Far North. With the coming of the missionaries, Matthews, and other Pākehā who migrated to the area from 1800 onwards, were influential toward promoting these changes. The chiefs soon realised that unless some direct action to preserve the history and tikanga took place, then much of their values and inherent rights would be displaced by the Westerners' imposed values.

It seems as if there was a spontaneous revival for more Pre-European teachings of the wānanga and a concerted attempt was made to begin recording this tikanga as it related to the people of Tai Tokerau.

Some of this concern might be better illustrated by an incident between Hone Ngāpua, one of the fighting chiefs and tohunga of Ngā Puhi, and Wiremu Karuwhā – Henry Williams the missionary - who on approaching him, offered himself up for the Mihinare Priesthood. In reply Williams' said that he was a man whose hands were polluted with the blood of his fellowmen and his teeth polluted with human flesh. Hone Ngāpua's reply was, "Well if your God won't have me, then I'll return to my own."

There were also people like Āperahama Taonui who foresaw the rapid disintegration of Māori Tikanga with the impact of Western culture. He advised against the signing of the Treaty and began his own wānanga which largely denigrated Pākehā and sought to promote Māori religious values in opposition to Christian ones, so much so that he was banished from Ōmanaia. Leaving with a large contingent from the Hokianga, he came into the Northern Wairoa, where he was given land by the local Chief, and settled. This contingent from Hokianga settled in the Aratapu area.

It was against this sort of general background that the hapū of Tai Tokerau decided to form a wānanga with the specific purpose of preserving for posterity, their history, tikanga and traditions.

Tai Tokerau Communication Systems

A proclamation went out throughout the territory for hapū to appoint people, experts from their areas, to meet together and begin to collate information pertaining to their hapū.

For example, *pūrākau, waiata* and *haka* that recounted the historical events of the waka that landed in Tai Tokerau, their people, and where they eventually settled. The history of the heated battles and the gifts exchanged during peace pacts, these were all recalled and duly recorded.

The earliest written records that I've seen myself were compiled in 1857. And by my calculations it took three or four years for the people to organise themselves so, I'd put the revival of the wānanga between 1850 and 1853.

From then on they met as a confederation representing their hapū annually at least twice sometimes up to three or four times a year, depending on the need. Sometimes tohunga chose a specific place to meet. In Te Rarawa men like Wairama Marsh, Terei Puku, Ngākuru Pene Haare and others had a small wānanga in which they collated information specific to their region, and this insured that the knowledge of these areas was kept maintained.

Te Aupóuri, Ngāi Takoto and Ngāti Kurī met regularly to wānanga and every so often Te Rarawa, Ngāti Kahu and Ngāi Takoto met together when times came to collect information pertaining to the Kaitaia area. That's how closely related they were.

Te Wānanga o Tai Tokerau, as it was known, comprised of two or three official members who met together with the other members of the confederation, once or twice a year, in order to gather the information collated for the entire area.

These Hui took a particular form. A pānui was sent out notifying hapū representatives of the venue, the day of the hui and the agenda or the kaupapa of the wānanga, depending on the season. The wānanga, in the main, extended over a period of three or four days, and long weekends were favoured as were the weekends.

Generally they gathered as a group at the designated marae on a Thursday or perhaps a Friday night, where the locals welcomed them in. After dinner in the evening we had usual Evensong followed by mihimihi. After performing these customary practises, only then, was the first session of the hui convened.

Ngā Tikanga Whakahaere o Te Wānanga o Te Tai Tokerau

The steering committee comprised of the Chairman, and the Secretary. All the tohunga were the Committee members and the Tiamana, as he was called, regulated the meeting. In the case of his absence, then the chief of the locals would Chair the hui or otherwise an appropriate person that the wānanga appointed.

I remember taking Dr Maharaia Winiata; of Ngāi Te Rangi to the wānanga in Mangamuka in 1957 in which he later recorded some of the talks for NZBC. I took him as a guest because at that specific hui we were to discuss Ngā Waka - Ngātokimatawhaorua, Māmari, Kurahaupó, and Mātaatua, in that order. The specific purpose of this wānanga was to resolve controversial issues, accounts and conflicting viewpoints regarding certain episodes relating to Ngā Waka and Ngā Puhi. The meeting was scheduled to discuss Ngātokimatawhaoroa and Māmari on the Thursday evening and the whole of Friday, then Kurahaupó on the Friday evening and most of Saturday, followed by the Mātaatua on the Saturday evening and most of Sunday morning before dispersing after karakia and lunch.

So here we were discussing these waka. I'll give you an illustration of the way these hui were conducted. It fell on those bringing outside guests the responsibility to caution them regarding the wānanga protocols and guidelines. So I said to Maharaia, "If he wished to speak, and only if the situation presented, then he was to consult with me first and I'd make his request known to the tohunga on his behalf." I added that only if they permitted him to speak, would he be allowed, and only then when the discussions on Mātaatua came up.

And so, on the Saturday evening we began discussions on the Mātaatua and the tohunga of the wānanga began to relate their knowledge of the waka.

Māori generally accepted that for certain ceremonies - such as taking the tapu off the canoe after launching - a tohunga with his karakia was indispensable, but for navigation and general running, the captain, and his karakia were indispensable. So, accepting this premise, then the logic of Toki Pāngari's contention, that Puhi was the captain of the canoe, was self evident. I remember Dr Winiata's comment to me afterwards he said, 'Well, I've done a doctorate in anthropology and social studies in the Pākehā wānanga but I can't argue against this logic."

I'd like to make the point - that from my own experience, the procedure as far as possible, aimed at arriving, after debate and discussion, at the truth of the subject.

Now turning to my involvement in the whare wānanga - let me just say that in ancient

Te Oneroa-o-Tohe, Ninety Mile Beach

times the original wānanga concerned two main schools - the *Whare Kura* and the *Whare Maire*. The *Whare Kura* was concerned very much with the things that we were concerned with in the wānanga. Whereas the *Whare Maire* was concerned with more esoteric types of knowledge. In Pākehā terms, witchcraft, but it wasn't witchcraft in the Pākehā sense - it dealt with the occult and the mystic.

The Tai Tokerau wānanga, because of its immediate concerns, took a pragmatic approach to safeguarding their culture and tikanga, evolved its own prototype becoming more trainer orientated. The earlier conditions of the Whare Kura or Whare Maire - to give a modern day analogy - were like specialised laboratories in the further advancement of knowledge in the Natural World and the World of Ultimate Reality – Criteria? Experts only. While the Tai Tokerau wānanga specialised, it covered a broader field which included elements from both schools, however, emphasis was more on the teachings of the Whare Kura.

My own entry into the wānanga resulted largely from an early age, exhibiting interest in these sorts of subjects. When I was young I attended many hui together with my father, and at that time every marae had several elders - *kaumātua* - and the majority of them were steeped in their culture. Many of these kaumātua were uncles, my father's cousins.

My grandmother, Ere Awarau, had a very large family and most of them in turn had large families, so that in my father's generation, in those two generations there would have been well over 100 in just my grandmother's immediate family, and in their descendants, their children, and by my generation, they numbered several hundred in those three generations.

They were mainly, my great grandfather Awarau and the Awarau whānau. By the time I was born it was quite a big whānau, especially if you included in amongst them, second and third cousins and all his sisters' descendants as well. Amongst these, as a child, there were at least a dozen outstanding orators, speakers, truly knowledgeable men. My grand uncles, of whom there were about a dozen, were lay readers in the Church. They were extraordinarily knowledgeable in the Scriptures.

Four of Dads brothers were Anglican priests. We also had several school teachers who were trained in the Mission Station at Kaitaia and at the mission school in Awanui. Generally speaking, most my father's uncles and cousins, were above average in terms of Pākehā education.

They all spoke fluent Māori, Māori being their first language. I remember many of them had gone away to secondary schools such as St. Stephens, Te Aute College and other schools and quite a number had gone to Theological school in Te Rau Kahikatea, Gisbourne.

The people of Ngāi Takoto, in Pākehā terms, had a high standard of education. This tradition continues to this day.

Besides these kaumātua from our own people, my grandfather on my fathers' side was one of the chiefs of the Ngāti Kahu people and one of the signatories.

Both Tupu (grandfather) and my great-grand tupuna, Rāwiri Awarau, Tupu's father-in-law, were signatories of the Treaty of Waitangi, and was from the Ngāti Kahu people. His hapū was Te Patu Kōraha. In addition, the Te Pātū people were very closely related to Ngāi Takoto. In fact they had, after the return of Te Aupōuri, gone up to Takapaukura in the North Cape and lived there for three or four generations.

Then the Pākehā began to make a real impact, and the Māori in the Awanui-Kaitaia area were beginning to sell off land to the Pākehās. Ngāi Takoto, Pātū, and Patu Kōraha returned immediately to Awanui and Kaitaia area in order to prevent any legal sales of their lands.

There was a close relationship between Ngāi Takoto, Aupōuri, Te Pātū and the Patu Kōraha, both by blood and by virtue of the fact that they had lived together for so long. Amongst these Patu Kōraha and Te Pātū people were also a large number of elders who were orators and knowledgeable men.

So my early life was spent amongst these people and my father being an Anglican Priest ministered all around these areas so it wasn't long before I became known to many of these elders.

One of the things that impressed me about the elders were that they knew exactly how they were related, their kinship ties, their whakapapa - genealogy - their social status, the pecking order, and their wider relationships. There was a closeness amongst them, there was an affinity with each other, and their positions in terms of *tuakana-teina* were clearly demarcated in their minds.

They also had an immediate interest in the community. Of course they were their own immediate whānau and hapū. They had a large interest also with the wider community in terms of their affiliations within the iwi - Ngāti Kurī, Aupōuri, Ngāti Kahu, Rarawa and Ngā Puhi, they knew their relationships.

My mother Hana Toi, on her father's side, belonged to the Ngāti Korokoro, Ngāti Whārara people which occupy the southern side of the harbour mouth of the Hokianga River.

Her father Toi lived with Ngāti Whārara in the Ōmāpere/ Pākanae area, Ngāti Korokoro in the Waimamaku Valley, extending into Te Roroa in the Waipoua to Ngati Whātua and on to Parawhau, Whāngārei, and through her Dads mother, into North Hokianga.

Her mother Hiraina, my grandmother, came from Ngāti Kuta. She actually lived in Russell and was affiliated to the Ngāi Tawake-ki-Te Takutai Moana and Ngāti Hine and extended over into the Ngāti Wai and Ngāti Tautahi people of Kaikohe. She was also closely connected with the Ngāti Rangi of the Ngāwhā area. So as an individual I had connections with most of the peoples of the Tai Tokerau. Because of listening to my elders at an early age and to my own parents, I soon became aware of my affiliations, and in my mind I began to identify and feel akin to these people.

Later as I travelled extensively to these marae, with my parents, I came to know many of the elders on these marae. More and more I began to identify with these marae and with these people, and of course with my father's and mother's connections. They accepted me as part of themselves, partly because of my genealogical knowledge and partly because of my actual physical presence on these marae. I felt at home. That was the background which moulded me and fitted me for the wānanga itself when it eventually came.

My entry into the wānanga happened in this manner. Wesley College was Methodist, and there I met people who were elders of the Ngā Puhi people. For instance there was Eru Te Tuhi who was a Methodist minister and an elder in his own right both in Ngāti Whātua and in Hokianga. There were people like Hira Rogers, whose sons had been educated at Wesley. They had two sons there during my time so they were frequent visitors to the College. There were numerous others, parents of the students whom I met at College which helped to extend the range of my acquaintances amongst the elders of Ngā Puhi and later elders of other iwi and Te Moananui-a-Kiwa.

As I moved out of Ngā Puhi amongst the other iwi, and later as I went into the Ministry in Waikato and Taranaki, I travelled to do missions in various parts of the country or attend hui and became known to the elders of many other iwi. After leaving College, it was my father's hope that I go to University. At that particular time I was too young to be enrolled, so I stayed home for a year.

During that time war broke out and my older brothers - I had six of them - enlisted in the 28th Māori Battalion. That left the main burden of the family decisions to me, even though my father was still alive, he began to delegate a lot of his functions to me. Soon I found that I was speaking on the marae at the age of 15, nearly 16. Two of us in the hapū, from about 8, had been taken in hand by the elders and taught the genealogies of the Aupōuri, Ngāi Takoto and Ngāti Kahu peoples. When I spoke on the marae, it soon became apparent to the elders that I had a bent for this sort of thing. So three of the elders, relations of my fathers, approached him to ask me to come onto the wānanga or at least for me to attend, so that they could gauge my reactions.

I went to my first wānanga with my main sponsor, a cousin of my father's, Nōpera Ōtene from Mangamuka. My reactions were favourable so these three elders - two from Ngāti Kahu, Perei Tauhara, Tuki Shepherd, and Nōpera Ōtene - decided to initiate me. I'm not going to discuss the initiation ceremony - anyway, they vary from hapū to hapū. Different elders had their own modes of initiation. Sufficient to say, I was put through an initiation ceremony similar to baptism in water. That was the only meeting I attended, then I joined the Māori Battalion. Father died that year it was 1940.

One of the main reasons for the depletion, was that it was common practice for a person who felt death was close, to sponsor an understudy, choosing a younger man from the hapū to accompany him to the wānanga and when he bowed out, it was understood that the pupil he sponsored would take his place as a member of the wānanga so there was then continuity of a member for that particular hapū.

They were guardians of the tikanga of that hapū and in a wider sense the guardians of the Tai Tokerau wānanga. They together advised the wānanga. These elders were fairly careful in choosing young men and knew their attitudes, generally speaking, looking for qualities of humility, integrity, and charity.

These are the qualities they expected in a pupil or disciple they chose, who would best guard and promote the interests of their people. The person who took up this position as the official representative on the wānanga received status and mana. They could use or misuse this position.

My own elders drummed into me the fact that I was to use the knowledge that I received as a means of knitting the members of the hapū together and to generate harmony amongst the members. One of the tasks that I understood from my association with these elders, especially the three who sponsored me, was that in land matters I was to put interests of the hapū first, never my own.

So elders of the various hapū became prominent. They were storehouses for the knowledge and because of the mana that they had been given, though they understood their function, to be that of guardians of the tikanga for their people, and to teach members of their own tribe the knowledge especially in the historical aspects of the wānanga. Many of them did not disseminate the knowledge very widely.

Human nature being what it is, they were jealous of their positions. Many did not fulfil the roles and responsibilities for which they were originally sponsored. If you recall, I said at the beginning that there was a concern at the erosion of cultural values due to culture contact being the motivation for setting up the wānanga. By this means of teaching, this general knowledge could be disseminated more widely amongst the people through the hapū representatives.

The wānanga wasn't for everybody. It was selective. Representatives were expected to use their discretion in regard to what they imparted. It was clearly understood they would impart general knowledge to promising or interested youth who came on to the scene, showing potential. They were later expected to move into the deeper levels of the tikanga of the wānanga. Sad to say, many of them didn't and as a result future generations have been deprived of their heritage.

In regard to this, being the only surviving member of the Tai Tokerau wānanga, I was recently approached by elders of Ngā Puhi, to resurrect the wānanga that went into recess in 1958. Tahu Kamira called the meeting at Taha Ruka's home in Mt Albert. There he put the proposition to us. There were half a dozen of us left at that time being asked whether we should go into recess. We decided at that point to agree, with the proviso that the records of the wānanga be distributed to their specific hapū. Apart from the six of us, where certain hapū lacked representatives, we selected people to whom the Tiamana Tahu Kamira could give the books in the hopes of one day resurrecting the wānanga and recover the books from those to whom they'd been given.

The wānanga now was set up for purposes that differed from the original wānanga, in that it was now for the specific purpose of meeting an urgent need. It evolved along different lines from your ancient *whare kura* and *whare maire.*

Now the question is - what form should it take for the present day, Ngā Puhi? How far should we go in? Should we use the same format and procedure of the ancient wānanga or do we create new rules and adapt to modern conditions? In itself the Tai Tokerau wānanga was an adaptation of the earlier ones. Is it time to adapt to another form of wānanga that's applicable, relevant to present day demands?

 The Achievement of Authentic Being

Wisdom is a thing of the heart.
It has its own thought processes.
It is there that knowledge is integrated
for this is the centre of one's being.

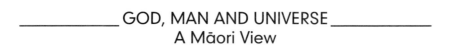

GOD, MAN AND UNIVERSE
A Māori View

The route to Māoritanga through abstract interpretation is a dead end. The way can only lie through a passionate, subjective approach. That is more likely to lead to a goal. As a person brought up within the culture, who has absorbed the values and attitudes of the Māori, my approach to Māori things is largely subjective. The charge of lacking objectivity does not concern me; the so-called objectivity some insist on is simply a form of arid abstraction, a model or a map. It is not the same thing as the taste of reality.

I like to use a descriptive method to explore the features of consciousness found in Māori cultural experiences. So I shall describe the religious, philosophical and metaphysical attitudes upon which Māoritanga is based. While I will also do a formal analysis of some of the basic concepts out of which these attitudes arise, it is important to remember that Māoritanga is a thing of the heart rather than the head. For that reason analysis is necessary only to make explicit what the Māori understands implicitly in his daily living, feeling, acting and deciding.

I am concerned, then, with viewing attitudes from within the culture. To do this, the writer must unmask himself for he can only interpret his culture to another in terms of what the institutions, customs, mores and traditions mean to him. From there I must ask, 'Is this a view held by my Māori people generally? Do their actions, their words, their oral traditions express the same general attitudes which I find in myself?'

So this study is presented from a point of view that begins from an analysis of the meaning that a particular cultural element holds for me, then goes on to consider whether the same meaning is true for other Māori. For what is Māoritanga? Briefly, it is the corporate view that Māori hold about ultimate reality and meaning.

Our point of departure is found in the words of the formal welcome:

Haere mai te ihi,
haere mai te wehi,
haere mai te mana,
haere mai te tapu.

Draw near o excellent ones,
draw near o awesome ones,
draw near o charismatic ones,
draw near o sacred ones.

This is a formal welcome used on special occasions to greet especially eminent guests on to a marae. It serves as a welcome and as a warning. As a welcome, it pays tribute to the dignity and status of the guests, acknowledging that they are the 'chosen' of the gods - charismatic people to whom the gods have delegated authority and power, to manifest the will and operation of the gods in the natural world. As a warning, it serves notice on those assembled that since these are the chosen of the gods, they are *tapu* people, set apart and dedicated to the service of the gods. As such, they cannot be treated with indignity and impunity without incurring the wrath and retribution of the gods.

It is the last consideration which makes the ritualistic observance of *marae* protocol (kawa) so formal and even rigid. For both guests (manuhiri) and hosts (tangata whenua), the formal observance of local *kawa* ensures the avoidance of transgression and the giving of offence. An analysis of the concepts which underlie this formal welcome reveals the basic themes and approach of the Māori to questions of ultimate reality and the relationships among God, man and the universe.

Ihi

The *ihi* has a close affinity with the Greek word 'arete'. *Arete* was derived from Aries, son of Jupiter. He was the god of war. Arete denoted the spirit of strife. By natural association, it came to mean manliness or vigour in battle. It later came to mean excellence in battle, and developed to include the idea of excellence or virtue blended with the impression of force. In Māori, for example: 'Haere ake ana te ihi me te mana o ngā toa.' ('A sense of vital force and power preceded the advance of the warriors.')

3

Ihi may be defined as 'vital force or personal magnetism which, radiating from a person, elicits in the beholder a response of awe and respect'. The closest English equivalent is 'personal or animal magnetism'. It is a psychic and not a spiritual force. Psychic force is an intrinsic quality in human being, a personal essence which can be developed more highly in some than in others; spiritual force (mana) is a gift endued by the gods.

Mana

Mana means spiritual authority and power as opposed to the purely psychic and natural force of ihi. In a theological sense, it may be translated as charisma. To understand the full implications and connotations, we can borrow two more Greek words, 'exousia' and 'dunamis'. *Exousia* is derived from the verb 'exesti' which means, 'lawful or permitted'. It is normally translated as 'authority'. In the Greek sense, authority means 'lawful permission delegated by the superior to the subordinate'.

In the Māori sense, since authority is derived from the gods, mana as authority means 'lawful permission delegated by the gods to their human agent to act on their behalf and in accordance with their revealed will'. Since authority is a spiritual gift delegated by the gods, man remains always the agent or channel - never the source of mana.

Dunamis is the other aspect of mana. From it we derive the words dynamic, dynamite, dynamo. It is derived from the Greek verb 'dunamai' which means 'to be capable or to have power'. It denotes the ability or power to perform. Thus dunamis meant 'power, might, strength; the power to perform'. It meant also (in the New Testament sense) 'power in action, power to perform miraculous works, and the power of the spoken word'. To the Māori, mana includes all these ideas, but essentially it means 'that which manifests the power of the gods'.

Mana in its double aspect of authority and power may be defined as 'lawful permission delegated by the gods to their human agents and accompanied by the endowment of spiritual power to act on their behalf and in accordance with their revealed will'. This delegation of authority is shown in dynamic signs or works of power.

Authority and power in this sense must be clearly distinguished since it is clear that to exercise spiritual power outside the limits delegated is to abuse the gift, and results either in its withdrawal or in that power running rampant and causing harm to the agent and others.

A simple analogy will make the distinction clearer. A person approaches a traffic crossing and the lights turn red. He has power to cross but no permission. The lights turn green but his car stalls at that moment. He has permission to cross, but no power. His car starts and the lights remain green. He has both authority and power to proceed.

Tapu

The Māori idea of *tapu* is close to the Jewish idea translated in the words, 'sacred' and 'holy', although it does not have the later ethical connotations of the New Testament of 'moral righteousness'. It has both religious and legal connotations. A person, place or thing is dedicated to a deity and by that act it is set aside or reserved for the sole use of the deity. The person or object is thus removed from the sphere of the profane and put into the sphere of the sacred. It is untouchable, no longer to be put to common use. It is this untouchable quality that is the main element in the concept of tapu. In other words, the object is sacred and any profane use is sacrilege, breaking of the law of tapu.

From the purely legal aspect, it suggests a contractual relationship has been made between the individual and his deity whereby a person dedicates himself or an object to the service of a deity in return for protection against malevolent forces and the power to manipulate his environment to meet needs and demands.

The idea of manipulating environment is based on the Māori view that there are three orders of reality, the physical or natural, the psychic and the spiritual. Whilst the natural realm is normally subject to physical laws, these can be affected, modified and even changed by the application of the higher laws of the psychic and spiritual.

By applying psychical laws (intellectual and emotional consciousness) in a scientific manner, man now manipulates that environment to suit his own purposes. This principle is no less applicable in the spiritual realm. In the Māori view, the application of spiritual laws to this end is dependent upon man's cooperation with the gods. This is brought about by entering into the contractual relationship already mentioned.

The method of entering into this relationship was by the *tohi* or sacramental rite of initiation. This consisted of two complementary acts: the dedication and the consecration. The act of dedication (tāpae) consisted of offering up a person, place or thing to the service of the deity, a declaration of the purpose intended and a definition of the future role of the object dedicated. It was henceforth sacred and untouchable, the object was now tapu. It could not be put to profane use. The profanation of tapu was regarded as a transgression (takatakahi) of the gods to whom the object had been dedicated, and such transgression incurred vengeance.

The act of dedication was followed by the act of consecration an act of praise extolling the power and virtue of the gods who were then invoked by name and petitioned to endue the person or object with mana. The prayers were accompanied by a sacramental act (tohi). Whilst the *tohunga* might participate in the consecratory prayers, the consecration was the prerogative of the gods. It was they who completed the rite, provided man fulfilled the conditions. The dedication was man's part, the consecration the response of the gods. Since the dedication was sacrificial, in the sense that it was offering a person's life or possession to the service of the gods, the sacrifice was accepted and consecrated by the bestowal of mana.

The bestowing of mana on people differed from that on things or places. In the former case, the spirit of the gods fell upon the person and filled or possessed him. The spirit of the gods guided and directed him, subject to his continuing assent. This was a covenant relationship which could be dissolved by either party not fulfilling the terms of the agreement. In the latter case, the gods placed guardian spirits over places or things to watch over the property dedicated to them. These guardian spirits (kaitiaki) manifested themselves by appearing in the form (ariā) of animals, birds or other natural objects as a warning against transgression, or to effect punishment for breach of tapu. The *Pākehā* idea of haunting is similar to the idea of this role played by guardians.

Two popular misconceptions should be cleared away. Early missionaries and anthropologists perpetuated the incorrect idea that mana was the positive and tapu the negative aspect of some vague psychic or spiritual force. As we have seen, tapu is the sacred state or condition of a person or thing placed under the patronage of the gods. Mana is the enduement of that object with spiritual power through the indwelling spirit over it. Humans thus became the channel through which the indwelling spirit of the deity was manifest.

Another error popularised by early anthropologists was that primitive man held an animistic view of nature, by which they meant that primitive man believed all natural objects to be animated by its own spirit. For the Māori, there was a clear distinction between the essence (mauri) of a person or object and the distinct realm of the spirit which stood over the realm of the natural order and was indwelt by spiritual beings. Since the natural order was not a closed system it could be infiltrated and interpenetrated by the higher order of the spirit. In fact, the Māori further distinguished between the essence of inanimate and animate objects. Whilst all the created order partook of *mauri* (life force, ethos) by which all things cohere in nature, in human beings this essence was of a higher order and was called *mauriora* (life principle). This essence (mauri) I am convinced, was originally regarded as elemental energy derived from the realm of *Te Korekore*, out of which the stuff of the universe was created.

In a secondary sense a tapu object may be classified as an accursed or unclean (poke) thing. The condition of tapu is transmitted by contact or association and a person can be contaminated and polluted by it.

Where contamination occurs through contact with sacred objects in the normal course of a tohunga's duties, he must cleanse himself before resuming his secular life if he is to avoid spreading this contamination or avoid offending the gods. But where contamination occurs through transgression, then a person must not only be cleansed from the pollution but the effects of the mana brought into action by it must be neutralised if the person is not to suffer its ill effects. It is in this contaminating and polluting sense that tapu is classified as accursed or unclean, a state in which the personality becomes wide open to either attack or invasion by demonic and other spiritual forces.

So, we may define tapu as the sacred state or condition in which a person, place or thing is set aside by dedication to the gods and thereby removed from profane use. This tapu is secured by the sanction of the gods and reinforced by endowment with mana.

Wehi

Wehi may be translated simply as awe or fear in the presence of the ihi of a person, or of the mana and tapu of the gods. It is the emotion of fear generated by anxiety or apprehension in case one gives offence to the gods, or a response of awe at a manifestation of divine power (mana).

The Pure Rites

To counteract the effects of tapu, the Māori employed what they termed 'pure' rites (purification rites). They were designed to cleanse from tapu, neutralise tapu, or to propitiate the gods. Where the intention was to cleanse from the contamination of tapu, the sacramental element used was normally water. For neutralising tapu or for the propitiation of the gods, the sacramental means was cooked food.

After a person occupied with sacred duties wished to resume his secular activities or after a person had inadvertently transgressed the tapu of an object, he washed himself in water dedicated to the god Rēhua. Thus water used for the purpose was called Te Wai-o-Rēhua (the water of Rēhua). Its function was the same as that of 'holy water' used by the Christian Church and an element of all major religions.

There is no forgiveness for deliberate transgression (takatakahi) since such transgression is a direct challenge to the mana of the gods. Such challenges were a common occurrence in Māori life and aimed at subduing the powers of the god of an opposing tribe or person. Should the mana of the opposing god prove too powerful, then the pure rite took the form of the 'pure whakanoa' designed to neutralise (whakanoa) or ward off the malevolent and debilitating effects of such mana.

Different types of food, ferns and other herbs were cooked in the 'umu pure' and after it became cold, the food was placed upon the person's head, the most sacred part of the body, and exorcism prayers recited over him. Popular belief held that by cooking, the mauri of the plant was released and thereby made common (noa) or neutralised, a state of things abhorrent to the gods, thus ensuring their departure. As tapu could be transmitted by contact, so could its opposite profane state be transmitted by contact with objects made *noa* (neutral, common, profane, sterile).

This belief accounts for an *ariki* (high chief) or tohunga being fed by servants, especially if they were engaged in projects of a very sacred nature. Contact with cooked food would neutralise their tapu and mana. It also accounts for other precautions practised by modern Māori of not ironing their clothes on a meal table, not washing their clothes with other linen such as tablecloths and avoiding placing their hats on a meal-table or passing food over a person's head. All such prohibitions are designed to avoid the depletion of mana.

One other form of *whakanoa* was employed in the official opening of a new building. During construction, a building was placed under the mana and tapu of Tāne, god of the forest, and of the various gods of construction and carving. Before the building could be put to common, secular and profane use it had to be freed from the mana and tapu of the gods. The *ruahine* or *tapairu* of the tribe (the senior woman by descent of the senior family) accompanied by the tohunga and other members of the tribe, entered to 'takahi' (trample underfoot) the tapu of the gods under whose mana the building had been placed during construction. This neutralised it and decontaminated it of tapu. It ensured that future users of the building would be unharmed.

The mana of the male differed from that of the female. Whilst the mana of the male was viewed as being positive, that of the female was regarded as negative. Hence the mana of a high-born female was regarded as particularly potent in negating or neutralising tapu. As a consequence, the act of a woman stepping over a man instead of going around him was highly improper and reprehensible since such an action depleted the male of his mana.

The pure as a propitiatory act, whilst remaining essentially the same in basic form, was applied on many different occasions. It proceeded on the principle that all created things were the property of the gods who, as the regents of Io the supreme god, were responsible for the departments of nature under which that object came. All animate things were regarded as children of the departmental gods.

The *pure rākau* was used to propitiate Tāne, god of the forest, before a tree was felled for canoe-making or house-building. A fire was lit under the tree and the first chip together with *mauku* fern was burnt. The scent, representing the essence of the tree, was offered up to propitiate Tāne for the slaying of this forest child of Tāne.

The same principle was applied in the harvesting of food crops, fruit, birds or fish. The food was cooked and whilst it was still steaming hot, it was elevated in the hands and 'waved' to and fro before the gods so that the essence symbolised by the rising steam could return to the gods. They were then petitioned to accept the essence while man consumed the substance. Thanksgiving for the bounty of the gods was given, after which the tohunga ate a morsel and buried the remainder. Only when this rite was completed could the harvest proceed.

Other propitiatory rites were connected with the ritual of the dead. They were known as the *pure tūpāpaku* (funeral rites), *pure hahu* (exhumation or disinterment rites), and the *pure kōiwi* (interment of human bones). All persons on death came under the jurisdiction (maru) of the gods of the *Pō* (for example Whiro, Maru, or Hine-nui-te-pō). The tapu of the dead was particularly virulent and a person contracting such tapu through contact had to be purified and neutralised. The practice continues in modern times.

In most tribes, it is still the custom to wash oneself after returning from a funeral. In modern times, the *pure whakanoa* at a *tangi* has largely been replaced by the *hākari* (feast) which follows the funeral. Amongst some tribes, it is still the practice to *mihi* (pay verbal tribute) to the gods of the Pō and exhort them to accept the essence of the food as their portion whilst allowing men the substance. This mihi has been largely replaced by the Christian grace.

In some places sextons at a particular funeral eat apart from the main body of the people. Their meal is laid out in the place where the corpse has lain during the tangi. This is to neutralise the tapu, both on the place contaminated by the tapu of the corpse, and that on themselves.

Times and customs change. The ancient reason for certain ritual acts can fade with the passage of time, or considerations of convenience and practicality can force changes. A practice creeping into some areas of Ngā Puhi is holding the hākari before the funeral service, to avoid the inordinate amount of time taken up by it and thereby facilitate the departure of guests who have to travel long distances on their return journey.

I wonder whether this is the original reason for the hākari fading with the passage of time, or a question of convenience, or both. Whatever the reason, the winds of change enforced by acculturation continue to blow and bury some institutions under the sands of time, or temper the regard and value of others.

The post-funeral hākari of modern times must be viewed within the tangi. Though the element of local pride enters into it, the elaborate preparations and prodigious amounts of food devoted to the tangi remain for the Māori part of their ritual and social obligations to the gods and to the *manuhiri*. Hence no efforts are spared to fulfil obligations, on the premise that only the best is good enough for the gods, and that tribal honour is at stake before visitors. These considerations encourage locals to exceed the conventional demands of hospitality.

It may seem that the modern tangi retains some of its pre-Christian associations. This is true. But it must be remembered that the significance of the various rites is only partially understood or totally forgotten. Again, the various rites, whilst to a large extent retaining their traditional form, have been so Christianised that offerings once made to the gods of the Pō are now made to *Ihowa* (Jehovah) or to Jesus Christ as Lord of the dead and the living. Other elements adopted from Christianity (the totally Christian church and funeral services) have become an integral part of the tangi. However these changes may occur, the general traditional form and underlying principles remain.

Tohi Rites

A dedicatory act placed a person or thing under tapu. The consecratory act was the means by which the person or thing was endued with mana. Earlier, we saw that whilst persons were filled with the spirit of the gods themselves to endue them with power, places and things were not filled or possessed, but brought under the patronage of the gods who consigned guardian spirits to oversee the object or place. The consecration of a person was accompanied by a sacramental act and these acts were called 'tohi'. This word means literally 'to endue'.

It is not generally realised that prior to the advent of Christianity, the Māori possessed a sacramental system which included sacraments parallel to those of the Christian church. This probably explains why Christianity was so readily accepted by the Māori and further explains his strong allegiance to the sacramental churches. Because of the parallel between the systems, we can make comparisons between them to help us understand the principles underlying both.

According to the Augustinian definition of Western Christendom, a sacrament is 'an outward visible sign setting forth and pledging an inward spiritual grace'. To the Māori, a sacrament is simply 'the means by which mana (charisma, grace, spiritual power) is transmitted to humans'. The means used could be a specific element (water) from the created order, or another person by tactile transmission. The personal agent instrumental in this act must himself have been previously endued with the spirit of the gods since he can only impart what he himself already is.

Baptism with Water

Iriiri, rūmaki and *uhi* are alternative names for the rite of baptism. *Iriiri* describes the purpose or function of the rite. It means literally, 'to place upon, to endow' and signifies that baptism was the rite of enduement with authority. Uhi (to sprinkle) and rūmaki (to dip into) describe the method.

A child was held over flowing water or the sea, which symbolised living waters, and the gods ruling over the different departments of nature were petitioned to endow the child with the mental and physical qualities desired. As the names of the different gods were invoked, should the child sneeze, cough or yawn, it was taken as a sign that the spirit of that god had alighted (iri) on that child. The child was then dedicated to those particular gods by immersing it in the water or by sprinkling it with water from a branch dipped in the stream or sea.

In this way, the child was incorporated into those gods to whom he had been dedicated and this gave him authority to invoke the names of those particular gods in times of crisis. Since the name signifies the extension of the personality, the god must come to the aid of the suppliant.

Secondly, the child was placed under the tapu of those gods. In other words, he was now removed from the sphere of the profane into the sphere of the sacred. His life was to be lived in the service of those gods in return for their blessing. In the Christian sense, it signifies the 'dying of the old life, and its burial, and arising to a new life in Christ'. Here is part of the dedication used, according to tradition, at Māui's birth:

> *Tihē Mauri ora! Ki te Wheiao, ki te Ao Mārama.*
> *Ka tū kei runga, ko wai koe?*
> *Ko Tū, Ko Rongo koe, ko Tāne koe.*
> *Ko te manuhiri i ahu mai i Hawaiki, nau mai.*

> *This sneeze is the sign of the new life, in this world.*
> *And when you are mature, who shall you be?*
> *You shall be Tū, (god of war),*
> *Rongo (god of vegetation), Tāne (god of man and forest).*
> *To you who come from Hawaiki*
> *We welcome your presence.*

Here we see that the sign of the coming of Tū, Rongo and Tāne was apparent when Māui sneezed during the invocation of each of the names of these particular gods. Other gods such as Tangaroa, god of the sea, did not adopt Māui and bring him under their patronage. The dedication of Māui to these three gods carried the implication in the second line that when Māui matured he would not only be under the tutelage, but would have authority to invoke them in times of crisis. There is also the consecration in which these gods who have come from *Hawaiki-tapu* (abode of the gods) are exhorted to fill Māui with their presence (nau mai).

Tohi Whakahā
Tohi whakahā, or *tohi mauri*, is the enduement of mauri (life principle) by infusion (whakahā) of the breath (manawa). It was used on two main occasions:

after neutralisation of a person's mana and vitality through the use of cooked food (umu pure); or at the initiation of a novice into the order of tohunga. In the former case, after a person had transgressed the tapu of the gods he went through the 'pure whakanoa' in which cooked food was placed on his head and the spirits causing his sickness were exorcised. This not only neutralised the mana and tapu of the opposing gods, but also the mana and tapu of his own tutelary gods, as well as debilitating his vital force. Sickness and death resulted from the depletion of the natural vital force through the agency of the gods or evil spirits, and this *mauriora* had to be replaced through the tohi mauri.

In the case of initiation, the tohi mauri was designed to give a novice learning the arts of tohunga extra mauri, since the work he would take up would require inner strength in the battle against alien spiritual power and for the task of bearing his people's burdens. For this role he needed a double function of vital life force (*mauriora*) for his physical and psychic health.

The method was the same for both. The *tohunga ahurewa* (high priest) bit the hollow of the head, (regarded as the spiritual mouth of the body) in order to open it up symbolically and then infused his breath (manawa) as the vehicle for mauri into the person by breathing on him. He thereby imparted his own vital life force into the novice.

Te Tuha

Te tuha was the tohi of the 'sacred spittle' employed by the *tohunga taura* (as distinct from the tohunga ahurewa), to impart mana. The *taura* were the *tohunga* of the dark powers and in order to impart their mana to their disciples, they spat upon the disciple's head and invoked the spirits of the dark powers to possess the disciple and empower him with the dark arts of *mākutu* and *whaiwhaiā* - the casting of spells to bring sickness and death on their enemies

Te Whakapā

Te whakapā was a *tohi* employed by a father before his death to impart the family mana to his eldest son. The eldest son could be by-passed by the father, however, and the family mana given to a younger son. It was also employed by some chiefs to institute the eldest son into the office and functions that he himself had held. In both cases, the intention was the same; to establish the son in the position of the father as head of the family or head of the tribe. The method was to assemble the family and elders as witnesses and then the father or chief laid his hands upon the son's head and pronounced over him both the office and functions he was to assume, and then pronounced his blessing. This laying on of hands was normally accompanied by the tohi mauri.

For the other members of the family, the whakapā was also used as a means of blessing, although the tohi mauri was not employed in these cases. A similar method was employed by the ancient Israelites to impart the father's blessing to their children. The corresponding rite in the Christian church is the rite of confirmation.

Kairarawa

A means to replenish mana was the rite of *kairarawa* or cannibalism. The word 'rarawa' in this context means with violence or with force. It is a term used to denote the forces that underlie the whole range of divine powers implied in the terms 'mauri' 'ihi', 'tapu' and 'mana'. Kairarawa denoted the consumption of the life force and the psychic and spiritual forces of the enemy which replenished one's own powers.

Like concepts such as tapu, which included an opposition of ideas within the same concept, (for example sacredness and uncleanness), so the concept of kairarawa had its contrast in the concept of *kaitoa*. All warriors going into battle were dedicated to the god of war and were specially consecrated. When a warrior fell in battle, especially if he was of aristocratic lineage, he was regarded as a person who, because of his rank and the tohi rites he had been subjected to, was a person of great mana, as well as of ihi. So the conquerors cooked him and ate certain selected portions of his body where they believed his mana resided. By eating his flesh they consumed his mana and ihi, and thereby replenished their own.

Eating the enemy's mana not only depleted the mana of the opposing tribe, it also brought the gods of those tribes under the subjection of the conquering tribe. In one sense it seems as if the fickle gods deserted the weak and sided with the strong. This eating of the enemy thus degraded the conquered tribe who were now treated with contempt by their conquerors. Degradation of the conquered tribe was termed 'kaitoa'. It signified that the toa (courage, strength) of the conquered had been eaten. Kaitoa means literally 'to eat the strength and courage of another'.

So cannibalism served two functions: first to replenish one's own powers (kairarawa); and second to deplete the enemy of their mana and thereby degrade them (kaitoa). During Hongi Hika's last battle in the Houhora area in the far north against the Te Aupōuri, one of the war leaders, Te Houtaewa, was finally slain. During Te Houtaewa's lifetime he was regarded as the greatest warrior of the Te Aupōuri. He was famous for his speed and agility in battle and it was commonly said that his mana resided in this thighs and legs. After his death, Te Houtaewa's legs were severed and cooked and certain portions eaten by Hongi and his warriors to gain his mana. The rest of his body was untouched out of respect for his bravery and because he was related to Hongi himself. His body was returned to the Te Aupōuri by Pōroa, who had for some time been associated with Hongi in his battles, but who was also a close relative of Te Houtaewa. In this instance, the purpose was solely that of kairarawa, not kaitoa, as evidenced by the return of the body for burial.

As the ancient Māori ate their enemies in order to replenish their vital force and take in the mana of the gods, so the modern Māori Christian goes to communion to take in the vital life force and mana of Jesus Christ by means of the 'ariā' of bread and wine.

An interesting sidelight to cannibalism is the incident by which the Ngā Puhi tribe received its name. Several generations before the migration of the Ngātoki-mata-whao-rua canoe to New Zealand, one of Nukutawhiti's ancestors, an ariki called Arikitapu, was betrothed (puhi) to Kareroa-aitu, the ahurewa of the tribe. She wanted a human heart to eat, so they chose her niece because of her high rank, and by magical arts slew her and removed her heart. The corpse was taken to the lagoon of Moanarua and by occult powers she was transformed into a taniwha. When Arikitapu's son was born, he was named Puhi to commemorate the event and was variously called *Puhi- taniwha-rau* (Puhi of the many taniwha) and *Puhi-moana-ariki* (Puhi of the sea of nobility) to denote his association with Moanarua, reputed to be the stronghold of the mana of the ancient Polynesians.

The Tohunga
The word *tohunga* is often translated as 'expert' (for example *tohunga-tā-moko* is rendered in English as 'expert carver'). Such use is wrong and stems from the mistaken idea that because the Māori used this term in association with recognised experts in a particular field the word must mean expert. The word tohunga is derived from the stem 'tohu' which as a verb means a sign or manifestation. Tohunga is the gerundive of tohu and means a 'chosen one' or 'appointed one'.

The tohunga was a person chosen or appointed by the gods to be their representative and the agent by which they manifested their operations in the natural world by signs of power (tohu mana). The choice of the tohunga in an official capacity as either an ahurewa to the tribe or as a leader in a particular field, rested with the gods and with the tribe. As young men developed, the seers of the tribe watched for signs to manifest themselves in these youngsters, such as being constantly drawn towards a group occupied in a particular pursuit, an inordinate preoccupation with a particular facet of life, a keen student in a particular field. Signs such as these were considered as the attraction and drawing of the gods to a particular vocation. These indications were put to the test by use of certain spiritual or occult rituals, and the young man was accepted or rejected. If accepted, he was dedicated and consecrated to the gods who empowered him for that particular office and function.

The function of a tohunga was defined by the qualifying adjective. Those who fulfilled the office and function of priests to the tribe were known as 'tohunga ahurewa'. As the name indicates they were the chosen ones (tohunga) of the 'higher way' (ahurewa). Their function was to mediate between the gods and the tribe to ensure the welfare of the tribe. They gave advice on the best time to engage in certain activities: where the best fishing grounds were at certain seasons; what the best methods were for ensuring success in economic activities. On the spiritual level, they were experts in propitiating the gods in the various religious rites and also in the sacred lore, traditions and genealogies of the tribe.

The second class of tohunga were the *taura*. They operated in the related field of the occult and black arts. It was recognised that they were inferior in mana to the ahurewa and less learned because they were denied access to the sacred lore of the *kauae runga*. In fact, many of the taura were drop-outs from the *wānanga*. They had failed the tests that each *pia* (novice) as required to undergo before being initiated into the lore of the upper wānanga; being rejected, many of these resorted to black magic in their search for power. Thus they were also known as *tohunga whaiwhaiā*, an adjective meaning 'pursuer'. By their black arts, they cast evil spells on others and set the demonic spirits to pursuing their victims. Another name for them is *tohunga mākutu*, tohunga who cast evil spells.

Some tohunga of this class developed out of the spirit of strife and jealously that existed between rival families. To exact vengeance they sold themselves to the dark gods and conducted their nefarious activities in secret. Hence the name taura (rope) signifying their ability to bring people into bondage under the dark powers.

Specialist tohunga were experts in various fields of artistic activity: carvers, tattooers, and so on. Here the concept was similar to the Greek idea of the spirit of muses coming upon a person to endow him with their artistic abilities. This is how the mistaken idea arose that a tohunga-tā-moko meant 'an expert tattooist'. It means a person chosen by the gods of tattooing and empowered with mana to suit him for this task.

The office and functions of the Christian priest are the same in principle for the welfare and benefit of the people. The choice and the consecration remain the prerogative of the divine one: 'You have not chosen me, but I have chosen you.'

We have ranged over the basic concepts of ihi, wehi, mana and tapu, studying their implications in the religious and cultural milieu. We have glanced at related concepts such as mauri, noa, kaitoa, and the basic religious and sacramental rites associated with these. A comparison between the Māori and Christian sacramental systems has been made to show that certain spiritual principles are universal in application. It remains for these concepts to be placed within the context of the metaphysical, philosophical and religious thinking out of which they originated.

The Gods and Creation

In considering the place and role of gods, we are on less firm ground as various tribes have different traditions. Those who hold a common tradition do not agree in detail. For this reason, it is necessary to balance tradition with the body of oral literature used on formal occasions to sanction customs or to justify a particular course of action. A semantic approach will also help. By analysing the root meaning of words, the relationships between words in stylised sentences, the symbolic and evocative value attributed to each, and by a study of grammatical constructions peculiar to Māori, the inner thought and psychological thinking responsible for such constructions and methods of expression become explicit and highlight cultural values.

For this study, I will be taking the tradition of the Ngā Puhi wānanga, modified by the tradition of my own tribal elders and my observations over the years of variations in detail in tribal custom and oral literature of other tribes expressed on the marae.

Io, Supreme God

In the beginning, *Io* existed alone in the realm of Te Korekore, in his passive state as *Io-matamoe, Io-mata-ane, Io-kore-tē-whiwhia* (Io of the slumbering countenance, Io of the calm and tranquil countenance, Io the unchanging and unadulterated in whom there is no confusion and inconsistency). Nothing existed before Io, for he alone was pre-existent as *Io-matua-kore,* 'the parentless', as *Io-matua,* 'the first parent', as *Io-mau,* 'the precursor', as *Io-pūkenga,* 'the first cause', as *Io-taketake,* 'the foundation of all things.'

He held intercourse within himself, between the *ihomatua* of his active and positive thought, and between the *ihomāriri* of his passive and negative self. So Io alone had a double *iho* (essence). He was both Io-mata-ane, of the passive countenance, and *Io-mata-kākā,* of the flashing active countenance.

He was truly supreme god for he was *Io-moa,* 'the exalted one', *Io-tikitiki-o-rangi,* 'the supreme one of heaven', *Io-te-toi-o-ngā-rangi,* 'the pinnacle of heaven', *Io-nui,* 'the infinite one', *Io-roa,* 'the eternal one', *Io-uru,* 'the omnipresent', *Io-mata-kana,* 'the all-seeing one', *Io-wānanga,* 'the all-wise', *Io-mata-aho,* 'of the glorious blinding countenance.'

Io dwelt tranquilly in the void of Te Korekore. He roused himself and stirred up his activity and communed within himself, for apart from his passivity and negativity, nothing existed. His essence flowed forth to fertilise Te Korekore. Then he spoke his command and the iho of the night was increased. He spoke again and the iho of *Hawaiki* in the night regions blossomed, and on succeeding commands the iho of the heavens, of light, of the rock foundation of the earth, and of the waters were increased. Thus were the essential foundations of the universe laid.

At that time, only the seed of potential being was established and there was no form or substance for this seed of creation gestated in Te Korekore. Then Io activated himself once more and he recited (tapatapa) the names of the different foundations of things: of the night and of light, of the earth and sky and waters, of the depths and heights, of the expanse of the skies and borders of the seas. Thus things became differentiated and took form.

Io called into being the night realms, and divided them into various planes of the great night (Te Pō-nui), the extensive night (Te Pō-roa), the enveloping night (Te Pō-uriuri), the intensive night (Te Pō-kerekere), the night streaked with light (Te Pō-tiwhatiwha), the night streaked with broad light (Te Pō-haehaea), the night of unseeing (Te Pō-tē-kitea), the night of hesitant exploration (Te Pō-tangotango), the night of groping (Te Pō-te-whāwhā), the night inclined towards day (Te Pō-namunamu ki Te Wheiao), the night that borders day (Te Pō-tahuri-atu).

Then Io illumined the nights with soft light so that they glowed like twilight (kakarauri). He divided the *Pō-tahuri-atu* from the dawnlight (wheiao) with a veil (te ārai) and beyond the dawn light he placed *Te Ao Mārama* - the broad daylight.

In the night regions of soft light, Io established the several Hawaiki: *Hawaiki-nui, Hawaiki-roa, Hawaiki-pāmamao, Hawaiki-tapu* (great Hawaiki, extensive Hawaiki, far distant Hawaiki, and sacred Hawaiki) in which Io chose to dwell with his divine assistants. The Hawaiki became the abode of gods and heroes. But no one, other gods included, could enter Hawaiki-tapu for it was sacred to Io. The other Hawaiki were also sacred and in ancient times were not mentioned in common talk except by oblique reference as *Tawhiti-nui, Tawhiti-roa, Tawhiti-pāmamao*.

Having created the nights and the Hawaiki, Io brought into being the first gods, *Rangi-awatea* and *Papa-tua-nuku*, the male and female principles out of which all things derived. *Awatea* was the god of 'space and light' (wātea and awatea) and the first heaven was created by him on the foundations established by Io. It was known as the heaven of Wātea (Te Rangi-a-Wātea). But having completed the first heaven, he looked below him and saw the spirit of Papa-tua-nuku (Mother Earth) and descended to cohabit with her. Out of this union sprang their first-born, Tāne and the other gods after him: *Tangaroa, Rongo, Tū-mata-uenga, Haumia-tiketike, Ru-ai-moko*, and *Tāwhiri-mā-tea*.

But Rangi continued to cling to Papa-tua-nuku and gave up his task of completing the heavens. By this act, he doomed his offspring to dwell in perpetual darkness. Io the omniscient stirred his activity and sent the spirit of rebellion to stir the children to revolt. After consultation among the brothers they decided, with the exception of Tawhiri-mā-tea, to separate their parents and allow light into their world. After several abortive attempts, Tāne conceived the idea of standing on his hands on Papa and thrusting against Rangi with his feet. His manoeuvre succeeded and Rangi was flung into the skies.

Tāne was summoned by Io and after elaborate pure rites, he descended to the borders of Hawaiki-tapu where the sacred winds, the mouth-piece of Io, commissioned him to continue with the task of completing the heavens. So the heavens were completed and became known as the great heavens of Tāne (Rangi-nui-a-Tāne). At the same time as Tāne received the mana to complete the heavens, Io delegated through Tāne various tasks for his brothers. So they became the regents of Io to continue creation in the departments of nature. Thus Tangaroa became the god of the sea, Rongo the god of vegetation. Ru-ai-moko divided the lands asunder, Tāwhiri took over the meteorological department and Tū took over the war office. Tāne reserved two departments for himself on earth, the forest and birds, and the creation of man. The first human created was *Hine-ahu-one* (the maid that emerged out of the dust). Tāne took clay, moistened it with water and sculptured the form of a female. He then infused the breath of his nostrils (hongi) into her and she came alive. Meanwhile, Awatea had been summoned by Io (prior to Tāne's commission), deprived of his mana and banished into the Night Realm. It was the mana from Awatea that was given to Tāne.

It is said that Io, the omnipresent one, established temples at Hawaiki-tapu in the Pō regions, at the pinnacle of the heavens, at *Whitianga* in the east, at *Hikurangi* in the west, at *Tokerau* in the north and at *Rarotonga* in the south. These places were beyond the horizon, and were sacred to Io.

Thus the nights and the heavens, the earth and the water, were created, and all things in them. But it was Io who laid the foundations and delegated continuous creation to the offspring of Rangi and Papa.

Io had his divine assistants in the heavens and the night regions. Those of the heavenly realm were called *Te Whānau-a-Rangi*, the company of heaven. These included the *apa* (spiritual beings) called the *whatukura* and *māreikura*, the male and female. And with them the *pou-tiri-ao*, who were all male. These were the personal assistants of Io. In the night realms, Io's assistants were the *mairehau*. Their functions were similar to those of the whatukura in the heavens, in that they were the sacred wraiths who transmitted Io's commands.

Maru was Io's chief assistant in the realm of Pō and seems to have been a beneficent overlord of that region, since he is invoked in some areas during the *pure* feast at funeral rites to receive the spirit of the departed into Hawaiki. Hine-nui-te-pō. a female attendant, guarded the entrance to the night realm and directed spirits of the departed along the path of Tāne (te ara whānui a Tāne i te Muri-wai-hou ki te Pō-tiwha). Whiro was the other overlord of the night region and while her functions were not clear, she seems to have been connected with the mourning rites and ceremonies symbolised by the greenery of leaves worn as a garland by visitors. These were deposited at the feet of the corpse and later buried with him. This garland was called 'te rau wharawhara o te aroha' (the wharawhara leaves of compassion), or 'te rau parekawakawa o te aroha' (the kawakawa garland of compassion). The Waikato and Taranaki tribes favoured the *kawakawa* as the symbol of love and compassion for the departed, while the Ngā Puhi tribes favoured the *wharawhara*. Today any greenery serves the purpose.

Besides these three, innumerable other spirits dwelt in the night realms. The departmental gods lived in Hawaiki, as did the spirits of departed heroes. Besides these there were a whole host of other spirits beneficent or malevolent. The malevolent spirits were called *hautupu*. Other demonic spirits were called *maitū*, but these were sometimes invoked as familiar spirits who became guardians for members of a *whānau*, and in this role were known as *kaitiaki*. Their counterparts in the natural world were *taniwha*. These dragon-like creatures dwelt in certain localities and could be independent and unattached from the local tribe. As such, they were devourers of men. But where they were attached to the local tribe, they acted as guardians and manifested themselves as animals, fish, birds or reptiles. Strictly speaking, these were not spirits but occult powers created by the psychic force of ancient tribal tohungas and by the mana of their creative word, given form and delegated as guardians for the tribe.

The other occupants of the night regions were the spirits of departed humans called *wairua*. They descended along the path of Tāne to the different Hawaiki in the night realm where they continued life and followed occupations little different from those on earth. The spirits of the departed that lingered on earth after death were called *kēhua* (wraiths, ghosts) who haunted the living. Other wraiths who haunted the living were not of human origin but demonic spirits known as *taipō* (inhabitants of the dark).

Not all wairua of departed humans went to the Pō. There was also a belief that many of them went to the realms of Rangi and others dwelt amongst the stars. But whether it was in the Pō, in Hawaiki or in the Rangi, all these were regions in the spirit world. A path from earth led to the Pō (te ara whānui a Tāne) and another led to the Rangi (te aratiatia a Tāne). Beyond the horizons and the stars, surrounding the earth, the night realms and the sky realms joined together.

The Māori Worldview

As we have seen, the created universe is divided into Te Pō and Te Rangi, which in themselves are divided into twelve planes. In between floats the earth sphere or sphere of day (Te Ao Mārama). The Pō and Rangi are in turn encompassed by the realm of Te Korekore.

How did the Māori view the origin of the universe? What is its basic element? Is it material, spiritual, or both? Is it static or dynamic? Is history cyclic or lineal? Some of the answers to these questions are obvious. For instance we have seen that Io is the first cause from which all things originated. It is also obvious that the Māori does not, and never has accepted the mechanistic view of the universe which regards it as a closed system into which nothing can impinge from without. The Māori conceives of it as at least a two-world system in which the material proceeds from the spiritual, and the spiritual (which is the higher order) interpenetrates the material physical world of Te Ao Mārama.

We may also conclude from the concepts of mana and tapu, and the nature of the creative acts of Io and his regents, that while the Māori thought of the physical sphere as subject to natural laws, these could be affected, modified and even changed by the application of the higher laws of the spiritual order.

In some senses, I suspect the Māori had a three-world view, of potential being symbolised by Te Korekore, the world of becoming portrayed by Te Pō, and the world of being, Te Ao Mārama.

Te Korekore

One is tempted to translate Te Korekore as the 'void'. But the traditional religious and theological ideas associated with the concept have hardened into such a rigid framework that one hesitates to use the term. Whilst it does embrace ideas of emptiness and nothingness, this by no means exhausts its meaning.

The word 'kore' means 'not, negative, nothing'. When the root of a word is doubled in Māori, it intensifies its meaning. For example 'kai' is to eat, 'kaikai' is greedy. Again, kore is an absolute concept. How is it possible to intensify that which is already absolute? By means of a thorough-going negativity, that which is negative proceeds beyond its limits and assumes the characteristics of the positive. While it does not entirely emancipate itself from the negative, it does become relatively positive. This is one of the characteristics of Io. He contains within himself all that is negative and positive, all that is passive and active.

Thus Te Korekore is the realm between non-being and being: that is, the realm of potential being. This is the realm of primal, elemental energy or latent being. It is here that the seed-stuff of the universe and all created things gestate. It is the womb from which all things proceed. Thus the Māori is thinking of continuous creation employed in two allegorical figures: that of plant growth and that of gestation in the womb. The allegory of plant growth is as follows:

> *te pū, te more, te weu, te aka, te rea, te waonui, te kune, te whē.*
> *primary root, tap root, fibrous roots, trunk, tendrils, massed branches, buds, fronds.*

That for human birth proceeds:

> *te apunga, te aponga, te kune-roa, te popoko-nui, te popoko-roa, hine-*
> *awaawa, tamaku, rangi-nui a tamaku.*
> conception, the first signs of swelling, the distended womb, the distended
> vagina, contraction, membrane ruptured, first stage of delivery and final
> stage.

Both allegories are made explicit in the recital of the different realms.

> *Te Korekore i takea mai, ki Te Pō-tē-kitea, Te Pō-tangotango, Te Pō-*
> *whāwhā, Te Pō-namunamu ki te wheiao, ki Te Ao Mārama.*
>
> *From the realm of Te Korekore the root cause, through the*
> *night of unseeing, the night of hesitant exploration, night of*
> *bold groping, night inclined towards the day and emergence*
> *into the broad light of day.*

According to the Io tradition, at the border between Hawaiki Tapu in the Pō regions is *Te Waipuna Ariki* (the divine fountain of Io the fountainhead). This is the fountain through which the primal energy of potential being proceeds from the infinite realms of Te Korekore through the realms of Te Pō into the world of light (Te Ao Mārama) to replenish the stuff of the universe as well as to create what is new. Thus it is a process of continuous creation and recreation. Te Korekore is the realm of potential being, Te Pō is the realm of becoming and Te Ao Mārama is the realm of being. Through the great path of Tāne linking these three realms there is a two-way traffic: the spirits of the departed descending to Hawaiki and that which is in the process of becoming ascending to the world of being.

Two conclusions emerge from this: the idea of continuous creation and the idea of a dynamic universe. These ideas are inclusive. The universe is not static but is a stream of processes and events. This concept also includes the idea that history is not cyclical but lineal - it is an on-going process. But the Māori did not develop the idea of a goal of history. The only hint that he aspired towards a final goal is the story of Māui's final attempt to gain eternal life for man by conquering Hine-nui-i-te-pō, guardian of the portals of night. Perhaps because of his concept of Io's utter sacredness, he could not aspire to full divinity in that sense (though the Māori regarded himself as a descendant of the gods and many of his ancestors were demigods: man today can, by fulfilling certain conditions, still wield the mana of the gods).

Each man is an event within the one ongoing procession of nature and so is each created object. Man withdraws from the mainstream of the universal process by returning to the spirit realm of Hawaiki, there to continue a spiritual existence after the pattern of the earthly one. The idea of rewards and punishment was not developed by the Māori except in the limited sense of super-heroes and demi-gods dwelling with the gods in Hawaiki-nui. Further, since the universe is dynamic and the earth is not simply *Papa* (rock foundation) but Papa-tua-nuku (rock foundation beyond expanse, the infinite), the universe itself is a process or event within the cosmic process by which Io orders creation. The ultimate reality, therefore, is Io, and the expression of this reality is the cosmic process in which all things are immersed and find their reality. So the temporal is subordinate to the eternal, the material to the spiritual, for the situation below is ordered by an ideal determination from above by Io as origin of the cosmic process.

Whether this orientation is articulated or not, it remains the subconscious attitude of the Māori and is reflected in his whole mode of thinking and the expression of it in his language and its structure. For instance, there is no verbal tense in Māori. Time is a continuous stream. The temporal is subordinated under the cosmic process and denotes not time but sequences in processes and events which occur in the cosmic process. Hence the particles 'ka', 'e...ana' and 'kua' attached to simple verbs denote the initiation, continuation and termination of particular processes and events. Again, the prepositions 'i', 'kei', 'ki' and 'hei' when joined with verbs and participles denote either the static or dynamic state of an object in relation to other objects. This characteristic is applicable to other prepositions such as 'a', 'o', 'mā', 'mō', 'nō', which, while to some extent retaining their normal functions of denoting relationships among objects, assume the predominant function of denoting the static or dynamic state of an object.

Conclusion

Sufficient has been said to show that a detailed analysis of the underlying themes of the Māori culture has never been attempted. The major task consists not in analysis of outward institutional forms, a task adequately covered by Te Rangi-hi-roa (Sir Peter Buck) and others, but in penetrating into states of mind for some kind of evaluation and understanding.

Only an approach which sets out to explore and describe the main features of the consciousness in the experience of the Māori offers any hope of adequate coverage. For the reality we experience subjectively is incapable of rational synthesis. This is why so many Māori react against the seemingly facile approach of foreign anthropologists to their attitudes, mores and values, and the affective states of mind which produce them.

I believe only a Māori from within the culture can do this adequately. Abstract rational thought and empirical methods cannot grasp the concrete act of existing which is fragmentary, paradoxical and incomplete. The only way lies through a passionate, inward subjective approach. Only a few foreigners alien to a culture, men like James K. Baxter with the soul of a poet, can enter into the existential dimension of Māori life. The grasp of a culture proceeds not from superficial intellectualism but from an approach best articulated in poetry. Poetic imagery reveals to the Māori a depth of understanding in men which is absent from the empirical approach of the social anthropologist.

The integration of an individual into full membership of society takes place over a long period of time. Not in formal schooling, but in his living situation. The process of learning, by which the raw material of the young is transformed into full citizenship, is inherent in the workings of each institution so that the instilling of values, norms and attitudes is effected by the apprenticeship to tribal life, that is, by existence in the cultural milieu. Remembering that the cultural milieu is rooted both in the temporal world and the transcendent world, this brings a person into intimate relationship with the gods and his universe.

THE NATURAL WORLD AND
_____ NATURAL RESOURCES _____
Māori Value Systems and Perspectives

Preface

The present Resource Management Law Reform being undertaken by Government is the most comprehensive yet attempted by a New Zealand Government. Granted that the system is in need of massive overhaul, the use and management of resources to which this reform is largely directed is being complicated by new and emerging factors.

The socio-economic impact of 'Rogernomics' has already had far-reaching effects on this nation. The impact is such that the socio-cultural fabric of New Zealand has been radically altered. The effects of Rogernomics has impacted more seriously upon Māoridom than any other sector. Already at the bottom of the heap, Māoridom has been shoved even further out on the socio-economic limb on to the dependency branch.

Since the creation of the Settler Government by the Crown with the 1852 Constitution Act, that Government and its successors have imposed a blatantly mono-cultural approach to legislation. By that process, the resources once owned totally by Māoridom have been appropriated by the agent of the Crown (government); which has resulted for Māoridom in 'the massive development of underdevelopment'.

Māoridom clearly sees that continued and persistent deprivation/ oppression/intrusion/imposition/manipulation of *tangata whenua* by the dominant culture/society/government, poses a serious threat to the self-esteem/

humanity/dignity/identity and very existence of present and future generations of tangata whenua.

The social disorders from which tangata whenua presently suffer are but symptoms of the mental, spiritual, organic disease, created by the colonisation process. This is demonstrated by the high-incidence and gross over-involvement of Māori in the negative areas of crime/unemployment/violence/mental and organic ill-health as confirmed by the negative statistics across the whole social spectrum.

Such deprivation and oppression has forced Māori to take an uncompromising stance on various issues to do with the Treaty of Waitangi. In terms of the resource management law reform, the Māori view would be that 'all people have a right to an environment that is adequate for health and well-being'. The objective for any authority that has to do with the environment and its resources is to ensure that resource management meets the needs of people **today** without compromising the heritage of future generations as to their needs.

This is the concern of Māoridom, under the present law review and general economic trends, the prognosis for the future generations of Māoridom, indeed of most New Zealanders, is grim indeed. Māoridom both in view of their past experience and foreknowledge of what could happen if they do not reverse the trends are saying, 'thus far and no further'.

The creation of the Waitangi Tribunal, Māori rights litigation, the maturation of Māori ideas beyond bicultural development and partnership and toward self-determination denote that they are no longer captive to the idea that patient suffering/ tolerance and so far unfounded hopes that justice and equity under the Pākehā system is a realisable goal. Having been freed from the myths created by Pākehā casuistry, they are now insisting on their guaranteed rights to 'tino rangatiratanga' which means self-determination as a realisable goal.

With the news that the United Nations will be issuing a proclamation regarding the rights of indigenous peoples to self-determination is an encouragement, and to Māori it reinforces their conviction that they were right all along.

The Māori Task Group of the Resource Management Law Reform would regard this review as crucial to defusing the likely conflict that could arise should Māori demands be once more ignored. Several basic principles are indispensable to the Review.

1.   That the general policy by which the review is ordered must not conflict with the fundamental objectives of the *tangata whenua*, for equity and justice.

2.   That we need to find common grounds on which to build agreements.

3.   That we need to have comprehensive agreement to affirm *tangata whenua* rights. These must be based on the Treaty of Waitangi and can be effected by attaching protocols to the Treaty. These protocols must define the exact meaning of the Spirit and the letter of the Treaty.

4.   Having affirmed the spirit and letter of the Treaty, then both Māori and Pākehā must work towards meeting the changing needs of all New Zealanders. A national formula for land quantum or a single settlement is not to be considered as a binding precedent for future agreements. Each agreement should vary according to the needs and potential of each iwi within their territories and for the Pākehā populace according to their needs. On this basis, we would work towards a society that meets the needs of all peoples.

5.   The process for negotiations with all the 'iwi' must be determined at the outset. This must be conducted by the Māori Task Group who, acting on the mandate of the various iwi, can negotiate with Government to reach agreements that are satisfactory to all parties.

6.   Negotiation is preferable and tidier than litigation, therefore consultation before policy decisions and legislation are determined, will avoid unnecessary conflict and litigation. Agreements, fairly negotiated and entered into freely, with the consent of all parties are far preferable to decisions imposed after lengthy, bitter and costly disputes.

7.   Before formal negotiations begin, early agreement be reached on the agenda, the timing for the negotiations, the funding for the *tangata whenua* group, for the process of ratification, and for the consultative task force.

This paper is designed to focus upon the Māori View. More specifically my brief is to define and give an account of:

-       The Māori view of the Natural World

-       The relationship between Māori and resources

-       The relevance and applicability of traditional measures employed by Māori in the use and management of resources in the present and for the future.

This subject may be approached on one of two levels:

- By isolating the various value systems inherent in Māori culture and lifting them out of context sufficient that it may provide a working brief for those responsible for formulating policy and legislation in the Resource Management Law Reform.
- Or by using the traditional holistic approach by which the Māori views the world.

Philosophy and Metaphysics

What is the nature of ultimate reality? Philosophy deals with 'the explanation that underlies all things without exception; the elements common to gods and men/to animals and stars/to the first whence and last whither/to the whole cosmic procession/the conditions of all knowing and the most general rules of human action' (W M James). More simply, it is the reach of thought beyond the foreground of life situations, to understand all time and existence, and that effort itself. It pursues answers to the three fundamental questions: What is the nature of reality, the nature of right and wrong and the grounds of valid belief? These are called respectively: metaphysics, ethics and epistemology.

As we think we live, and how we live is a pretty good indication of how we think. A man's metaphysics is the sum total of the beliefs out of which develop the basic convictions and assumptions by which he directs and guides his life. Metaphysics deals with first principles, especially those dealing with knowing and existence or being; and this metaphysics is connected with his centre.

All subjects, no matter how specialised must be connected with that centre where our most basic convictions are found. This does not mean that they are purely subjective or relative, or even mere conviction. They must approximate reality, whether in the Natural world, or the Real world behind that.

This centre is where a person must create for himself an orderly system of ideas about himself and his universe in order to give direction and purpose to his life. From that centre derive his basic convictions about the meaning and purpose of life in general and he will exhibit a sureness of touch that comes from inner clarity.

Science and Values

Science and technology produce 'know how' but it is nothing without 'know why' - a means without an end, a mere potentiality. The real problem is to turn the potential into reality in order to achieve authentic existence.

Education has devoted its efforts almost exclusively to 'know how'. To produce an integrated and well-rounded system education must include and transmit ideas of value. 'Know how' must take second place. Unless metaphysics is part of the education system, education cannot help us to choose between different options and pick our way through life. Values are more than mere formulae and dogma. They are instruments by which we view/ interpret/experience and make sense of the world.

Man is looking for abundant life and it is not true that 'knowledge is sorrow' as Ortega thought. It is poisonous error that brings unlimited sorrow - the failure to keep alive one's basic convictions. Owing to faults in metaphysical analysis the general populace is confused as to what those basic convictions were.

A truly educated person is not one who knows a little about everything, or everything about something but one who is truly in touch with his centre and has no doubts about his basic convictions. If he has faced up to the ultimate questions posed by life, his centre no longer remains in a vacuum which ingests everything that seeps into it. Those ideas are likely to lead to a denial of the meaning and purpose of life which in the end leads to total despair and meaningless. Fortunately, the heart is often wiser than the head. So he is saved from despair but lands in confusion. Only by fronting up to the questions of his fundamental conviction will he create order out of disorder.

Western Views of Ultimate Reality

These fall into three main categories: the Scientific, the view of the New Physicists and the Spiritual.

The Scientific

This view achieved its zenith in the 19th century at which time it came to rival Christianity as the worldview of ultimate reality. It spawned in its train other philosophies under the general term of Humanistic Views. The major tenets of the scientific view were:

- The universe is composed of indestructible atoms of inert matter existing in infinite space and absolute time.

It conforms to strict mechanical laws operating in an absolutely predictable manner. This was the mechanistic view which conceived of the universe as a machine or clock ticking on remorselessly.

- Since space is infinite and time absolute, the natural universe contains the whole of reality and therefore nothing can intrude or impinge upon it. It follows therefore that there is no such thing as spirit.

28

Methodology

Its methodology as based on 'observation'. We 'observe' some event, we ask what caused it to occur and we propose a tentative solution, a 'hypothesis'; we test our hypothesis ideally under controlled conditions and if our test (experiment) bears out our hypothesis, we have a theory; if we subject our theory to further exhaustive testing and we obtain the same result under all conditions at all times, we may have a general law.

Humanistic philosophies

The scientific method underlies an important assumption no longer regarded as tenable; namely, that no knowledge is genuine unless based on observable fact.

- Positivism: Valid knowledge is obtainable only through the scientific method. No knowledge is genuine except that based on observable fact.
- Evolution: Organisms evolve from lower to higher forms by the process of natural selection in which only the fittest organisms are capable of survival.
- Freudian Psychology: The higher manifestations of human life are but the dark stirrings of the subconscious mind resulting from the unfulfilled incest wishes of childhood. All higher manifestations of human life, art, religion etc. are but phantasmagorias in the brains of men.
- Relativism: Denies all absolutes/norms/values/standards

Humanism denies:
- the existence of the spiritual dimension
- all absolutes
- Norms, standards, and ethical values to which human conduct should conform
- that speculation, the methodology of the New Physicists, is valid.

The New Physicists

Towards the end of the 19th century, the validity of the Mechanistic view was being seriously questioned. Since traditional science was based upon observation, how do we apprehend those things beyond the range of human observation - in the Microcosm and Macrocosm? Can we assume that the laws that apply there are of the same order as those that apply in the Natural World? What about those intractable factors that refuse to fit into the traditional framework?

These difficulties were compounded by the New Physicists who were forced to propound ideas at variance with the accepted theories - Max Planck's Quantum theory (1900); Einstein's Relativity (1905); Heisenberg's Uncertainty principle (1926).

Reality
The New Physicists ask us to conceive of three worlds: 1. Sense-perception; 2. Real World; 3. World of Symbol. In the world of Sense-perception the methodology of traditional science obtains.

The Real World
Though we cannot directly prove its existence by observation we are compelled to assume its existence behind that of the world of sense-perception. It exists independently of us and though we cannot apprehend it by direct means we may grasp it by 'speculative' means. By this means, the New Physicists have accelerated development of new technologies, the production of an atom bomb, etc, - powerful arguments for the validity of their 'speculative' methodology.

World of Symbol
Symbols are a deliberate creation of the human mind. They are an indirect reference to some other reality, a representation of it. They are the means by which the mind creates maps/models/formulae as a means of representing/grasping/interpreting/reconciling/integrating the different orders of reality.

According to this new view, we are to conceive of Ultimate Reality as:

- a space-time continuum in which space and time are relative to each other and cannot be understood apart from each other (relativity theory).
- the universe is finite in extent and relative in time.
- reality can no longer be conceived in terms of solid atoms of inert matter but as a complex series of rhythmical patterns of energy
- in that continuum, there is no absolute rest, size, motion, and simultaneity
- under these conditions, the atom obviously needs only minimal space and time in which to exist. In other words, the universe is 'process'. If it is process, then it is more akin to mind and spirit than it is to matter. Therefore the universe is not a closed but 'open' system.

Māori Worldview

Like the New Physicists, the Māori perceived the universe as a 'process'. But they went beyond the New Physicists idea of the Real world as simply 'pure energy' to postulate a world comprised of a series of interconnected realms separated by aeons of time from which there eventually emerged the Natural World. This cosmic process is unified and bound together by spirit.

Their World of Symbol

The ancient Māori seers like the later modern physicists created sets of symbols to provide them with their maps/models to portray each state in this evolutionary process. These representations were the means by which they could apprehend/grasp/interpret/reconcile the various worlds; and grasp what they perceived as ultimate reality.

These symbols were encapsulated and couched in story/myth/legend/art/forms/proverb/ritual and liturgical action. The institution of ancestral genealogy, portrayed in minor thematic symbols as the tree developing from seed to fruit/or the sexual act culminating in the birth of the child out of the darkness of the womb into the light of the natural world were some of the main ways by which the real world was represented. Just as human genealogical tables denoted successive generations of descent, by analogy every living organism in the natural world, every tree, fish, bird or object is the result of a prior cause, of a chain or procession of events.

Each thing whether in the real or natural world has its own root foundations in the 'cosmic tree' which was sometimes depicted as having its roots in heaven and its crown on earth. But whatever symbolic representation was chosen the methodology was to recite first the actual genealogy itself and then to embed it in narrative form. The genealogy was learned by rote and provided the frame or skeleton, and the narrative form clothed it in flesh. This latter provided the explanation.

Genealogy of Creation (see Appendix Three.)

Io-taketake, creator, root-cause

Void Abyss Night

Shoot Taproot Laterals Rhizome Hair root

Seeking Pursuit Extension Expansion Energy

Primordial Memory, Deep Mind

Sub-conscious wisdom

Seed-word Breath of Life

Shape Form

Time Space

Heaven Earth (The Natural World)

Narrative Form

Io-taketake - the Ground of Being, Root Cause, Creator - stood alert in his intense and awesome *tapu*. Then he stirred himself, uttered his word into eternity and the Void, the Abyss and the Endless Night came together to form the spiritual framework in which the Cosmic process could begin to operate. Thus the seed-bed of creation, the realm of the Potential or Becoming was established.

Io-wānanga, uttered his word and the root foundation of all things were established - the seed, the shoot and the various roots. In Te Kākano, the original seed, pulsed the life-principle (mauri) impelling the shoot to emerge and branch forth as roots seeking, pursuing, extending, enlarging, spreading, increasing, urged on by its mauri from behind in its quest for being. After aeons of time that insentient movement reaching critical mass burst forth into pure energy (hihiri).

How can the potential achieve being and the process assume a meaningful purpose? Out of Te Hihiri was birthed primordial memory, which developing through deep mind, the subconscious, and consciousness achieved wisdom. Thus definite order, direction and purpose guided the process.

Transition from the world of spirit into the world of the material was now possible. Forces and events were gathering beyond the Veil (Te Ārai) which divides Night and Day.

The Breath of Life (Hau-ora) was infused into the Void and the veil was lifted to allow the Dawnlight to enter. It shattered the darkness and freed the bounds of Night to release the richness of life conceived in the womb of Te Kore and Te Kōwhao. Shape and Form came into being in Time (Wā) and Space (Ātea). Thus Heaven and Earth were formed. *Tihē Mauriora! Ki Te Wheiao, ki Te Ao Mārama!* The Life-principle emerges into the dawnlight, the broad light of day. The Natural World.

Processes of a new order now began to operate in the space-time continuum in which the world of sense-perception was located. Out of the Black Hole (Te Kōwhao) Rangi and Papa emerged clinging to each other. Dim light alone filtered between them. Into this constricted space were born their seventy children, the lesser gods who chafing at their incarceration resolved to part their parents. Under the leadership of Tāne their efforts were successful and they too emerged into the broad light of day and they became the departmental gods over natural resources. From them the myth heroes descend and from these *tupua* our *tupuna* descended.

Ultimate Reality (Māori)

- That ultimate reality is *wairua*-spirit
- The Universe is 'Process'
- *Io Taketake*, is First Cause, Ground of Being, Creator and genesis of the cosmic process.
- Spirit is ubiquitous, imminent in the total process; upholding/sustaining/replenishing/regenerating all things by its *hau* or *mauri* (Breath of Life-principle).
- As a corollary of the above, the All is One and interlocked together.
- Man is both human and divine an integral part both of the cosmic process and of the natural order.
- The Māori approach to life is holistic. There is no sharp division between culture, society and their institutions.

Because of his holistic approach the Māori avoids the disjunction between the secular and spiritual, the compartmentalisation and isolation of one institution from another, and the piecemeal approach to problem and conflict resolution.

The piecemeal approach has one major weakness. It prescribes for the symptoms rather than the real causes. The solutions are temporary and partial because the real problems are either not understood or simply ignored. Eventually the problem flares up in a more virulent form. Political legislation is particularly prone to this weakness since it is based on the adversarial system and often decisions are based upon what is expedient. A holistic approach aims at the harmonisation, integration and reconciliation of the various elements of the situation.

This piecemeal approach is clearly evident in the present Law Reform Review. Each government department does its own thing; different groups delegated the task of reviewing the different Acts proceed each from its own base and its particular brief and views. The review lacks a common integrating element which can reconcile the various groups which this review will affect. We have already witnessed this in the Fisheries controversy. The various reactions exhibit an air of hysteria. The Rogernomics thesis has produced a volatile antithesis in which it is hard to envisage an ordered satisfactory synthesis.

Culture

Culture may be defined simply as the way of life accepted and adopted by a society. Māoritanga, the term adopted by *tangata whenua* to denote his culture, means the way in which he views life and responds to life in contrast to the way other ethnic groups do. In Māori terms then, culture is that complex whole of beliefs/attitudes/values/mores/customs/knowledge acquired, evolved and transmitted by his society as guiding principles by which its members might respond to the needs and demands dictated by life and their environment.

Culture is the most powerful imprinting medium in the patterning processes of the individual. The interiorised patterns/images/stereotypes/symbols and convictions which motivate members to action organises communal activity, established social institutions and standards of behaviour. All arise out of the cultural metaphysics.

Whilst socio-cultural elements are subject to change, within this flux remains a corpus of basic convictions about reality and life. This corpus provides the thread of continuity which integrates and holds together the social fabric of a culture. Hence, despite cultural erosion and genocide as imposed by colonialist processes tangata whenua has never totally surrendered the core beliefs and value systems of their culture.

Cultural Comparisons

Dr Ranginui Walker[1] distinguishes between indigenous and metropolitan culture in the following ways:

Indigenous Culture:

- Has a universal set of principles held in common.
- Small scale in size ranging from basic family unit through extended family, to tribal confederations

- Their mythology and spiritual beliefs credit them with divine origins and descent through culture heroes.
- Rule was exercised by the chiefs, elders, and priests; but the power that they held was tempered by kinship bonds and the need to validate leadership by generous and wise rule.
- Consensus decision-making was the method of operation for the achievement of social and political goals.
- They think of themselves as holding a special relationship to Mother Earth and her resources; as an integral part of the natural order; recipients of her bounty rather than controllers and exploiters of their environment. Therefore Mother Earth is to be treated with reverence, love and responsibility rather than abuse and misuse.
- Spiritual and social values, e.g. mana/tapu/generosity/sharing/caring/hospitality/service/fulfilling one's social obligations were the cardinal values.

Comments upon Rule and Policy

In Māori culture, rule by recognised leaders and consensus decision making were but two aspects of the one process. Determining social and political goals was a people process. Policy meetings were held in open forum on the marae where free speech prevailed.

These policy meetings took place at the levels of the whānau/hapū and iwi. Each was free at any level to agree or disagree.

- Whānau: At this level every adult was free to express his/her opinion and view.
- Hapū: At the tribal level the *māngai* (mouthpieces) presented the considered views of their particular whānau group
- Iwi: At the tribal confederations, the hapū representatives drawn from the whānau groups expressed the view of their tribe.

After much discussion, the consensus view would begin to emerge and minor differences would be reconciled until concord was achieved. But should a whānau or hapū disagree they signified their dissent with the words: "Waiho mai mātou ki waho" - leave us out. That decision would be respected. Once consensus was reached, the leaders committed their group to the *take* - policy and then set out organising their particular group to carry it out.

Democracy as espoused by its modern exponents in terms of 'one person one vote' is not 'rule by the people' as the term means, but refers rather to the means by which the electoral process is carried out. The voter's options are limited between two or more parties. Under the present system, that opportunity occurs once every three years. From this point the members of

Parliament and the bureaucrats become the policy and decision makers.

Māoridom by contrast ensured people involvement at each stage for the leaders had to report back and justify their stance should it be a departure from the original whānau or hapū policy.

Metropolitan Culture

- Macroscale aggregation of people.
- Infrastructure of centralised political power/legal system/judiciary/ military; and a bureaucracy through which power is devolved down to the regional/local level.
- Government, with the exception of dictatorships, is founded on the quasi-democratic principle of 'one person one vote'. But this is for purely elective purposes. Policy is determined by government and the bureaucrats not by the people at large.
- Secular and spiritual disconnection leads to compartmentalisation of social and political institutions which produce ethical standards peculiar to that institution. This produces in turn a relativism, confined within the framework of 'situational' ethics - legal/church/business/professional etc. Many of these are concerned with ensuring group solidarity and protectionism, group interests and power rather than with ethical considerations.

Orientation of Metropolitan Culture

Because of the influence of humanistic philosophies, especially Relativism, Metropolitan cultural bases are in a state of continual flux.

Whilst these theoretical changes continue to occur, an unchanging constant is the idea that the most important thing in life is achievement. The majority no longer asks who a person is but what is he in his work/calling/status/position.

This modern approach finds it roots in the Calvinistic idea of election or predestination - that some are elected to eternal happiness and others to damnation. Stress was laid on everyday works, the duty of one's calling; and success in these as the stamp of divine approval and proof of one's election. (My comment is that in the fact of rising unemployment, limbo is going to be somewhat crowded).

This attitude became pervasive and the more the modern economic system prevailed the more did unremitting diligence/strict discipline/achievement and success become the cardinal virtues of secular man. All round ability became the supreme virtue/profit, the object of ambition, struggle and worship. And achievement the prime value of the modern efficiency orientated society.

In a dynamically developing world, western man attempts to realise himself through his own achievements. By achieving something, he 'is' something - work/career/earning money; producing/expanding/consuming; growth/efficiency/improvements in living standards; - this is the meaning of life.

Values that revolve around economics rank uppermost. This value overrides human/neighbour/race considerations; restricts vision to self as centre of the universe; allows and/or condemns a person to the prison of the anonymous, impersonal mechanised techniques/powers/organisations of the system. The greater the so-called progress, the more deeply enmeshed a person becomes in the socio-economic process.

The network of norms/sanctions evolved under the system controls him mercilessly in his calling/work/leisure. Prohibitions/laws/precepts, like those under the present law reform review no less, seek to meet the demands of a life thoroughly organised/regulated/bureaucratised/computerised. So a person loses his autonomy/spontaneity/initiative/identity/humanity. His life has become an achievement game. He justifies his existence in terms of his achievements and performance before his society/boss/himself rather than before the judgement seat of God.

Can he be happy in this way and remain human? TV programmes like Dallas/Falcon Crest/Dynasty demonstrate graphically that a person may be a marvellous organiser/executive/manager/director and fail miserably as a human being. What I am really saying is that whilst achievement has value, it is 'not decisive'.

Though not against achievement as such, Jesus was firmly opposed to making 'achievement' in itself the measure of being human. He did not claim any special privileges on the basis of who he was or had achieved. He let God justify him in the fact of the defenders of pious works. Applying this principle to the Colonisation process and the systems derived therefrom; Māoridom has decided to oppose strongly a monocultural system that condemns him to the loss of self-esteem, humanity and dignity. The resurgence in Māoridom is a direct response to that threat.

Māori Values

'How do you legislate for spiritual values?' This question was posed to the Royal Commission on Social Policy by a member of Treasury. A study of the Bible especially in relation to Mosaic Law is the short answer. But I suspect the poser of the question was being deliberately obtuse. This is one of those catch-questions which reflects a negative attitude to spiritual things generally. On the premise that the universe is 'One' and that spirit being immanent in all things is 'ultimate reality', then no real distinction exists between spiritual, socio-cultural and socio-economic values.

Taonga

'Where your treasure is, there will your heart be also.' These words of Jesus sum up the Māori view of the link between desire and end denoted by the phrases *manawa-pā* and *ngākau-pā* - Objects which touch the soul or heart; that is, the soul or heart's desire.

Generally speaking it is customary to denominate those ends which are desired for their own sake as values. States of mind which are 'good' in themselves are therefore those which consist in the pursuit, apprehension or enjoyment of values.

Definition: There is no specific term in Māori for the word value. With his holistic view of the Universe the Māori idea of value is incorporated into the inclusive holistic term 'taonga' - a treasure, something precious; hence an object of good or value. The object or end valued may be tangible or intangible; material or spiritual. *Taonga*, e.g. a *mere pounamu* - greenstone *mere* is so regarded for its utilitarian, cultural, social or simply its aesthetic value.

- utilitarian; as a weapon
- historico - social; as an heirloom of historical associations with people and events.
- cultural and social; as a tangible symbol to seal a peace pact, or an alliance between tribes; or to commemorate an important social occasion or event.
- spiritually, to denote the 'mana' of those ancestors who wielded it with distinction.

Taonga then, denote the 'end' or 'good', which are desired for themselves, as values. In this context of Taonga as value, the whole range of cultural elements bequeathed by their forebears to their descendants as legacy or birthright are classified as:

Ngā taonga a ngā tūpuna - ancestral treasures
Taonga tuku iho - treasures bequeathed
Ohaaki a ngā tūpuna - guidelines, maxims of the ancestors

These taonga refer to the cultural tradition, lore, history; corpus of knowledge etc, with which the descendants can identify and which provide them with their identity, self-esteem and dignity; that which provides them with psychological security.

Even death was regarded as a taonga for that is the 'greenstone door' that led to ultimate reality and rest. Processes of assimilation and cultural genocide imposed upon *tangata whenua* have robbed them of much of their taonga resulting in the loss of dignity, self-esteem, and identity. This loss results in the displacement due to cultural erosion, under assimilationist policies, of the basic metaphysics by which members of a culture guide their life. Cultural genocide produces spiritual and psychological insecurity manifested in negative social behaviour whose outward symptoms are crime, violence, mental ill-health and other social disorders.

Now the cultural metaphysics or basic convictions which provide a people's guidelines to life evolve over generations of life experience in which succeeding generations add their quota of knowledge and fresh discoveries to the corpus of their cultural heritage. The customs and traditions of previous generations based on their beliefs and attitudes regarding the nature of ultimate reality, of the universe, and of man are the foundation stones upon which the mores, standards and values of the culture are founded. The mores, standards and values comprise the body of the cultural metaphysics.

Categories of Value
Values may be divided into three major categories corresponding to the needs relative to the various levels of the human personality - spiritual, psychological and biological. Primacy of value in descending order is accorded respectively to the spiritual, psychological and biological.

Spiritual values
Spiritual values are always beyond the full grasp of mortal man. They are ultimate and absolute in nature and yet always beckoning man onwards. The closer one approximates to the ideal the greater the satisfaction. There is always a gap between the ideal and practice; between becoming and being; but towards that excellence all things strive. The Māori expression is, 'Kia eke ki tōna taumata' - that it may attain to the excellence of its being; or, to authentic existence. This refers not only to humans but to all created things.

Now, the goal of human endeavour is to achieve 'atuatanga' - divinity, This is the meaning and purpose of life. The two major attributes of divinity are mana and tapu - authority and power, holiness. Mana and tapu are spiritual qualities to which all may aspire and they are therefore ends which may be denominated as values.

Psychological
Psychological security as sense of belonging/sense of safety/source of approval as prerequisites to self-esteem, identity and dignity are provided by the members of one's society. But such benefits demand reciprocal response from beneficiaries. Thus the psychological values of a culture are viewed as social in nature - sharing, caring, fulfilling one's obligations to society.

Biological

Since man needs food, shelter, clothing to meet his basic needs, material resources and goods are valued as the means by which those needs which enable man to survive are met.

Cardinal Spiritual Values

> *Haere mai te mana!*
> *Haere mai te tapu!*
> *Haere mai te ihi!*
> *Haere mai te wehi!*
> *Welcome to the authorities!*
> *Welcome to the sacred ones!*
> *Welcome original charismatic ones!*
> *Welcome original awesome ones!*

This is a traditional welcome accorded to the authorities and dignitaries of Māoridom. It accords honour to those divinely chosen people invested with the divine gifts of authority, power, charisma and sacredness and whose presence carry an aura of the numinous eliciting awe in the beholder.

Mana is divine authority and power bestowed upon a person divinely appointed to an office and delegated to fulfil the functions of that office. This divine choice is confirmed by the elders, and initiated by the tohunga under the traditional consecratory rites (tohi) by which the divine spirit is called down to empower the person with authority (mana) and hau (breath of spirit) and mauri (the life-principle).

From a social perspective, mana enhances a person's prestige giving him authority to lead, initiate, organise and regulate corporate communal expeditions and activities; to make decisions regarding social and political matters.

Tapu may be defined generally as the sacred. It is a concomitant of mana, for a person of mana is ipsofacto a tapu person. Any person, place or thing invested with divine mana is 'set aside' for a specific purpose being placed under the divine mantle. Thus tapu removes a person, place or thing from ordinary secular association and use. This element of 'separation' or being 'set apart' is a basic element of tapu. Under Israelite law, strict prohibitions related to their prophets or priests under the decree; 'Touch not my anointed'. This is the prohibitive element of tapu.

Tapu has an 'unclean' aspect. Burial sites, the dead, those things under the dark gods and demonic influence are unclean. Tapu, whether sacred or unclean, is ingested by association or contact. Hence a person who touches a corpse, builds a house on a burial site or enters a cemetery becomes unclean or contaminated. To resume normal secular activities and avoid contaminating others, that person must undergo ritual cleansing.

Because of this prohibitive aspect, tapu persons, places or things may not be interfered with or transgressed. Such transgression invites divine retribution - illness, death, mental ill-health, misfortune. Persons under tapu must observe strict laws of behaviour and conduct in regard to both their personal lives and in the conduct and operation of sacred ritual. To act carelessly in such matters weakens or results in the loss of personal mana and tapu.

Ihi is psychic force in contradistinction to spiritual power. A person may operate at either one or both levels. Ihi is not mental power but mental force. The former is akin to a person's IQ, the latter is related to the will. Ihi then is will power, a psychic force which through the charisma that character-ises it, marks out a true leader, confident and decisive in his actions; or a carver secure in his technical ability to produce a work of art to portray and reflect the reality which his vision perceives; or a warrior confident in his ability and skill in battle. Like mana and tapu, ihi engenders awe because of its numinous qualities.

Wehi is the sense of awe or fear generated by the mysterious and numinal forces that emanate from a person of mana, tapu and ihi. These numinal qualities together form the basis upon which the divine sanctions of a culture operate within society to regulate behaviour.

Together with hau, mauri, wana and other spiritual properties of a similar kind they form a powerful interlocking system which provide socio-cultural mechanisms of control in regulating behaviour, motivating, guiding and managing corporate activities; ensuring that tradition is observed; stress-ing the importance and the necessity for concentrated effort to be applied to different activities, or phases of it, e.g. kumara planting. The processes associ-ated with kumara planting - preparing the seed-beds/planting/weeding/har-vesting and storing; were conducted under strict laws of tapu with the appro-priate ritual prayers. Similarly the carving of a meeting house was a sacred task hedged about with prohibitive laws of tapu.

Social Values
Society provides its members with psychological security. For this provision, members are expected to reciprocate by contributing their skills, labour or goods to contribute to the social pool. Because the members were united on the basis of kinship ties the whānau or hapū group was regarded as organism rather than organisation. That is, that the group shared a corporate life and each individual an integral member of that body or organism performing a particular function and role. Therefore, to serve others is to serve the corpo-rate self. Thus loyalty, generosity, caring, sharing, fulfilling one's obligations

41

to the group, was to serve one's extended self.

These then, were the socio-psychological values - social in value because of the awareness of kinship and family ties; psychological in value because of the sense of security, of belonging to a group with which one was intimately united. The prime social values were summed up by the term *aroha* - charity, love; a concept general throughout Polynesia.

To operate in aroha reaped the rewards of social approval, honour, esteem and whilst this was a motivating factor, equally important was the sense of obligation which could entail sacrifice even unto death upon the part of a member.

Contrast with Hedonism

According to the hedonistic theory, there are not a 'number' of values but only 'one'; namely, pleasure or happiness. Our actions and aspirations are motivated by selfish desire for the sake of happiness which we expect to gain there from. A variant of this view is psychological hedonism which affirms that we are so constituted that we can only desire our own pleasure.

This philosophy finds its justification in the subjectivist view that what we desire and value are determined by forces and factors beyond our control. From this, the conclusion is drawn that we are in the final analysis controlled by our desires. Biology reinforces this view by portraying man as an organism of a particular species endowed with instincts, traits and drives appropriate to that species. Anthropology on the other hand, views man as a member of a group conditioned by the imprinting processes of his culture.

These theories run contrary to experience and the facts of life. Nelson Mandela cannot be happy being incarcerated in prison. His motives are not instinctive, nor those of the self-seeker, but of a person concerned for the plight of his people. He seeks to see the ends of justice being served.

Mother Theresa articulates her motives thus: 'The world lacks love and it is our duty to share our love with others, especially the poor'.

The characteristic ignored by the hedonists is that in addition to the desires and instincts which drive a person to do something, there is consciousness of something other which tells him what he 'ought' to do. In other words most people have a sense of 'moral obligation' - and in possessing that moral sense he is free, free from determination by natural circumstances. Values are not concerned simply with desires and wants but also with moral obligations - a sense of right, wrong, fairness, justice.

These are ethical attributes which, because man is not purely animal determined by instinct, but is intelligent and spiritual as well; are innate in human character and frees him to act above the pull of his lower nature, should he will to do so.

Hedonism can find roots only in a society where the disjunction between the secular and spiritual, between economic and theological disciplines, between the human and divine, between the family and nation have occurred. It happens in nuclear-type societies symbolic of metropolitan culture with its quarter-acre sections bounded by fences and hedges; by numbered tenement flats.

Māori social values are based on social obligations which always entail a measure of self-sacrifice, a commitment not simply to one's family unit but to extended family (whānau), to the tribe (hapū), and to one's people (iwi).

Material Values

Material values are related to those material objects and natural resources which directly supply our basic needs and wants for food, shelter and clothing; or related to wealth and capital by which those needs may be supplied indirectly. Natural resources are drawn directly from our natural environment.

The means by which those resources are used and managed will depend on how we view and relate to our environment.

Before Pietism arose, Western Reformation theology paralleled Māori thinking in regarding all life as unified and their view of life was not fragmented nor were their institutions compartmentalised. Christian concern was not confined to the Church and its activities but embraced politics, economics, education, science, industry, commerce, welfare, health, etc.

The Pietists, reacting against formalism, adopted the Platonic dualistic view of the universe and partitioned life into the secular and spiritual. This view was reinforced by scientific methodology which isolated component elements or particular fields for intensive study. This process of isolation carried over into the partitioning of social institutions. Meanwhile the Pietists retired into their ivory castles and exclusiveness. Much of western religious activity and mission became irrelevant to those concerned with the everyday concerns of meeting basic biological needs.

The unifying thread, the spiritual dimension had been withdrawn. Institutional, political, social, professional, class differences arose to divide and fragment life. As Metropolitan Culture continues to become more complex so the potential for social fragmentation increases proportionately. Māori culture with its emphasis on spirituality offers both a philosophy and theology to provide that unifying element to reconcile the disjunction between the secular and the spiritual created by the mental attitude endemic in Western culture. By this means harmony and balance may be restored to the Natural Order.

The Natural Order
Mauri

Immanent within all creation is *mauri* - the life-force which generates, regenerates and upholds creation. It is the bonding element that knits all the diverse elements within the Universal 'Procession' giving creation its unity in diversity. It is the bonding element that holds the fabric of the universe together.

A synonym for mauri in certain contexts is 'hau' (breath). 'Hau-ora' - 'the breath of life' is the agent or source by and from which mauri (life-principle) is mediated to objects both animate and inanimate. *Mauri-ora* and *hau-ora* as applied to animate objects are synonymous. Mauri without the qualifying adjective 'Ora' (life) is applied to inanimate objects; whilst hau is applied only to animate life.

A popular misconception that Māori culture held an animistic view of the world needs to be corrected. It arose because Western anthropologists were not aware:

a. of the fine distinction between the terms mauri and hau;

b. that because mauri and hau, both spiritual in nature, indwelt all things it was assumed that the Māori regarded all material objects as being indwelt by spirits.

c. Māori did believe that certain trees, or spots, or other objects had guardian spirits dwelling there. This did not mean that that spirit was the spirit of the tree, and animated it. Rather, a spirit could use a tree or place, a river, or even a person as a home. For this reason such spirits could be driven out.

Mauri was a force or energy mediated by hauora - the breath of the spirit of life. Mauri-ora was the life-force (mauri) transformed into life-principle by the infusion of life itself.

Papatuanuku

Like the Greek 'Ge or Gaia', a personification of Earth, the Māori term *Papatuanuku* - 'Land from beyond the veil; or originating from the realm beyond the world of sense-perception', was the personified form of *whenua* - the natural earth.

Papatuanuku was conceived by tangata whenua as the Primordial Mother who married Rangi (Sky Father) and became the female parent who birthed the departmental gods and humankind. These gods were of a lower order delegated to take charge over the elements - winds, forest, cultivated crops, etc.

Whenua was the term for Natural Earth. It was also the term for 'after-birth' - placenta. This use of the term 'whenua' served as a constant reminder that we are born out of the womb of the primeval mother.

Papatuanuku is our mother and deserves our love and respect. She is a living organism with her own biological systems and functions creating and supplying a web of support systems for all her children whether man, animal, bird, tree, grass, microbes or insects.

Papatuanuku's children live and function in a symbiotic relationship. From unicellular through to more complex multicellular organisms each species depends upon other species as well as its own, to provide the basic biological needs for existence. The different species contribute to the welfare of other species and together they help to sustain the biological functions of their primeval mother, herself a living organism. They also facilitate the processes of ingestion, digestion and waste disposal... they cover her and clothe her to protect her from the ravages of her fierce son, *Tāwhiri* the Storm-bringer. She nourishes them, they nourish her.

Because Papatuanuku belongs to the older primeval order, her sustenance derives not only from the mauri active within her but is supported by members of that order. Though she was separated from Rangi the sky father by their first children, he still weeps for her and the rain of his tears provides the moisture for her cleansing and drinking. He gives her light, air, warmth, elements needed for her sustenance.

Papa's Consciousness

The genealogy of creation occurs in stages in which one order, after it has reached its culmination takes a giant leap forward to be succeeded by a radical departure resulting in the introduction of a new stage. That process is illustrated by the stages, void--root foundations--energy-consciousness--spirit--form--a new space/time continuum--*Ranginui* and *Papatuanuku*. (See Appendix Three.)

This process of cosmic change is discernible as natural and biological evolution in the natural world, rock--quartz--crystal, or in the biological mutations that can occur. Each stage of the change occurs in a time-frame which may be likened to a compartment. In the natural world, these compartments contain distinctive elements of particular orders of being; inanimate--animate--consciousness--spirit.

What is the goal of the cosmic process? In order to understand what a thing is, we do not go to the lower but to the higher. If we want to understand what a quartz is, we do not go to the rock from which it was formed but to the crystal into which it is becoming. A ploughed field is understood when a shoot of corn appears in it. It is understood by the entry into it of something higher, of life itself.

The end to which man is moving is towards perfect spirituality when consciousness has achieved omega point and spirituality comes into its own, freed from the restrictions and constraints of time and space.

The conditions by which this happy event may occur is latent within the milieu of our environment. On our realisation of this truth and adjusting to it will depend the speed by which mankind will achieve its omega point when he will move into a higher consciousness. This will mean a change in attitude towards ourselves and to our environment - our relationship with our universe, and others. In our relationship with Mother Earth we must understand that we are:

- the conscious mind of Mother Earth and our contribution is to enhance and maintain her life support systems
- to treat her with love and reverence as our primeval mother.
- that we are not owners or despots over mother earth but recipients and therefore stewards

We are, however, rapists, despoilers, pillagers of mother earth. We waste, exploit, denude and pollute the earth. We exploit the natural resources, denude the forests, pollute the air and the seas apart from the land, scar the earth, and abuse and misuse the gifts she gives us. Cyclone Bola demonstrated dramatically that to abuse and misuse the earth for the sake of a 'fast buck' invites mother earth to present the bill and force us to pay.

A new sense of awareness, new attitudes are required to turn us completely round. Attitudes to counter the organisation/regulation/bureaucratic/consumer /production/expansionist/materialistic mentality. Awareness, that we are an integral part of the cosmic process, of the unity within all creation, that we are an integral part of the natural order which is no less sacred than the spiritual order, that we are to flow with the cosmic process rather than oppose its legitimate course for our own selfish ends. Only then can we restore and maintain the harmony and balance which successive generations of humankind have arrogantly disrupted.

The function of humankind as the envelope of the noosphere - conscious awareness of Papatuanuku - is to advance her towards the omega point of fulfilment. This will mean a radical departure from the modern concept of man as the centre of the universe towards an awareness that man's destiny is intimately bound up with the destiny of the earth.

He will recognise then that what is less than human, both the inanimate and animate, is also sacred. Thus will he embrace a holistic view which encompasses all life. He will thus learn to flow with and ride upon the vibrant energies of the Cosmic stream. He will then learn the hidden truth that in him we live and move and have our being. So will he overcome his sense of isolation, that estrangement which breeds despair - the encounter with nothingness. Only then will he recognise inwardly that he has come home.

Traditional Measures (their relevance and applicability)
Introduction
We are now in a position to answer the question posed earlier, "How do we legislate for spiritual values?" I doubt that it is possible to legislate for spiritual values. The letter kills. It is the spirit that gives life. Certain measures may be introduced, and legislation may be promulgated to regulate the use and management of resources but it is an inherent tendency within man to either evade or actively oppose legislation that militates against his self-interest.

The spirit gives life. The spiritual aspects behind legislation that has to do with the ownership, use and management of natural resources are:

- the awareness that all life, including what is less than human, is sacred
- that in our relationship with other users that they have rights, that considerations of justice, equity, sharing, caring and aroha must be taken into account

In other words, there must be a commitment to the principles behind that legislation which will not be achieved by enforcement but by a change of attitude effected through intensive continuing education. Commitment to truth and to higher values is a way of life which makes legislation superfluous.

Ecosystems and Kawa
Wairua (spirit) or *hau* (the breath of the divine spirit) is the source of existent being and life. Mauri is the elemental essence imparted by wairua:

- to give uniqueness and being to each individual object; and it is that element that is immanent in all things knitting and bonding them together. Out of this double function of mauri is created unity within diversity.
- it is the basic building block of the universe around which *hihiri* - elemental energy coalesces and with which it merges to generate and bring the process into the actuality of existent being.

Kawa, to borrow theological terminology, is 'liturgical action'. It is applied to the way in which the progressive steps of a religious ritual is ordered. Strict rules were applied to the conduct of kawa and any mistake or contravention of the ritual or failure to complete the ritual was a transgression (hapa) and

47

was taken as an ill-omen.

Now the various species and orders partook of mauri and for that reason were tapu to a greater or lesser degree. Each class, type, species and genus was under the protection of its tutelary deity - Tāne of trees and man, Rongo of crops and vegetation, Tāwhiri of the weather, Ruaumoko of minerals, volcanoes and so on.

For these reasons the tapu of a thing had to be removed and the tutelary deity of a tree, fish, etc, had to be propitiated before it could be freely utilised. Trees, birds, fish and other resources each had its kawa. A meeting house or marae had its kawa both to remove the tapu and to dedicate them. In other words, kawa was the ritual approach to all things.

Behind the institution of kawa and its use lay a host of attitudes, ideas, and cultural perspectives. A sense of reverence for life, of the fitting and proper way of treating things, an awareness of the spiritual essence, of the wana (aura of splendour, the glory) that radiates from all animate life and a sense of their numinal qualities.

These perceptions prevent the careless, inconsiderate and wasteful use of resources, the careless disposal of wastes and the extravagant and prodigious wastage, exploitation, pillaging, despoilation, destruction, denudation and pollution of our environment.

Before any corporate activity or expedition, any work was undertaken, it was customary to say prayers, to conduct the kawa at the beginning, during the course and at the end of a particular activity. It gave pause to reflect upon the intention and outcomes of a particular enterprise, the onerous responsibilities involved and the personal discipline required to achieve the outcomes desired.

Such practices are still observed by tangata whenua. But I am cynical about its adoption and feasibility in Pākehā culture. The 'go-get-'em' belligerent consumer mentality and the capitalistic values that drive its adherents in the obsessive pursuit of increased production, expansion, consumption, growth and efficiency as advocated by 'Rogernomics' and Treasury is fast becoming endemic in Western capitalistic society. Time is money and who's going to waste time on the intangibles of spiritual and cultural values. 'A bird in the hand is worth two in the bush.' It is a case of the 'survival of the fittest'. Efficiency, ability, profit, achievement; these are the laws and gospel of the modern efficiency-orientated society.

Perhaps we have gone beyond the point of 'no return' and now Papatuanuku the earth mother will herself take a hand in the destruction that man is perpetrating upon his fellow-man. If immediate outcomes do not come about through prayer, at least its practice could give us pause to reflect and help modify and restrain our self-destructive tendencies.

Kawa can and may provide the means by which the balance and harmony within the ecosystem may be sustained.

Rāhui and Mauri

The institution of rāhui fulfilled two main functions:

a. For the purpose of conserving or replenishing a resource - fish, birds, etc - a rāhui was imposed upon the area affected, a river, forest, lake, harbour which banned people from utilising the resources within the prohibited area. The area was monitored and when it was considered that the resource had regenerated itself sufficiently, the tapu was lifted in accordance with the appropriate kawa and the resource restored to general use.

b. Rāhui was imposed on the occasion of drowning and/or an accidental death on a harbour or place where the death occurred for perhaps a month or whatever period was determined. It was an appropriate way of observing the proprieties surrounding the occasion – of the loss of a member of the whānau – of paying respect to his memory, of conveying in concrete terms to the family their support and sympathy and also allowing time for the tapu associated with the death to be dispensed naturally by the cleansing powers of the natural elements of air, sun and rain.

The concept of Mauri (Life-force), plays a vital role in the institution of rāhui. The relationship between them rests upon the following principles.

- The cosmic process as designed by the creator is a movement from the 'lower' to 'higher', from potential to authentic being. There is therefore a meaning and purpose inherent within it. That final purpose is yet to be fulfilled.
- Mauri as life-force is the energy within creation which impels the cosmic process onwards towards fulfilment. The processes within the physical universe aretherefore 'pro-life' and the law of self-regeneration latent within creation will, if not interfered with, tend towards healing and harmonising the eco-systems and biological functions within Mother Earth.
- We have seen that in the movement from lower to higher each stage of the process occupies aeons of time and when it has achieved its 'omega' point it makes a giant leap forward and a radical departure occurs at the time of transition like a bud bursting into bloom.
- Since the transformation occurs at the apex of each stage; namely, its

high-test point of achievement, then the next stage has to do with the transformation of the conscious into the 'super-conscious' – from *Whakaaro* to *Wānanga*. (See Appendix Three.)

From the Māori point of view, that transition and transformation will result in the perfect comprehension of the higher spiritual laws ever sought by the ancient seers (tohunga) to enable mankind to flow in union with the universal process and thereby become fully creative. This is man's transition from the purely human into *atuatanga* (divinity) whose manifestation has already become evident in the lives of the saints and seers of various peoples and religions.

This *atuatanga* will mean the perfect blend and union of mind and spirit in which the gift of *matakite* (enlightenment) will allow man to exercise mana (authority, power) responsibly in perfect wisdom and freedom. Thus will he creatively lift up and transform creation itself.

Rāhui in this context points to the double function that mankind must exercise as stewards responsible for his environment.

a. To prohibit exploitation, denudation, degeneration and pollution of the environment and its resources beyond the point of no return where the latent 'pro-life' processes within the biological functions and ecosystems of Papatuanuku collapse.

b. That man, as the conscious mind of Papatuanuku, aids the pro-life processes of recovery and regeneration by focussing the mauri of particular species within that area. The means of accomplishing this was the task of the tohunga who by his knowledge and art drew forth the mauri of the universe and concentrated it within a stone or some other object which was then secretly placed within the area – forest, sea, river. From this source, the aura of the mauri would radiate outwards both to the environment and more specifically to the particular species for which it was intended. Thus mauri created benevolent conditions within the environment to harmonise the processes within earth's ecosystems and aid the regeneration process.

Those with powers of spiritual insight and perception (matakite) perceived mauri as an aura of light and energy radiating from all animate life. It is now possible to photograph this mauri in living things.

Summary
Our previous outline of the various worldviews and comparative studies of cultural values summarise man's relationship to the physical universe.

1. That man is answerable to a creator for the manner in which he treats the natural world and exercises his power over the use and management of resources.
2. That the universe has a spirit and life of its own, a spirit and life (wairua and mauri) immanent within creation which must be respected and supported. Man's well-being corresponds with the well-being of the earth. One and two may be viewed apart or combined as one entity.
3. That the universe is physical and material and that man is autonomous and answerable only to himself. There is no real restriction on his actions except that which is self-imposed or that imposed by his society which may hold differing value judgements.

Man's relationship to the universe will thus be determined by which of the foregoing views he adopts. He will regard his role and function according to that choice. Hence he may regard himself as steward, guardian or lord respectively over the universe. Māoridom subscribes to the first two views whilst Westerners subscribe to the third.

Western man either because he holds to the traditional scientific view, or because of the pietistic disjunction between the secular and spiritual, approaches his environment with the idea that there are no constraints on his powers to exploit the natural resources to serve his private needs and ends. Resources are regarded as a commodity whose value is judged by its price in the market place. This attitude is being increasingly challenged. In the New Zealand situation the challenge is coming not only from Māoridom but from Pākehā Conservationists.

Contemporary Environmental Problems
Metropolitan Culture is confronted by a plethora of problems relating to the use and management of resources. The problems are recognised but the solutions are a matter of controversy. There is a conflict between economic and ethical values, between the scientific, pragmatic and the theological, moral, between the value systems of one culture and another.
As regards the environment, the problems relate to those of damaging residues relating to industrial wastes and pollution, to the use of natural resources and sustainability, the conservation of nature for the sake of its well-being, and the problems of population growth and depletion of resources.

Thus central to the environmental problem is the question of ensuring that the various value judgements are given due regard and the right decisions are made. On the view that environmental and Māori cultural concerns are a luxury, the Department of Treasury, reflecting the Rogernomic economic approach, promotes the view that resource conservation is to be considered according to the laws of the market place or those of supply and demand or when the economy is right. For instance, though the inshore fishery is on the verge of biological collapse, it is argued that because the economy is self-regulating, when the price of fish has dropped then demand will also drop. Hence, self-regulating measures will be imposed automatically thus conserving the resource. This is a pipe dream.

But the avoidance of environmental concerns or the flippant attitude of Treasury will not eliminate the problems. Nor will the avoidance of basic issues relevant to the Treaty. Our responsibilities are not simply to satisfy private interest groups, or simply to overcome immediate economic problems. Our responsibilities are personal, moral, socio-cultural.

Environmental problems are not new. They are as ancient as man himself. What is new is:

1.   The development of modern technology whose sophistication and efficiency has enormously accelerated the rate by which natural resources are drawn off and expended thus threatening to:

- deplete and exhaust non-renewable resources
- disrupt ecosystems by changing the face of the earth in flagrant disregard for the consequences
- build up non-degradable wastes difficult to eradicate
- sterilise the earth by destroying organisms essential to the maintenance of the equilibrium of earth's organic and biological functions through the use of chemical wastes and highly effective pesticides

2.   Population growth and spread of mankind whose demands for the supply of its basic biological needs and improvements of living standards exacerbate the pressures already imposed upon the environment and natural resources. At present rates of exploitation, the collapse of much of earth's biological systems is a real threat to the quality of life we leave for future generations and the existence of man on earth.

Conclusion

In the final analysis the real problem stems back to man himself. He is in disharmony with the cosmic process, with this physical universe; and what is more pathetic, within his own ranks internationally, nationally, locally, culturally, socially, economically, politically, legally, philosophically, metaphysically, theologically and religiously.

Only a massive turn around of attitudes and a commitment to the best and highest within him can redirect his course towards an affirmative life-style free from the seeds of destruction inherent within his present systems.

It will only be effected when we break out of the strait-jacket of the pragmatic, materialistic and positivistic ideologies based upon the capitalistic value systems which hold that the positivist ideology is the basis for rational planning and control. It has two basic weaknesses:

- In its consensual aspect it makes no allowance for other alternatives and allows the world 'as it is' to remain unquestioned whether it is right or wrong, just or unjust thereby confirming the status quo. Its very limited parameters have an inhibiting effect upon the solutions offered. Secondly, education must not neglect the teaching of metaphysics concerning the fundamental questions and convictions of life. It must break out of its strait-jacket.

- Liberal studies have plunged us into a morass of confusion in which mind and heart are at war with one another and reason beclouded by an extraordinary and unreasoning faith in its reasoning powers spawns sets of fantastic life-destroying ideas. Sciences are taught without adequate awareness of the presuppositions of science; of the meaning and significance of scientific laws; and the place of science in the totality of human thought.

- Economics is taught without reference to a basic view of human nature.

- Political thinking is unrelated to metaphysics and the moral and ethical problems involved.

- Social theory is based on a pragmatic approach to human nature and symptoms rather than causes and prescribed for.

Only a metaphysic that provides an integrative element across the whole spectrum of life, which produces a holistic approach to life, can unify its diverse elements and allow us to achieve a balance and harmony conducive to life abundant.

Endnote
1. This paper is both undated and unpublished. It was written during the late 1970s or early 1980s. Personal correspondence from Dr. Ranginui Walker.

KAITIAKITANGA
A Definitive Introduction to
the Holistic Worldview of the Māori

Introduction

The purpose of the Resource Management Act 1991[1] is to promote the sustainable management of natural and physical resources (Section 3(1)). By definition, 'sustainable' management includes the protection of the community's enjoyment of those natural and physical resources. In achieving those purposes, matters of national importance are specified. One of those matters is a requirement to recognise and provide for the relationship of Māori and their culture and traditions with their ancestral lands, water, sites, *wāhi tapu* and other *taonga.*

One of the major concerns for Māori is that the cultural and spiritual decisions of Māori concerning their taonga were left to the discretion of local authorities and the Planning Tribunal.[2] By the ground rules provided in Parts I and II of the Act, they are not. However, if the ground rules are misunderstood or ignored, then they are.

The intention of the Act, in its definitions and in the matters specified as being of national importance, is unambiguous. There is a mandatory obligation upon all persons exercising powers under the Act to recognise and make provision for Māori cultural values in all aspects of resource management, in the preparation and administration of Regional and District Plans. Section 7 reiterates the cultural emphasis.

The reference to *Kaitiakitanga* in Section 7(a) is specific. It applies to traditional Māori 'guardianship' over such resources as native forests and *kaimoana*.

Part II of the Resource Management Act 1991 deals with the 'purpose and principles' which provide the ground rules for everyone exercising powers under the Act. It concludes with Section 8 which requires that the 'principles of the Treaty' be taken into account in the management of natural resources. This acknowledges the Crown's obligation under Article II of the Treaty of Waitangi to preserve for Māori their culture and traditional way of life. The Act lays down the ground rules by which these obligations are to be met in the preparation and administration of plans for the management of New Zealand resources.

Section 8 provides that: 'In achieving the purpose of this Act, all persons exercising functions and powers under it, in relation to managing the use, development, and protection of natural and physical resources shall take into account the principles of the Treaty of Waitangi'.

This provision introduces the Treaty partners into the management of our natural resources. This is an acknowledgment that there is a separately identifiable interest of one of those parties, that is Māori which must be taken into account. 'In achieving the purpose of this Act', application of the principles of the Treaty of Waitangi in management by the Crown, or its delegated authority (Regional and Local Bodies) of natural resources needs to take place.

Despite these provisions there are concerns amongst the tribes that local authorities may misunderstand and even ignore the Māori perspective. This paper is written in order to provide a background against which the relationship of Māori and their culture and traditions with their ancestral lands, water, sites, wāhi tapu and other taonga may be understood with special emphasis and focus on 'Kaitiakitanga'.

Fundamental Knowledge

Myth and legend are an integral part of the corpus of fundamental knowledge held by the philosophers and seers of the Māori and indeed of the Polynesian peoples of the Pacific from ancient times. Indeed, there are remarkable parallels and similarities between the extant myths and legends held by the various Polynesian groups who have been separated from each other for time spans ranging from eight hundred to two thousand five hundred years.

For instance Māui as a myth hero, Tangaroa as the 'god' of the sea, Tāne, Rangi, Papa and the stories that revolve around them have a common thread or theme running through them. The concepts which underlie the various legends also exhibit a common motif and focus. Modern man has summarily dismissed these so called myths and legends as the superstitious and quaint imaginings of primitive, pre-literate societies. That assumption could not be further from the truth.

Myth and legend in the Māori cultural context are neither fables embodying primitive faith in the supernatural, nor marvellous fireside stories of ancient times. They were deliberate constructs employed by the ancient seers and sages to encapsulate and condense into easily assimilable forms their view of the World, of ultimate reality and the relationship between the Creator, the universe and man.

Cultures pattern perceptions of reality into conceptualisations of what they perceive reality to be; of what is to be regarded as actual, probable, possible or impossible. These conceptualisations form what is termed the 'worldview' of a culture. The worldview is the central systematisation of conceptions of reality to which members of its culture assent and from which stems their value system. The worldview lies at the very heart of the culture, touching, interacting with and strongly influencing every aspect of the culture.

In terms of Māori culture, the myths and legends form the central system on which their holistic view of the universe is based.

Western culture, whose major focus on the natural universe assumes that it is comprised of indestructible atoms of solid matter and conforms to strict mechanical laws in an absolutely predictable manner, goes on to further assume that the world can be understood and is scientifically describable. Western culture therefore applies scientific methodology to understand and describe cause and effect.

Other cultures start from other assumptions concerning the universe and arrive at different conclusions. Their logic may be just as good or as bad as Western cultures and the way that they reason from assumption or hypotheses to conclusion may be very similar particularly in regard to the natural world, but their basic assumptions may be very different. Other cultural assumptions may be just as valid, but focused on a part of the data that western cultures may ignore. For instance westerners may focus on the 'how' or 'immediate why' of events but seldom concern themselves with the 'ultimate why' of such occurrences.

The 'legend' of Tāne ascending to the highest heaven in a bid to obtain the 'Baskets of Knowledge' from *Io,* the creator, demonstrates the principles outlined above.

The legend relates how Tāne, after he had successfully organised the revolt that led to the separation of their parents Rangi (Father Heaven) and Papa (Mother Earth) and having concluded the various purification rites, wended his way through the heavens until he arrived at the penultimate heaven. He was again sanctified by Rehua the 'Priest God' of exorcism and purification who then allowed Tāne entrance into the twelfth heaven, the abode of Io. There he received the three Baskets of Knowledge together with two small stones one white and the other a predominantly red coloured stone. The former white stone was named *Hukatai* (Seafoam) and the latter red stone was called *Rehutai* (Seaspray).

He descended to the seventh heaven where his brothers had completed the *Whare Wānanga* (House of Learning or Wisdom). After the welcome, he had to undergo more purification rites to remove the intense *tapu* (sacredness, restriction) ingested from his association with the intense sacredness of Io. Having completed the purification rites, Tāne entered the Whare Wānanga named *Wharekura* and deposited the three Baskets of Knowledge named *Tuauri, Aronui* and *Tua-ātea* above the *taumata* - the seat of authority where the seers and sages sat - then deposited the stones Hukatai and Rehutai, one on either side of the rear ridge pole.

On the surface, such a story may be regarded as a fairytale, a fantasy to tell to children by the fireside in the evenings. Nothing could be further from the truth for this legend is part of the corpus of sacred knowledge and as such was not normally related in public. Furthermore, the way in which it was couched ensured that even when related in public, its inner meaning could not be understood without the key to unravel it. And unless all the parts were known and understood it was impossible to make sense of it.

It was a basic tenet of Māoridom that the inner corpus of sacred knowledge was not to be shared with the *tūtūā* - the common herd - lest such knowledge be abused and misused. Such sacred lore was not lightly taught and was shared only with selected candidates who after a long apprenticeship and testing were deemed fit to hold such knowledge. Such an incident occurred in my experience when the seriousness of imparting such knowledge to tūtūā was brought home to me.

After the war, I returned to the Wānanga and was questioned by the elders of the Wānanga about my war experiences. In the course of my sharing our experiences I mentioned the atom bomb. One of the elders who had of course heard of the atom bomb asked me to explain the difference between an atom bomb and an explosive bomb. I took the word *hihiri* which in Māoridom means 'pure energy'. Here I recalled Einstein's concept of the real world behind the natural world as being comprised of 'rhythmical patterns of pure energy' and said to him that this was essentially the same concept. He then exclaimed "Do you mean to tell me that the Pākehā scientists (tohunga Pākehā) have managed to rend the fabric (kahu) of the universe?" I said "Yes" "I suppose they shared their knowledge with the tūtūā (politicians)?" "Yes" "But do they know how to sew (tuitui) it back together again?" "No!" "That's the trouble with sharing such 'tapu' knowledge. Tūtūā will always abuse it."

The Worlds of Māori Cosmogony
The Lore of The Wānanga
The legend of Tāne's ascent into the heavens provide the sanctions, protocols and guidelines upon which the Wānanga was to be conducted and determined

the subject content to be taught. In the genealogy of creation, *te whē* (sound) was always associated with Wānanga. Wānanga when standing alone means to discuss, debate, impart knowledge. When associated with te whē, it means wisdom.

Now Te Whē (sound) represented the word in embryo, or the seed word. It was the *kahu* (dress) in which alone the seed word could be clothed and articulated, then thought may be conceptualised and expressed in word. Te Whē and Wānanga were each indispensable to the formation and existence of the other. Ancient Māori seers and sages were well aware of the ancient conundrum which other cultures also posed when thinking about the existence of thought itself: namely, 'Is it possible to think without words?' For Māori, the answer was in the negative. One cannot exist without the other.

Wānanga, as the institution of higher learning, was termed *Te Kauae-runga* (Literally, 'The Upper Jaw'). Other institutions of learning such as the *Whare Maire* were concerned with occult lore and certain forms of *karakia* (liturgical chants) and other matters were termed *Te Kauae-raro* (Literally, 'The Lower Jaw').

Prior to entry into the Wānanga, selected and screened candidates or pupils (tauira) were required to go through certain initiation and purification rites which also included dedication to a particular tutelary deity such as Tangaroa, Tāne and Rongo in accordance with the major specialisation that he wished to pursue. His first action when he entered into the Wānanga house was to proceed to the rear ridge pole, pick up and place *Hukatai* (sea foam) - the white stone - in his mouth and symbolically swallow it, after which he replaced it. This was a reminder that all knowledge was sacred and therefore to be nurtured and treasured. Only then could they be fed with the sacred food of the baskets of knowledge.

Sessions were normally held during the slack periods of the year especially during the winter months when the activities of hunting, fishing, planting and harvesting were over and their help not required. Normally, learning was a life long pursuit and even after graduation most of the members continued to attend wānanga.

On approaching graduation, the students were required to undergo some searching tests. Those dedicated to Tāne were, for instance, ordered to go to the forest without any food supplies, sometimes for several weeks and were expected to fend for themselves, living off the bounty provided by Tāne. It was a period of meditation and/or fasting in which they were not only expected to practice their bush craft but also to learn to commune with the spirit of their tutelary deity and return with some original knowledge. Their graduation depended upon their passing the rigorous tests and examinations imposed by the sages. If they passed the tests then they were initiated into the new grade or order of *taura* (masters, teachers).

When a student graduated he then returned to the rear ridge pole where he took up *Rehutai*, the red coloured stone and symbolically swallowed it. These symbolic ritualistic acts brought home some important truths. At the beginning when he swallowed Hukatai - the white stone he was acknowledging that he was entering upon a search for knowledge (mātauranga).

Now knowledge and wisdom are related but different in nature. Knowledge is a thing of the head, an accumulation of facts. Wisdom is a thing of the heart. It has its own thought processes. It is there that knowledge is integrated for this is the centre of one's being.

All things, no matter how specialised must be connected to a centre. This centre is constituted of our most basic convictions - ideas that transcend the world of facts. This does not mean that they are purely subjective or relative, or even mere convention. But they must approximate reality whether in the world of sense perception or the real world behind that. Such ideas without this approximation inevitably lead to disaster.

A truly educated person is not one who knows a bit about everything, or everything about something, but one who is truly in touch with his centre. He will be in no doubt about his convictions, about his view on the meaning and purpose of life, and his own life will show a sureness of touch that stems from inner clarity. This is true wisdom.

How is the transition made from knowledge, *per se*, to wisdom? The swallowing of Rehutai is symbolic of how this state may be achieved. Hukatai (sea foam) and Rehutai (seaspray) are metaphors taken from a canoe *en passage* on the sea. The sea foam or wake generated by the canoe in motion symbolises the pursuit of knowledge as an accumulation of facts picked up along the way. Of itself, such facts constitute an unorganised set of ideas unrelated to his centre.

The centre is where he must create for himself an orderly system of ideas about himself and the world in order to regulate the direction of his life. If he has faced up to the ultimate questions posed by life, his own centre no longer remains in a vacuum which continues to ingest any new idea that seeps into it. The swallowing of Rehutai is the answer to the problem.

Rehutai depicts a canoe heading into the sunrise. As the sea foam is thrown up by the bow, the rays of the sun piercing the foam creates a rainbow effect as you peer through it. By meditation in the heart, the centre of one's being, illumination comes suddenly in a moment of time, and the unorganised sets of ideas suddenly gel together to form an integrated whole in which the tensions and contradictions are resolved. Knowledge is transformed into wisdom. This is essentially a spiritual experience. Illumination is from above, a revelation gift from God. When it occurs, it acts as a catalyst integrating knowledge to produce wisdom.

The Baskets of Knowledge

The three baskets of knowledge obtained by Táne were named *Tua-uri*, *Aro-nui*, and *Tua-átea*.

Tua-uri literally translates as 'beyond in the world of darkness'. There were twenty seven nights (Pó) each of which spanned eons of time. This is the 'real world' behind the world of sense perception of the natural world.

It is the seed bed of creation where all things are gestated, evolve, and are refined to be manifested in the natural world. This is the world where the cosmic processes originated and continue to operate as a complex series of rhythmical patterns of energy to uphold, sustain and replenish the energies and life of the natural world.

Four related concepts must be held in balance although they occur at different stages and are divided by other elements in the genealogical table of the birth and evolution of the various stages of the cosmic process. They are *mauri*, *hihiri*, *mauri-ora*, and *hau-ora*.

Mauri occurs in the early stages of the genealogical table. It is that force that interpenetrates all things to bind and knit them together and as the various elements diversify, mauri acts as the bonding element creating unity in diversity.

Hihiri is pure energy, a refined form of mauri and is manifested as a form of radiation or light, and aura that radiates from matter but is especially evident in living things.

Mauri-ora is the life principle. As the word implies, it is that bonding force which is further refined beyond pure energy (hihiri) to make life possible.

Hau-ora is the breath or wind of the spirit which was infused into the process of birth to animate life.

The genealogy of creation is quite specific and develops logically from the early stages of the root cause implanted within the cosmic space-time continuum of the void - abyss and nights in its primordial beginnings evolving into the highly specialised and variegated objects of the natural world. When each stage in this evolutionary process reached its high or 'Omega' point, the process took a huge leap forward to initiate a new stage and series.

To sum up, the three baskets of knowledge deal with the three world view of the Máori in which Tua-uri is the real world of the complex series of rhythmical patterns of energy which operate behind this world of sense perception.

Though we cannot prove its existence by logical argument, we are compelled to assume its existence behind that of the world of sense perception. We cannot apprehend it by direct means. But in the Máori view and experience we have other faculties of a higher order than the natural senses which when properly trained can penetrate into the 'beyond'. It is still accepted by the modern Máori that our *tohunga* which were specially trained and gifted in this field were *matakite*, literally 'seers'; which reminds me of the words of that seer mentioned above regarding the exploding of the atom bomb: 'They've torn the fabric of the universe, but do they know how to repair it?'

Te Aro-nui translates literally as 'that before us', that is, 'before our senses'. This is the natural world around us as apprehended by the senses. Like any other race, Māori observed the world around us; noted recurring cycles and events, their regularity, deduced cause and effect and came to the same conclusions that most people come to. That knowledge and lore became part of the corpus of general knowledge and was transmitted from one generation to another.

An example of this was my own father born in 1862 and brought up in the traditional ways of our people. As children we often went fishing both in the harbour and in the open sea with members of the tribe. My father was always consulted. He would quickly calculate the day according to the Māori lunar calendar, the state of the tide, the direction of the wind and other phenomena. He would then advise us what reefs, or grounds to fish and the best times according to the state of the tide. He would advise against going to other grounds which were handier or more popular as a waste of time. He would give us the reasons. By the time we were young men we had imbibed a lot of this traditional lore. Often we tested this knowledge and found it trustworthy.

Such lore was carefully stored and transmitted. But over and beyond that they used other extra sensory faculties and techniques to test their environment and new phenomena. They had techniques for testing poisonous plants and trees; those that were good for healing and for food; ways by which highly poisonous berries such as the karaka could be rendered harmless and utilised as food. Some of those techniques are still used to this day.

Genealogy as a tool for transmitting knowledge pervaded Māori culture. Every class and species of things had their own genealogy. This was a handy method for classifying different families and species of flora and fauna, of the order in which processes occurred and the order in which intricate and prolonged activities or ceremonies should be conducted.

According to a typical classificatory genealogy, Tāne the 'god' of the forest married several wives to produce different families of children. From one wife was born the healing trees, from another the building trees and so on. Tangaroa, the god of the sea, also married several wives from each of which the different species and generations of fish, shellfish and seaweed were born. The same techniques were applied to herbs, to root crops, berries, birds, soils, rocks and so on. Everything had its *whakapapa* or genealogy.

Te Ao Tua-ātea is the world beyond space and time. *Ātea* is the word for space, it is usually combined with *wā* (time) to form *wātea* (space-time). They saw space and time as conjoined together and relative to each other.

The final series of the *Tua-uri* genealogy is recited as: *Te Hauora* begat shape, shape begat form, form begat space, space begat time, and time begat Rangi and Papa (heaven and earth). Thus the space-time continuum became the framework into which heaven and earth were born.

According to this concept, the universe is finite in extent and relative in time. This is in contrast to the realm of Tua-uri, the realm in which the universal processes were founded in the space-frame of the void and abyss and set in the time-frame of the eons of the nights.

Tua-ātea is the world beyond any space-time framework. It is infinite and eternal. This is the realm of Io, the supreme God whose attributes were expressed in the various names attributed to him, *Io-taketake* (first cause), *Io-nui* (almighty), *Io-roa* (eternal), *Io-uru* (omnipresent), *Io-matakana* (omniscient), *Io-mataaho* (glorious one), *Io-wānanga* (all wise) and others.

This is the eternal realm which as before Tua-uri and towards which the universal process is tending. The worlds both of Tua-uri and Aronui are part of the cosmic process. And if the universe is process, it is more akin to life, mind and spirit which are obviously processes. Therefore the world of sense perception, the natural world around us is unlikely to be ultimate reality. For the Māori, Tua-ātea, the transcendent eternal world of the spirit, is ultimate reality.

The World of Symbol

To the three baskets containing the knowledge of the three worlds we must add a fourth world, the world of symbol.

The world of symbol is a deliberate creation of the human mind. Man creates symbols to depict, represent and illustrate some other perceived reality. Words, formulae, forms, ritualistic ceremonies, legend and myth are created by the human mind as maps, models, prototypes and paradigms by which the mind can grasp, understand and reconcile the worlds of sense perception and the real world behind that.

In every culture, there are exclusive groups who disseminate their knowledge by means of secret symbols known only to the initiates. Secret societies, professional groups and certain religious groups use secret signs, rituals and legends to safeguard that knowledge from the general public. And unless one knows and understands the keys to unlock that knowledge, then the reality to which the symbols refer remain a mystery.

On the other hand, there are symbols created by and for the general public. But these symbols must approximate to the reality to which they refer before a society will accept and give assent to them. Only then are they incorporated into the corpus of that culture's general knowledge and become part of that culture's traditions and customs.

Some Conclusions

We have seen how the seers and sages of Māori society deliberately created their myths and legends as symbols to portray some other perceived reality. Those symbols were deliberately couched in these forms in order to facilitate several desired objectives.

Legends and Myths

Legends and myths have been used from time immemorial as a graphic means of creating word pictures and scenarios as a framework into which the basic elements of the realities perceived may be set in summary form.

The Use of Legendary Myth and Story

The use of legendary myth and story imprinted upon the mind, acted as pegs to which the finer details could be attached in progressive order to reconstruct the component features of that body of knowledge.

Aid For Ease Of Recall

On the one hand legend and myth provided a mechanism for aid ease of recall. On the other hand, they were selected as a camouflage to hide inner meanings from the uninitiated. This thereby preserved the integrity of such sacred lore and mediated abuse and misuse.

Sanctions

The legend itself, by virtue of its association with the pantheon of gods, provided the sanctions by which *kaupapa* (first principles) were authorised and out of which *tikanga* (custom) could flow and be validated.

Genealogy

Genealogy as an important symbolic mechanism has already been demonstrated above. As a cultural institution it pervaded much of Māori culture. One of its primary functions was to trace family and tribal ancestral lines. But even here, there was an element of symbolism. Man's early ancestry traces back through its myth heroes to the gods to Mother Earth. This truth is also featured in the Māori carved meeting house where the ridge poles of the house, embedded in the ground and sustaining the ridging, symbolises the Cosmic Tree. The ridging is perceived as representing the dome of heaven - *Te Tāhuhunui-o-te-Ao*, and the floor represents Mother Earth - Papatuanuku. Thus man is perceived as a citizen of two worlds with his roots in the earth and his crown in the heavens. Man did not evolve from the primates but was born out of the seed of the god Tāne, impregnated into the dawn maid *Hineahuone* who was formed and shaped out of the red clay - *onekura* - of Mother Earth.

In terms of the knowledge deposited in the three baskets concerning the three worlds we have traversed in the inner world of our minds, we find another application for the use of genealogical tables. Genealogical tables of creation trace the logical sequence of the evolution of the processes that occurred in Tuauri. That same principle is applied in the world of sense perception, in a multitude of ways. Thus, keeping in mind the symbolic nature of many of these genealogical tables, we have the key by which we can open the door to an area of knowledge which can reveal many of the basic concepts latent within Māori culture.

The Holistic View

The seers and sages of Māoridom did not hold either to the eighteenth century view of the earlier natural scientists, nor did they accept the view held by the modern physicists that the real world behind the world of sense perception is composed solely of complex series of rhythmical patterns of energy.

Natural Science

Under the eighteenth century view of the natural scientists:

1. The universe was composed of indestructible atoms of solid matter existing in infinite space and absolute time.
2. It conforms to strict mechanical laws operating in an absolutely predictable manner.
3. Since space is infinite and time is absolute, the universe is a closed system and nothing can impinge upon it from without or disturb its regularity. The whole of reality is confined within its borders. There is therefore no room for concepts such as spirit and the higher manifestations of life.

Positivism: Valid knowledge is obtainable only through the scientific method. No knowledge is genuine unless based upon observable fact.
Relativism: Relativism denied all absolutes, norms, values and standards.
Freud: All the higher manifestations of human life are but the dark stirrings of the subconscious mind resulting from the unfulfilled incest wishes of childhood. Art, religion, spirit are but phantasmagoria as in the brains of men.

The New Physicists[3]

The New Physicists changed the rigid framework of the earlier scientists. People like Marie Curie (radium), Max Planck (quantum theory), Albert Einstein (relativity), Werner Heisenberg (uncertainty principle) and a host of others at the beginning of the 20th Century introduced entirely new concepts.

1. The universe is finite in extent and relative in time; and in it there is no absolute rest, size, motion, simultaneity.
2. Matter can no longer be conceived as indestructible atoms of solid matter but rather as a complex series of rhythmical patterns of energy.
3. Under these conditions, the atom obviously needs only a minimal space and time in which to exist (the uncertainty principle). In other words, it is 'process'.
4. If it is process rather than inert matter it is more akin to life, mind and spirit which are obviously processes.
5. If this is true, then the world of sense perception is unlikely to be ultimate reality. It follows that the universe is not a closed but an 'open' system which therefore allows for the incursion of such things as spirits.

The New Physicists then proposed a new construct for the universe by proposing the existence of a 'Real World' behind the world of sense perception. It may not be apprehended by direct means through the senses but may be grasped by 'speculative' means and the use of symbol (eg. $E = mc^2$) to portray events in that real world (Tua-uri).

Our Polynesian seers and sages came to similar conclusions many centuries ago with this difference, that besides pure energy, there were many other elements such as the primordial embryo and roots of all things containing mauri as the bonding force; the primal force developing into hihiri (pure energy); and later, the impartation of the word of power and wisdom, and the infusion of the breath of the spirit, all these were active elements in the directing and ordering of the cosmic process.

To conclude this section:

Open System: If the universe is an 'open' system into which the spiritual dimension may impinge, then it is possible that man, who is also a spiritual being, may discern spiritually the processes that occur in Tua-uri and Tua-ātea.

Integrated Whole: More importantly, the Māori world which sees the three realms as an integrated whole, is the basis for the holistic approach of the Māori to his environment.

Mother Earth and Man

The first woman, Hineahuone, was formed out of the clay of Mother Earth and impregnated by Tāne to produce *Hinetitama*, the dawn maid. Tāne cohabited with her to produce more children. These were the progenitors of

65

the human race. The Māori thought of himself as holding a special relationship to mother earth and her resources. The popular name for the earth was *whenua*. This is also the name for the 'afterbirth'.

Just as the foetus is nurtured in the mother's womb and after the baby's birth upon her breast, so all life forms are nurtured in the womb and upon the earth's breast. Man is an integral part therefore of the natural order and recipients of her bounty. He is her son and therefore, as every son has social obligations to fulfill towards his parents, siblings and other members of the whānau, so has man an obligation to Mother Earth and her whānau to promote their welfare and good.

Kaupapa and Tikanga

Kaupapa is derived from two words, *kau* and *papa*. In this context 'kau' means 'to appear for the first time, to come into view', to 'disclose'. 'Papa' means ground or foundation. Hence, kaupapa means ground rules, first principles, general principles.

Tikanga means method, plan, reason, custom, the right way of doing things.

Kaupapa and Tikanga are juxtaposed and interconnected in Māori thinking. When contemplating some important project, action or situation that needs to be addressed and resolved, the tribe in council would debate the kaupapa or rules and principles by which they should be guided. There is an appeal to first principles in cases of doubt and those principles are drawn from the creation stories of Tua-uri, the acts of the gods in the period of transition following the separation of Rangi and Papa, or the acts of the myth heroes such as Māui or Tawhaki and numerous others. The methods and plans they used in a similar situation are recounted and recommended. Alternative options are also examined and a course of action (tikanga) is adopted.

There may be an appeal to general principles which originally derived from the 'first principles' tracing back to the sanctions derived from the gods and myth heroes and have now become established as custom and a traditional way of doing certain things as being sufficient sanction for a certain course of action. In the latter case there is no need to appeal to original kaupapa but to *Tikanga Māori.*

Tikanga Māori translates as Māori custom. They denote those customs and traditions that have been handed down through many generations and accepted as a reliable and appropriate way of achieving and fulfilling certain objectives and goals. Such proven methods together with their accompanying protocols are integrated into the general cultural institutions of the society and incorporated into the cultural system of standards, values, attitudes and beliefs.

Kaitiakitanga
Definition

The term *tiaki*, whilst its basic meaning is 'to guard' has other closely related meanings depending upon the context. Tiaki may therefore also mean, to keep, to preserve, to conserve, to foster, to protect, to shelter, to keep watch over.

The prefix *kai* with a verb denotes the agent of the act. A *kaitiaki* is a guardian, keeper, preserver, conservator, foster-parent, protector. The suffix *tanga*, when added to the noun, transforms the term to mean guardianship, preservation, conservation, fostering, protecting, sheltering.

Kaitiakitanga is defined in the Resource Management Act as guardianship and/or stewardship. Stewardship is not an appropriate definition since the original English meaning of stewardship is 'to guard someone else's property'. Apart from having overtones of a master-servant relationship, ownership of property in the pre-contact period was a foreign concept. The closest idea to ownership was that of the private use of a limited number of personal things such as garments, weapons, combs. Apart from this all other use of land, waters, forests, fisheries, was a communal and/or tribal right. All natural resources, all life was birthed from Mother Earth. Thus the resources of the earth did not belong to man but rather, man belonged to the earth. Man as well as animal, bird, fish could harvest the bounty of mother earth's resources but they did not own them. Man had but 'user rights'.

Spiritual Guardians

The ancient ones (tawhito), the spiritual sons and daughters of Rangi and Papa were the *Kaitiaki* or guardians. Tāne was the Kaitiaki of the forest, Tangaroa of the sea, Rongo of herbs and root crops, Hinenui-i-te-pō of the portals of death and so on. Different *tawhito* had oversight of the various departments of nature. And whilst man could harvest those resources, they were duty bound to thank and propitiate the guardians of those resources. Thus Māori made ritual acts of propitiation before embarking upon hunting, fishing, digging root crops, cutting down trees and other pursuits of a similar nature. When fishing, the first fish caught was set free as an offering to Tangaroa and when felling a tree, the first chips were burnt and their essence offered up to Tāne. Only then could man use the substance. When a meeting house was completed, the tapu of Tāne was removed to enable the people to use it freely. Kumara or fern root was dug and the first fruits cooked and then waved as an offering before Rongo. The steam rising from the cooked food was sweet smelling savour offered to the *tawhito* (ancient ones) as a thanksgiving and the substance of the food retained for man.

From the above outline we see how first principles (kaupapa) derive from the myths and legends associated with Mother Earth as the primeval

Mother and from her children regarded as the ancient ones.

Western Values

By contrast, in Western culture, there is a disjunction between the material and spiritual, between the secular and sacred. This disconnection is linked to the capitalistic mode of production and expropriates and commodifies the land, its resources and people. All have a price in the marketplace. In a market driven economy prime values are thrown out the window and values that revolve around economics rank uppermost. This value overrides spiritual and human considerations and the profit motive becomes the prime value.

Māori are therefore extremely sceptical regarding the government's resource management plans, its conservation policies and sustainable management efforts. Based as they are within a society driven by market considerations, conservation and sustainable management policies must eventually fail. So long as the prime values are based on economics, then the values implicit in sustainable management plans are diametrically opposed, and the latter must eventually succumb.

Mother Earth

Papatuanuku was the personified name for the earth and *whenua*, the common name. Papatuanuku was the primordial mother figure who married Rangi and birthed the departmental gods (tawhito) who were delegated to oversee the elements and natural resources - winds, storms, lightning, forests, cultivated crops, fish and so on.

Whenua was the term both for the natural earth and placenta. This is a constant reminder that we are of the earth and therefore earthly. We are born out of the placenta and therefore human. As the human mother nourished her child on the womb and then upon her breast after the child's birth, so does Mother Earth. Not only does she nourish humankind upon her breast but all life animals, birds, trees, plants. Man is part of this network and the other forms of life are his siblings. They share with each other the nourishment provided by Mother Earth.

Papatuanuku is a living organism with her own biological systems and functions. She provides a network of support systems for all her children who live and function in a symbiotic relationship. The different species and genera contribute to the welfare of other species and also help to sustain the biological functions of Mother Earth both in their life and death. Her children facilitate the processes of ingestion, digestion and excretion.

The streams of water are her arteries bringing the life giving waters for her to imbibe and share with her offspring. Those same streams act as alimentary canals and help in the disposal of waste.

Earth's Consciousness

Man is the conscious mind of Mother Earth and plays a vital part in the regulation of her life support systems and man's duty is to enhance and sustain those systems. The tragedy, however, is that when these first principles are forsaken and Mother Earth is perceived as a commodity and her natural resources seen as disposable property to be exploited, then there is no avoiding the abuse and misuse of the earth. Man becomes a pillager, despoiler and rapist of his own mother. Forests are denuded, the land, sea and air are polluted, her surface is scarred and the resources are depleted.

Until we relearn the lesson that man is an integral part of the natural order and that he has obligations not only to society but also to his environment so long will he abuse the earth. To realise that he is a child of the Earth will help him in working to restore and maintain the harmony and balance which successive generations of humankind have arrogantly disturbed.

Tikanga Tiaki (Guardianship Customs)

Out of the perceptions and concepts derived from the first principles emerged the tikanga or customs instituted to protect and conserve the resources of Mother Earth.

In order to conserve the resources and ensure their replenishment and sustenance the Māori introduced the tikanga or custom of *rāhui*. Rāhui was a prohibition or ban instituted to protect resources.

Within the tribal territory a certain area would be placed under rāhui and posted as being out of bounds to hunters, fishers and harvesters. Other areas would remain open for use. This was a form of rotation farming. When the resource was considered to have regenerated itself, then the *tapu* would be lifted and that area restored to general use. Another area might be placed under the tapu of rāhui in order to allow it to regenerate. Thus the rotation method ensured a constant and steady source of supply.

This type of rāhui must not be confused with another form which was applied when an *aituā*, misfortune resulting in death occurred. If a person was drowned at sea or a harbour, that area was placed under a rāhui because it had become contaminated by the tapu of death. After a certain period of time when those waters were deemed to have been cleansed then the rāhui was lifted and those waters opened for use.

Rāhui and tapu were at times used interchangeably to mean the same thing namely 'under a ban'. Rāhui in its basic meaning is 'to encompass'. A rāhui designated the boundaries within which the tapu as a ban was imposed. Tapu meaning 'sacred or set apart' denoted that a ban was in force over that area.

Rāhui and Mauri

To aid the process of regeneration, a mauri stone would be placed in the area accompanied by appropriate ritual and prayer.

Mauri-ora is life-force. All animate and other forms of life such as plants and trees owe their continued existence and health to mauri. When the mauri is strong, fauna and flora flourish. When it is depleted and weak those forms of life become sickly and weak.

Kawa

Ritual or liturgical action was termed *kawa*. Kawa had to be conducted carefully and meticulously. Any break in a ritual chant or a particular action left out of the traditional ceremony was regarded as an ill omen.

Normally the decision to rāhui an area was the prerogative of the tohunga, the expert in a particular field or custom. He was an expert in reading the signs that pointed to the depletion of resources in different areas of the tribal territory. He would consult with the chief (rangatira) and/or tribal elders and a firm decision and course of action was approved.

The tohunga would then conduct the appropriate ritual which invoked the aid of the appropriate departmental god; and then he would take a talisman stone and by his prayers concentrate the life force of the birds, fish or whatever in that stone and plant the mauri stone within the area encompassed by the rāhui, or on a fishing ground, or wherever the situation warranted it.

Sign posts with the appropriate symbols would be posted around the boundaries as a warning that the area was prohibited. The rāhui was then proclaimed to the people who were warned against trespass.

The Institution of Rāhui

The institution of rāhui was designed to prohibit exploitation, depletion, degeneration of a resource and the pollution of the environment to the point where the pro-life processes latent within the biological and ecosystems of Papatuanuku might collapse.

So that man as the conscious mind of Papatuanuku might aid the pro-life processes of recovery and regeneration, the tohunga would conduct the appropriate ritual, focussing and concentrating the *mauri* of the particular species within the area. Mauri is a form of energy and energy is a form of radiation. From this source, the aura of the mauri would radiate outwards both to the environment and more specifically to the species for which it was intended. Thus mauri created benevolent conditions within the environment both to harmonise the processes within the Earth's ecosystem and to aid the regeneration process.

An Aside

An incident comes to mind. When the *toheroa* canneries were built near the Ninety Mile Beach and the elders of the tribe discovered that the toheroa was to be canned and sold, they met to consult together and their opinion was that the mauri of the toheroa would depart from the Ninety Mile Beach and there would be no toheroa left in about fifteen to twenty years. Their predictions both about the departure and the length of time for it to occur proved to be exactly right.

To summarise, Kaitiakitanga was the word used by Māori to define conservation customs and traditions, including its purpose and means, through rāhui.

Kaitiakitanga and *rangatiratanga* are intimately linked. As outlined above, the rangatira proclaimed and enforced rāhui since he was the rangatira over the tribal territory.

This concept of rangatiratanga is demonstrated in the cutting down of the flagstaff at Kororāreka by Hone Heke. Governor Fitzroy had imposed excise duties and customs upon Pewhairangi Harbour in the Bay of Islands. Heke demanded that Fitzroy remove them since Heke was the chief over that territory. When Fitzroy refused Heke cut down the flagstaff three times and when Fitzroy proved to be recalcitrant, Heke cut down the flagstaff a fourth time and then proceeded to overthrow the garrison and sacked Kororāreka.[4]

He contended that the Crown had a centralised authority but he exercised local authority as guaranteed under Article Two of the Treaty of Waitangi. Heke was right. *Tangata whenua,* under the guarantees of Article Two, have the authority to control and manage the resources within their territory. Under the institution of rāhui, tangata whenua have the right to control the access of other people and their own tribal members to the resource and the use of that resource.

Other Terms

Under the principle of *Mauri Manaaki,* derived from the mauri of a meeting house in which the mauri was implanted by Tāne in *Wharekura* (the first *whare wānanga*) came the custom (tikanga) of *tuku rangatira* (noblesse oblige).

Tāne planted three mauri in Wharekura: *Mauri Atua* (life force of the gods), *Mauri Tangata* (the life force of tangata whenua) and *Mauri Manaaki* (the life force of the guests and visitors.) The word *manaaki* means to bestow a blessing. The presence of visitors was equivalent to the bestowal of a blessing upon the hosts. On the part of the hosts, they bestowed a blessing upon the guests by giving them the best of their provisions in the *hākari* (banquet) and hospitality provided. This was a reciprocal relationship which could be extended by the exchange of gifts.

Taiapure, Mātaitai

Applying this principle to the use of resources, the coastal people would set aside a portion of land for the use of inland tribes to build *papakāinga* houses where they could reside during the fishing season and prepare dried fish for winter provisions and so on. They also set aside *taiapure* reserves such as a stretch of coast, a reef, a fishing ground where the inland tribes could gather shellfish (mātaitai) or fish on fishing grounds (tauranga-ika) and reefs (toka).

Tuku Rangatira

This *manaaki* (blessing) was initiated under the custom (tikanga) of *Tuku Rangatira* (noblesse oblige). A magnificent example of this tikanga was the gifting by Ngāti Maru of Harataunga (Kennedy's Bay) to Ngāti Porou as a staging area to prepare themselves for trading in the Auckland markets.

Conclusion

We have traversed over a wide range of interrelated topics from fundamental knowledge, through the Māori Worldview and the value systems derived from them, to try to understand the holistic approach to life and the application of the fundamental principles (kaupapa) to life situations through Māori customs (tikanga) integrated into the value systems of their culture.

We have further taken *Kaitiakitanga* as a particular cultural institution to show how those first principles may be applied through Tikanga Māori to resolve the rights of tangata whenua and their role in determining how environmental and conservation policies may be applied to achieve positive results. It is hoped that the information contained herein may help the decision makers to determine how Kaitiakitanga may be expressed and applied to resource management. Further, it is hoped that the paper will provide alternatives that may be studied to find how a bicultural blend may be developed in order that all may benefit from the bounty that Mother Earth has so richly bestowed upon this nation.

Endnotes

[1] An Act of the New Zealand Parliament passed in 1991 to regulate environmental management in New Zealand.

[2] A judicial forum established to mediate conflicts in environmental management.

[3] For a discussion on the work of the New Physicists, see *The Tao of Physics* by Fritjof Capra (Shambhala, Boston 2000) and *The Dancing Wu Li Masters* by Gary Zukav (Bantam Books 1980)

[4] These events took place in *Te Tai Tokerau* (Northland, New Zealand) in the 1840s. Hone Heke was a chief of the Ngā Puhi people of the region who was prominent in conflicts against the British. Governor Fitzroy was an early Governor of the then nascent New Zealand Government.

MĀTAURANGA MĀORI, MĀTAURANGA PĀKEHĀ

Tangi kau ana ngā tai o te uru mō rātou kua ngaro i te tirohanga kanohi: ngā tōtara whakamarumaru, ngā poutokomanawa o ngā whare maire o ō tātou mātua, o ō tātou tūpuna. Tū kau mai ngā puhi o te tonga, o te whenua kua mahue, te tangata kua ngaro. Aue! Taukuri e!... E mihi tonu ana ki ō tātou mate, ngā mate kua hinga mai i waenga i a koutou. Anā, me pēnei te mihi i a rātou,

> *Huhua noa ana*
> *Rapurapu noa ana*
> *ka ngaro rā*
> *e taku manu tiutiu i te ata e*
> *Papā te whatitiri*
> *Kahukura ki te rangi*
> *tāwhano kau ana*
> *ko ahau ki muri nei e*
> *Tuwhera kau nei*
> *te riu o te whenua*
> *tau e nuku haere.*

Nā reira, haere koutou i Te Ara-whānui-o-Tāne, te tāheke roa ki Te Muriwaihou ki Te Pō-tiwha, ki Te Pō e aue ai te moe. Moe mai koutou i roto i te Ariki...Ā,

73

tēnā koutou, tēnā tātou. Me hoki tātou ki te taitara i tukua mai hei kōrerotanga māku. Nā, te mātauranga Māori me te mātauranga Pākehā. Ā, me tētahi ngarara e kiia ana, *epistemology*, arā, kia ake nei ko te āhuatanga o tēnei mea... ngā whakaaro mō tēnei mea mō te mātauranga. E rua ngā ngarara nei. Te mea tuatahi e ki ana te Pākehā, *metaphysics*, tuarua ko te *theory of knowledge*. Ae, e kore pono e āhei ki te kōrero ki tētahi, ki te kāhore tētahi. E whakaaro ana au me pehea taku timatanga kōrero ki a tātou... Nā, ko tāku haere he whāngai i a koutou ki ngā kai o ngā kete, me timata pea ki reira.

Te Pikinga-a-Tānenuiarangi

... e kore au e mōhio ki ngā kōrero i kōrerotia ki a koutou. Engari, i roto anō o ōku rohe, mō Tānenui-a-rangi, tana haerenga ki te tiki i ngā kete o te mātauranga. Ka haere ia, i mua atu i tana tomo i Te Toi-o-ngā-rangi, ka purea e Rehua. Nā, ka uru atu ia ki Te Toi-o-ngā-rangi, ka homai ngā taonga ki a ia. Ko ngā kete e toru, ko ngā whatu e rua. He kohatu...ā, nonohi noa iho nei. Kotahi he whatu mā, te ingoa ko Hukatai. Kotahi he whatu whero nei, nā, ko tērā, ko Rehutai. Nā, ka hoatu hoki te tātua o te mana ki a ia. Ka hoki mai ia.

Tae mai ia ki Te Rangi Tamaku, arā, ki Te Rangi Tuawhitu, i reira ana tēina, ana tuākana e tatari atu ana i a ia. Ka tangi ngā pūtātara, ā, ka karangatia a Tāne. Nā, ka whakamanuhiritia. Ka oti, nā, ka unuhia te tapu o Io i runga i a ia. Ā, ka tomo ia ki Wharekura. I a ia e ngaro atu nei, kua hangā e ana tēina, e ana tuākana, te whare wānanga tuatahi, ko Wharekura te ingoa. Ā, ka tomo mai ia ki Wharekura, ka huri ia ki te tara whāiti o te whare, ki te taumata, nohoanga a ngā tohunga... ka noho, ka whakairia e ia ngā kete e toru, Te Kete Tuauri, Te Kete Aronui, ā, me Te Kete Tuaātea, i te wāhi i runga ake i te nohoanga o ngā tohunga.

Ka huri ia, ka haere ia ki te poutuarongo. Tae atu ka whakatakotongia ngā whatu nei, kotahi ki te taha maui, ko Hukatai, kotahi ki te taha katau, ko mea, ko Rehutai.

Te Whare Wānanga

Tēnei mea o te wānanga, ko ngā wā o te Hōtoke, ngā wā kua mutu ngā hauhake kumara, me ngā mahi mātaitai mō te Hōtoke, ēnā mea katoa. Nō reira, ko ērā marama, ā, ngā wānanga noho ai. Nā, ka tae mai ngā tauira, ka tohia e ngā tohunga. Mauria ki te wai, nā, hei kuta. Mohio ana koutou ki tēnei mea ki te kuta? Nā, hei ā tou ki te wai, kua tohu i te taringa i te tangata, kia rongo ai i ngā korero, me ōna karakia. Nā, ka mutu, ka haere ngā tauira ka tomo ki te whare wānanga. Ka haere rātou ki te whatu tuatahi, ki a Hukatai, kua horomia e rātou. Kua meinga rā ki roto i ō rātou waha, ki reira kōrorirori ai ki te arero, ka mutu, ka tangohia mai, ka whakahokia te whatu. Ko te tikanga o tērā mahi ko tēnei, he whakatūpato i a rātou, ka tahi. He whakamahara i a rātou ko tēnei mea, ko te mātauranga, he mea tapu. Koia tērā, a Hukatai.

Nā, ko te mātauranga, hei ā kohikohi. Whakarongo i te kōrero, kua kohikohia, kia kī ai tāu kete. Tango mai hoki i ngā tohunga kua whāngaia ki ngā kai o ngā kete e toru. Tāu mahi, he kohikohi ki roto ki tāu kete.

Te Whakamātautautanga o ngā tauira

Nā, ka pau ōna marama, ōna tau pea e noho ai ngā tauira nei ki ngā waewae o ngā tohunga whakarongo i ngā kōrero. Ka tae ki te wā, e tohia ai rātou, e whakaarotia ai mehemea kua tohungatia rānei rātou, kua aha rānei. Ā, i reira, ka tonoa rātou kia whakamātautauria. He tohi kē anō tō tēnā tauira, he tohi kē anō tō tēnā. Ētahi hei ā tohi ki raro ki a Tāne, te maru o Tāne, ētahi te maru o Tangaroa, puta noa.

Mehemea kua tohia koe ki raro ki te maru o Tāne, kua tonoa koe ki te ngahere. Mehemea kua mau i a koe ngā kōrero mō Tāne, mohio ana koe he aha ngā kai māu i roto i te ngahere. Engari, ko te tino whai māu ko tēnei, kia whāia e koe kia nohopuku, whakatiki rānei i a koe. Engari, ko tō whai kia puta te wairua o Tāne ki a koe, ki te whakaako i a koe ki ngā mea o te wairua, kia mōhio ai koe ki te whakarāpopototanga o ngā kōrero katoa i kōrerotia ki a koe i raro i tērā tohi. Ā, tuarua, kia kitea e koe ētahi mātauranga hou.

Nā, ki te Pākehā, *original knowledge*, mō te ngahere, mō ngā mea a Tāne. Nā, ka haere tētahi, ka tae ki taua wā nei, ka tonoa tētahi ki te ngahere, ki te rapu ki te whai i te wairua o Tāne. Tae atu ki reira, ka noho te tangata nei. Ā, e rua pea wiki. Whai i tana mahi, he nohopuku. E, tirotiro haere, te rapu haere, koinei e titiro i ngā rākau. Ā, ka mutu, ka hoki mai (i) te wā i whakaritea e ngā tohunga.

Ka tae mai, ka whakamātautauria. Patapatai i ōna pātai, ka ea ērā pātai. Ka tae te pātai whakamutunga, "Tēnā, he aha te kōrero a te wairua a Tāne ki a koe?" Ka kī atu te tamaiti nei, "I a au e noho ana, i te ngahere, e nohopuku ana au i tētahi rā i raro i ngā kahika nei, ngā kahikatea nei, kātahi au ka whakaaro ki a au anō, he aha rā te kahikatea o ngā rākau katoa i tupu tōpū ai? Kahikatea ki kō, kei kō, kei kō, engari tā rātou tupu he tupu tōpū."

Tangohia e te rākau, ka kerikeria e ia. Ka kitea e ia, he pāpaku tonu te tupu o ngā taketake o tēnei mea o te kahikatea. Kātahi ia ka whakaaro he aha rā i pēnei ai? Ka tae mai te māramatanga ki a ia. Ka mohio ia ki te tikanga i tupu tōpū ai ngā kahikatea nei, koinei anō te rākau e pēnei ana tāna tupu. Ka mahara ia te kōrero i kōrerotia. Mahara ia i te… i ngā wā o te tūpuhi, ki te pupuhi te hau, ki te ngeri te hau, mehemea e tupu ana ia i runga o tana kotahi, te pāpaku o ngā taketake o te rākau, ka hinga te rākau. Engari, i a rātou e tū nei, kua tuitui rātou i ngā taketake, nā, kua powhiwhi ngā taketake i roto i ētahi o ngā taketake o te rākau, ka pupuhi e te hau, ka mea ki te hinga, kua puritia ngā taketake o tētahi. Nā, ko tērā te māramatanga i tae mai ki a ia. Ā, ki te tū tahi te tangata e kore e hinga. Ā, e ai te tū tōpū. Engari, ki te tū tahanga te tangata, ka hinga. Ka mea atu ngā tohunga ki a ia, "Pass."

Ko Rehutai ráua ko Hukatai

Ná, kátahi ia, ka haere ia ki te poutuarongo o te whare, e takoto ana a Rehutai. Tangohia e ia térá o ngá whatu, he kohatu whero, ka purua ki tana waha, kóroriroritia, ka whakahokia.

Ná, ko te tohu o térá ko ténei. Mehemea kei runga koe i te waka, e haere ana, i te atatú e anga ana te haere o te waka ki te púaotanga mai o te ata, ná, ka maiangi ake te rá, i muri, e kite ana koe i te huka o te wai, ná, ko Hukatai térá, *sea-foam*. Kua taea e koe ngá huarahi, kohikohia ai e koe te mátauranga, mai i te timatanga. Ae, áianei, e anga atu ana koe ki roto i te mea, i te púaotanga mai o te rá. Mehemea e titiro atu ana koe mehemea kua maranga mai te rá, mehemea e titiro atu ana i te hiku o te waka, ná, kei reira hoki te Rehutai. Ná, ka kokoti te ihu o te waka i te moana, ná, kua puta te Rehutai. Á, titiro atu koe, kua kite atu koe pénei i te ániwaniwa nei. Ná, koia térá. Ténei mea, rereké anó te mátauranga i ténei mea i te móhio. He mátauranga anó te mátauranga, he móhiotanga anó te móhio. Á, e ú ai te mohio ki roto ki te tangata. Ná te tae mai o te máramatanga o te wairua pénei i tá ó koutou mátua titiro. Kia puta te máramatanga o te wairua ki te hinengaro o te tangata, nó te mea, ko te mátauranga, he mea nó te máhunga o te tangata, ko te móhio he mea nó te ngákau, o te hinengaro o te tangata. Á, kia tae rá anó ki te wá e márama ai te wairua o te tangata, tana hinengaro, katahi anó ka kiia kua móhio ia.

Ngá Kete o te wánanga

Ná, he aha te tikanga o ngá kete nei? E toru ngá kete nei. Ko te mea tuatahi, ko Te Kete Tuauri, ará, ngá kórero mó Te Ao Tuauri. He Ao énei mea. Te Kete Aronui, ko Te Ao-tú-roa, e noho nei tátou. Ko Te Ao Tuaátea, ko Te Ao, ko Te Ao e kiia ake, Te Ao-mutunga-kore, *eternal world...*

Māori Knowledge, European Knowledge

Greetings. Let us return to the title that I have been asked to address, that is, Māori knowledge and European knowledge. There is an endeavour called *epistemology* which concerns thinking about knowledge. In fact there are two. The first is called *metaphysics* and the second is, *the theory of knowledge*. It is said that one can not be discussed without the other. I have been thinking about where I should begin...I should perhaps 'feed you with the food contained within the baskets'[1], let us begin there.

The Ascent of Tānenuiarangi

I am not aware of the traditions that have been discussed with you, however, in our region we speak of Tānenuiarangi, his journey to seek the 'baskets of knowledge'[2] Tāne embarked upon his journey and before he entered the highest heaven (Te Toi-o-ngā-rangi) he was cleansed by Rehua. Thereafter he entered the highest heaven and treasures were given to him: three baskets and two stones… very small stones (pebbles). One of the stones was white and was called Hukatai. The other was red and was called Rehutai. Tāne was also given the girdle of mana (spiritual authority). After that he returned.

He arrived at the seventh heaven called Te Rangi Tamaku and there his siblings were waiting for him. Conch shells were sounded and he was welcomed. Following this, the intense sacredness of Io was taken off him and he entered the house called Wharekura. While he was away, his siblings had constructed the first house of higher learning called Wharekura. Upon entering the house, Tāne turned to the left and narrower side of the house and arrived at the seat of the high priests. There he suspended the three baskets of knowledge above the seat of the high priests. The three baskets were called Te Kete Tuauri, Te Kete Aronui and Te Kete Tuaātea.

Following this he turned to the rear post of the house and deposited the two stones. To the left of the post he deposited Hukatai; to the right of the post he placed Rehutai.

Te Whare Wānanga: The House of Higher and Esoteric Learning

The House of Learning was convened in winter time after the harvesting of the sweet potato and seafood had been completed. It was in those times that the wānanga (house of learning) met. When the students arrive, they are baptised by the priests. They are taken to the water for the *kuta.* Do you know what the kuta is? It was a ritual whereby students were suspended in water to expand their capacity to hear so that they will be able hear, capture and remember the words of prayers, rituals and incantations. When this is finished, the students return to the House of Learning. They then go to the first stone, to Hukatai, and they place it in their mouths. The stone is rolled around inside the mouth for a while before it is taken out and returned. The first reason for this custom was to warn students and to alert them to the seriousness of what they are about to undertake. Secondly, it told them that knowledge was and is sacred. This is the meaning of Hukatai. Now, concerning knowledge, this is something we collect. One listens to stories and explanations and gathers these things into one's basket so that it may be full. One gathers together these things from priests and experts who have partaken of 'the food of the three baskets' (sacred knowledge). Your task is to gather together these treasures into your basket.

The Examination of the Student

Months or even years pass during which students learn at the feet of the priests and teachers. Following this, it is time for the students to again go through a 'baptismal' ceremony whereby the priests are able to determine whether a student has become the vessel of higher learning, illumination and spiritual authority or not. Hence, students are examined. Now, some students are dedicated to Tāne (under the mantle of Tāne), others to Tangaroa and so on.

If one is dedicated to Tāne, then one is sent into the forest. If you have learnt correctly the teachings concerning Tāne, you will know the correct foods of the forest. However, the real test is this: the student is sent into the forest to meditate and to fast. The goal is for the spirit of Tāne to come to you, to teach you things of the spirit so that you will know and understand all the things that have been taught to you under the aegis of your 'baptism'. Secondly, so that you may see and understand new knowledge.

According to the European, this is called 'original knowledge', in this case, concerning the forest and things pertaining to Tāne. Now there is one student who arrived at this point in his learning and was sent into the forest to seek the spirit of Tāne. He arrived and took his place in the forest for two weeks perhaps. He did what was required including meditation. He looked around about him and to the trees. After that, he returned to the House of Learning at the time arranged by the priests and teachers.

Upon arrival he was examined. Various questions were posed and he replied to all of them. Finally, they arrived at the last question: "Now, what was the teaching of the spirit of Tāne to you?" The student explained, "When I was in the forest meditating, I sat one day under some kahikatea trees. I asked myself, why do these trees grow together? One tree might be here, another might be there, but they grow together."
this seminar.

He looked at this and decided to dig around a little. Then he saw that the roots of the kahikatea trees are somewhat shallow, they do not grow deeply into the ground. He asked himself why this should be so. Then he had an illumination. He understood why the kahikatea trees grow together. This is the only tree that grows in this way. He recalled what was said (at the House of Learning). He understood…that at stormy times, when the wind blows, if the kahikatea tree should grow on its own, then it will fall over because of the shallowness of the roots. However, as they stand together, the roots have become interwoven with one another. When the wind blows and a tree should lean over, then it is held in place by the roots of another tree. This was the illumination that came to him. Further, if a person should stand on his/her own, then he/she will fall, according to the model of standing together. Upon hearing this explanation, the priests and teachers then said, "Pass".

Rehutai and Hukatai

Following this, the student then goes to the rear post of the house, to where Rehutai has been deposited. Again, that pebble, the red stone, is taken into the mouth. It is rolled around the mouth for a little while and then returned. The symbolism of this act is as follows. If one is upon a canoe, traversing the ocean at dawn, one see the rising sun. Now behind the canoe, you will see 'sea foam' or Hukatai. You have traversed and are traversing the pathways of knowledge, from the beginning. Now as you travel toward the rising sun and you look at the 'tail' of the canoe, at Hukatai, you will also see Rehutai, a rainbow within the sea foam that rises along the canoe. Now that is the symbolism. Knowledge (mātauranga) is different from knowing (mohio). When illumination of the spirit arrives (symbolised by the rainbow effect in the water), then one truly knows, according to your ancestors. When the illumination of the spirit arrives in the mind of the person that is when understanding occurs - for knowledge belongs to the head and knowing belongs to the heart. When a person understands both in the mind and in the spirit, then it is said that that person truly 'knows' (mohio).

The Baskets of the House of Learning

What is the meaning of these baskets? There are three baskets: the first is *Te Kete Tuauri* and concerns the world of *Te Tuauri* ('beyond in the dark'). These are worlds. *Te Kete Aronui* concerns the world that we reside in, *Te Ao-tū-roa* ('the long standing world'). *Te Ao Tua-ātea* is referred to as *Te Ao-mutunga-kore*, the eternal world…

Endnotes

1. The 'food contained with the baskets' is a metaphor for knowledge.
2. One translates the phrase 'ngā kete o te wānanga' as the 'baskets of knowledge' with caution.

Rev. Māori Marsden, Waipoua Forest, Northland
Photographer unknown.

The Quest for Social Justice

*It is poisonous error that brings unlimited sorrow
- the failure to keep alive one's basic convictions.*

HE PEPEHA MŌ ĒNEI RĀ

Tērā te uira te wāhi rua, i runga o Pōneke,
I te whare mīere,
Whare pou i te ture,
Pou Tinihanga.
Ehara ia nei he tohu nō te mate?
Kia mīere ko Ngāti Māori, uri tangata
Whare wāwāhi i te wairua o Te Tiriti
Kawenata tapu i herea e ngā mātua,
Ki te remu o te kahu o Wikitōria.

I hua hoki rātou ka maringi mai,
Ko te waiū, ko te mīere reka,
I puakina e te pukapuka a te mihinare
Waihoki te hua,
Te takahi mana, huti pouwhenua.

Topea ana e Heke te haki a te Kuīni
Rukuhia ana e Kawiti te Atua-o-te-pō.
Maea ake, he toto te kai,
Riro ana Ngā Puhi ki ngā niho o Tū.

Titiro whakarunga ki Ōrākau
ko Rewi Maniapoto,
Ki te maunga houhunga ko Tītokowaru,
Ki a Te Whiti-o-Rongomai, Tohu-Kakahi,
Tāroi-o-te-riri,
Kei Ngāti Toa ko Te Rauparaha,
Kei Tūhoe Pōtiki ko Te Kooti Arikirangi,
Ēnei pōkai tara, kāhui toa,
I whéke nei,
Kia toi-te-kupu, toi-te-mana,
Toi-te-whenua.

Te whenua kua mahea,
Te tangata kua ngaro,
Hinga ko ngā pou-toko-manawa
O ngā whare maire,
Tūpou ko ngā rau tītapu,
I hoaina ki taku tikitiki,
Te hou o te kōtuku,
O te toroa māpuna,
Te rau o te huia,
Tohu rangatira, tohu amorangi.

A Statement of Our Times

Forked lightning alights over Wellington
Above the house of honey,
House of laws,
House of honeyed deceit.
Is this not a portent of doom?
That Māoridom and her descendants be honeyed?
This house that divides the spirit of the Treaty,
Sacred Covenant bound by our forefathers
to the robes of Queen Victoria.

It was said
that milk and honey will pour forth,
A promise written in the Missionary's handbook.
Alas, the tainted fruits -
Mana trampled, our posts of authority removed.

Heke felled the flag of the Queen,
Kawiti submerged in the God of darkness.
He emerged having tasted blood,
and Ngā Puhi taken by the teeth of the god of war.

Look south to Ōrākau
to Rewi Maniapoto,
to the frosted mountain, to Tītokowaru,
To Te Whiti-o-Rongomai and Tohu Kākahi,
To the peacemakers.
Consider Te Rauparaha of Ngāti Toa,
and Te Kooti Arikirangi of Tūhoe-Pōtiki,
Warriors who urged us to
Hold to our Word, Hold to our Mana
Hold to our Land.

The land, desolate,
The people, lost.
The poles of this sacred house have fallen,
and our sacred plumes have wilted,
Plume of the White Heron,
Of the far-ranging Albatross.
Sacred feather of the Huia,
Symbols of chiefs and sages.

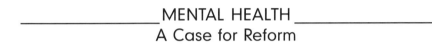

MENTAL HEALTH
A Case for Reform

Introduction

When asked to produce a paper on 'Māori Illness and Healing', I was tempted to produce an overview of Māori concepts/beliefs/attitudes regarding the subject, together with an analysis of specific areas of the subject under consideration. On further thought, I decided to change tack in order to present a contemporary point of view, in line with the seminar's general theme, and concern for reform.

This paper is therefore predicated on the thesis that continued and persistent deprivation/oppression/intrusion/imposition/manipulation/exploitation of the *tangata whenua* (indigenous peoples) by the dominant culture/society/government, poses a serious threat to the self-esteem/humanity/identity which leads to serious disorders - social/organic/mental/spiritual.

Social disorders are but symptoms of mental/spiritual dis-ease. In the contemporary New Zealand situation, the Māori is the major client/victim of the colonisation process as demonstrated by the high incidence and gross over-involvement of Māori in the negative areas of crime/unemployment/violence/mental health and confirmed by the negative statistics across the whole social/national spectrum.

But the recognition that problems exist for the tangata whenua does not guarantee that either legitimate studies of viable solutions will be implemented by the practitioners/psychologists/legalists/bureaucrats/high priests of the system in their delivery of services to the client/victim. Social/cultural/political conditioning of even well-intentioned *Pākehā* bound mentally by this cultural patterning process, together with various types of pressure to conform makes it difficult to imagine that political rhetoric will match concrete policy. To free the Māori, the Pākehā himself must be freed from his system. A lawyer, when challenged by me about his course of action in a certain case, said to me, "I can't help it, I'm only a servant of the system." Which is a cop-out if there ever was one. Something cannot be politically right, if it is morally wrong. My task then is:

- to deal with Māori illness and healing, not from an abstract/philosophical/elitist/academic standpoint, but from the sociological reality of his present plight as victim in a *milieu* of culture conflict.
- to ask basic questions, challenge assumptions, and analyse the real causes of modern Māori illness of which gross over-involvement in the negative areas of health/crime/education/employment/welfare, are symptomatic.
- to present specific examples of how the various apparatus and mechanisms of socio-political control operate under the modern form of colonialist domination.
- to show that the negative statistics affecting the Māori are directly related to deprivation etc. and not to those assumptions/rationalisations which flow from integrationist/assimilationist perspectives, couched in 'blame the victim' stereotypes.

The history of the colonisation process demonstrates that wherever it occurs, it portrays a highly predictable form, from which there emerges for the indigenous peoples the following pattern of domination and methods of socio-political control:

- Pacification by either treaty/paramilitary/military/legislative means.
- Appropriation of lands and resources
- Cultural Genocide
- Processes of assimilation past/present, resulting in the 'development of under-development' for indigenous peoples.

Conflict Model
For the above reasons, I have deliberately chosen a *conflict*, rather than a pluralist/consensus model (now termed multicultural/bicultural model) - models generally offered as best suited to an analysis of the relationship between the indigenous people and the colonial power. From the historical/economic/political perspective, this model offers a context to accommodate the past

experience of the tangata whenua (as above), and as illustrating the contemporary methods by which the Pākehā in the New Zealand situation utilises new apparatus and mechanisms of social control to ensure his continued dominance, and abort Māori aspirations in his struggles for social justice and the achievement of authentic being.

Indigenous versus Metropolitan Culture

Dr Ranginui Walker[1] distinguishes between indigenous and metropolitan culture in the following ways:

Indigenous culture has a universal set of principles held in common:

- small scale in size ranging from basic family unit through extended family, to tribal confederations.
- their mythology and spiritual beliefs credit them with divine origins and descent through culture heroes.
- rule was exercised by the elders/chiefs/priests, but the power they held was tempered by kinship bonds, and the need to validate leadership by wise and generous rule.
- consensus decision making was the method of operation for the achievement of social and political goals.
- they think of themselves as holding a special relationship to *Mother Earth* and *her* resources; as an integral part of the natural order, recipients of her bounty rather than controllers. Therefore this largess is to be treated reverently and responsibly, and not to be abused/misused/exploited/ravaged
- generosity/sharing/caring/hospitality/service/fulfilling one's social obligations were the cardinal values.

Metropolitan culture involves:

- macro scale aggregation of people
- infrastructure of centralised political power/legal system/judiciary/military; and a bureaucracy through which power is devolved down to the parochial level.
- government, with the exception of dictatorships, is founded on the democratic principle of one person, one vote, and the arbitrary convention of rule by simple majority.
- the secular and spiritual are disconnected and this disconnection is linked to the capitalist mode of production. Such disconnection produces double standards and situational ethics slotted into compartments - Christian/political/business/legal/medical etc. Such ethics

are largely professional, concerned mainly with ensuring group solidarity and protecting group interests.

- capitalism expropriates and commodifies the land, its resources and people. All have a price in the market place. Here, the god of mammon reigns supreme.

Basic Orientation of Metropole

Whilst many theoretical changes continue to occur in Metropolitania, an unchanging constant is the idea that the most important thing in life is achievement. We no longer ask *who* a person is but what is he in his work/calling/status/position. This modern approach is essentially a western idea. It finds it roots in the Calvinistic idea of election or predestination, that some are elected to eternal happiness and others to damnation. Stress was laid on everyday works, the duty of one's calling, and success in these as signs of divine approval and proof of one's election.

This attitude became pervasive and the more the modern economic system prevailed the more did unremitting diligence/strict discipline/achievement/success, become the cardinal virtues of secular man. All-round ability became the supreme virtue; profit, the object of ambition/struggle/worship; and achievement, the law of the modern efficiency-orientated society.

In a dynamically developing world, western man attempts to realise himself through his own achievements. By achieving something, his is regarded *as* something - work/career/earning money; producing/expanding/consuming - growth/efficiency/improvements in living standards; this is the meaning of life. Values that revolve around economics rank uppermost. This value overrides human/neighbour considerations; restricts one's vision to self as centre of the universe; allows and/or condemns him to the prison of the anonymous/impersonal mechanised techniques, powers and organisations of the system. The greater the progress, the more deeply enmeshed he becomes in the socio-economic process.

The network of norms/sanctions evolved in this situation controls him mercilessly in his calling/work/leisure. Prohibitions/laws/precepts sprout to meet the demands of a life thoroughly organised/regulated/bureaucratised/computerised. So he loses his autonomy/spontaneity/initiative/humanity. His life is an achievement game. He justifies his existence in terms of his achievement/performance before his society/boss/himself, rather than before the judgement seat of God.

Can he be happy in this way? Can he remain human? TV programmes like Dallas/Falcon Crest/Dynasty demonstrate graphically that a person may be a marvellous organiser/executive/manager/director and fail completely as a human being. What I am really saying is this: that whilst achievement has value, it is not *decisive.*

Jesus was firmly opposed to making achievement in itself the measure of being human, though he was not against achievement as such. The proud Pharisee who thought that his achievements counted for something in the sight of God and man and therefore to be justified both in his existence and position as a teacher and authority on Mosaic law went home unjustified. On the other hand, the sinner who made no claims concerning himself in the sight of God went home justified. He recognised that he was a recipient; that what he was and had, he owed to others. In that recognition and humble acceptance, his personality became open to receiving grace. The Crucified One did not claim any special privileges on the basis of who he was or what he had achieved. He let God justify him in the face of the defenders of pious works. Jesus is God's sign that the decision depends not on man, but on God who expects an unshakeable trust from man in his own passion.

Summary
Culture is the most powerful medium in the patterning processes of the individual's mind. The interiorised patterns/images/symbols/prejudices/stereotypes imprinted upon his soul are based primarily upon the value systems transmitted by his culture. In western culture, in which achievement/work/career/status/success/efficiency are the cardinal virtues, promoted by the educational system whose major emphasis is upon the achievement of exams; to be labelled a failure, according to arbitrary criteria, dooms a person to a future with no prospects. The resultant trauma is easy to imagine. Estrangement breeds despair, the encounter with nothingness.

Western View of Ultimate Reality
Nineteenth Century View
- The Universe is composed of indestructible atoms of solid matter existing in infinite space and absolute time.
- It conforms to strict mechanical laws operating in an absolutely predictable manner.
- Since space is infinite and time absolute, the universe is a closed system, nothing can impinge upon it from without or disturb its regularity. The whole of reality is confined within its borders.

From this 19th Century view emerged the scientific view and the pragmatic approach to life. The scientific method developed the following framework and procedure, based upon observation. You observe something happening, you seek its cause and you come up with a tentative solution (hypothesis); you put your hypothesis to the test by experiments, ideally under controlled conditions. If the results bear out your original hypothesis, you have a theory. And if after further experimentation, you obtain the same results under all conditions at all times, you may have discovered a general law.

Science and technology produce 'Know how' but it is nothing without 'Know why'. 'Know how' is a means without an end, a mere potentiality. The real problem is to turn the potential into reality (being) to achieve authentic existence. Western civilisation is in a state of permanent crisis. If this is true, then I suggest that there is something wrong with its educational system. Since it had devoted more energy and resources to organised education, with the exception of 'the arms and nuclear race', to complete its task, education must first and foremost transmit ideas of value. 'Know how' must take second place. It is foolhardy to put power into the hands of people unless they know what to do with it. The transmission of values is the major task of education. Unless it is integrated, part of the mental make-up, education cannot help us to pick our way through life, to choose between different options. Values are more than mere formulae or dogma. They are instruments by which we view, interpret, experience and make sense of the world.

Humanistic Philosophies

But Western civilisation has an almost impossible task to fulfil these ideals of education, because of its humanistic philosophies based solidly upon the scientific method and pragmatic approach which cannot answer the 'Why' of life. Until the views of the New Physicists percolate down to the masses and place the following humanistic ideas into proper perspective, there seems little hope for renewal. Humanistic ideas may be summed up as:

- Evolution is a movement from lower to higher forms.
- Natural selection, which purports to explain automatic and natural processes of evolution on the basis of 'survival of the fittest', produces a 'dog eat dog' mentality in politics/economic and life in general.
- All higher manifestations of human life – art, religion, etc are but phantasmagorias in the brains of men.
- Freud: The higher manifestations of human life are but the dark stirrings of the subconscious mind resulting from the unfulfilled incest wishes of childhood.
- Relativism – denies all absolutes, norms, values, standards.
- Positivism – Valid knowledge is obtainable only through the scientific method. No knowledge is genuine unless based upon observable fact, which is rubbish, in view of the findings of the New Physicists to which we now turn.

The New Physicists

By the turn of the century the validity of the mechanistic view and its whole philosophical base was being seriously questioned. What about those things beyond the range of human observation in the realm of the microcosm and macrocosm? Can we assume that the laws that apply there are the same as those which we obtain in the world of sense-perception? There are certain intractable factors that refuse to fit into the old framework. Further difficulties arose when a new breed of physicists propounded new theories at variance with accepted ideas – 1900, Max Planck – Quantum Theory; 1905; Einstein – With Relativity; 1927, Heisenburg – Uncertainty Principle[2].

They ask us to think of a Space/Time continuum in which space and time are relative to each other and cannot be understood apart form each other. According to this concept, the universe is finite in extent, relative in time; and in it there is no absolute rest/size/motion/simultaneity. Matter can no longer be conceived in terms of solid atoms but rather as a complex series of rhythmical patterns of energy.

Under these conditions, the atom obviously needs only a minimal space and time in which to exist. In other words, it is process. If it is process rather than inert matter, it is more akin to life/mind/spirit which are obviously processes. If true, then the world of sense-perception is unlikely to be ultimate reality.

Worlds

The New Physicists ask us to conceive of three worlds – Sense Perception/ Real World/World of Symbol.

-       *The World of Sense Perception* is a physical world around us as perceived by the senses.
-       *The Real World* – though we cannot prove its existence by logical argument, relativism compels us to assume its existence behind that of the world of sense-perception. This world is independent of us and cannot be apprehended by direct means. We grasp it by speculative means. Suffice it to say that by means of this new approach, many technological developments have taken place and an atom bomb produced. That is more powerful evidence than any logical argument.
-       *The World of Symbol* is a deliberate creation of the mind and refers indirectly to a perceived reality. The human mind creates maps/ model/formulae as a means of grasping/understanding/representing/ reconciling both the worlds of the senses and the real world postulated by the New Physicists.

Some Conclusions

We have seen that science cannot answer the questions of the why of life. Neither can education help us so long as it ignores metaphysics, our fundamental convictions about existence. Man is looking for life abundant and it is not true that knowledge is sorrow as Ortega thought. It is poisonous error that brings unlimited sorrow - the failure to keep alive one's fundamental convictions. Owing to faults in metaphysical analysis, the general populace is confused as to what those convictions are.

- Liberalism into whose morass we have been plunged recently in New Zealand is simply another name for confusion as to what our convictions really are. Mind and heart are at war with one another, and not as commonly asserted reason and faith. Our reason beclouded by extraordinary/blind/unreasoning faith in its reasoning powers (cf. Logical Positivism), spawns sets of fantastic life-destroying ideas.
- Sciences are taught without adequate awareness of the presuppositions of science; of the meaning and significance of scientific laws; and the place of the sciences in the totality of human thought.
- Economics is taught without reference to a basic view of human nature.
- Political thinking is unrelated to metaphysics and the ethical problems involved necessarily become confused and end in double-talk. Action becomes governed by expediency.

All subjects, no matter how specialised, must be connected to a centre. This centre is constituted of our most basic convictions – ideas that transcend the world of facts. This does not mean that they are purely subjective or relative, or even mere convention. But they must approximate reality whether in the world of sense-perception or the real world behind that. Such ideas without this approximation, inevitably lead to disaster. A truly educated person is not one who knows a bit about everything, but one who is truly in touch with the centre. He will be in no doubt about his basic convictions, about his view on the meaning and purpose of life, and his own life will show a sureness of touch that stems from inner clarity. The centre is where he must create for himself an orderly system of ideas about himself and the world, in order to regulate the direction of his life. If he has faced up to the ultimate questions posed by life, his own centre no longer remains in a vacuum which ingests any new idea that seeps into it. Those ideas are likely to be a denial of the meaning and purpose of life which leads to total despair and meaninglessness. Fortunately, the heart is often more intelligent than the head. So he is saved from despair but lands in confusion. Only by fronting up to the questions of his fundamental convictions will he create order where there is disorder.

What I am really saying is that in the west, metaphysics and philosophy generally have lost their way. There are as many philosophies as there are philosophers. Like a spinning catherine wheel whose sparks fly outwards fragmenting and dispersing into oblivion, so western philosophers tend to move away from each other. This is particularly the case with those whose views are founded on mechanistic views of the universe and cannot see beyond this world and the perceptions of their senses. They are the humanists/ logical positivists/liberals, who in effect reject the evidence of the New Physicists.

Māori View

The three-world view of the New Physicists, with its idea of a real world behind the world of sense-perception, consisting of a series of processes and complex patterns of energy, coincides with the Māori view. The Māori, however, goes beyond this schema and asks us to conceive of different levels of processes which together comprise the world of spirit which is ultimate reality. The world of sense-perception including all life is part of this process.

All existent being derives from a common centre. Everything depends for its existence, whether in this world, or in that behind it, upon *mauri* (lifeforce) which originates in *Io-taketake* (Io-the-first-cause). Io, whose mauri is primary and whose mauri both unifies all things and at the same time bestows them with unique qualities, provides for unity in diversity. Man is therefore an integral part both of the natural and spiritual order, for mauri animates all things. From this basic conviction derives the holistic approach of the Māori to all life.

The World of Symbol

The Māori developed his sets of symbols in the form of a genealogical tree (See Appendix Three) to portray the process by which the world of sense perception came into being. The series reads thus:

- *Io*, the Creator and First Cause, begat:
- *Te Korekore, Te Kōwhao, Te Pō* (Void, Abyss, Nights), the Realm of Potential Being, which begat:
- The seeking, pursuit, burgeoning, increase, elemental energy; i.e. the realm of energy and processes, which begat:
- Latent memory, deep mind, emerging consciousness, sound – the Realm of the Mind, which begat:
- Word and wisdom. Into that total milieu was infused:
- The Breath of the Spirit and of life – the realm of Mauri.
- Then was begotten light/shape/form; begetting in turn:
- Time and Space. Into this framework of the Space/Time continuum was born:
- Rangi and Papa – Sky Father and Earth Mother – the world of senseperception.

Māori Approach to Healing

The approach to life is governed by one's perception of reality. Since ultimate reality is for the Māori the realm of the spirit, this concept plays a major part in his approach to healing. The Western approach, based as it is upon the scientific method, deals largely with observable symptoms rather than with causes. Whilst western medical practice has recently taken on board the psychological aspect, in the Māori view psycho-somatic medicine is still deficient in that the spiritual element is not taken into account.

A large part of my thirty years in the ministry of the Church has been devoted to the healing ministry, primarily in the areas of the psyche and spirit without, however, neglecting the organic and physical aspects. On the results obtained through the application of spiritual principles, no one can convince me that the spiritual dimension is not a reality.

Scenario 1

A father and three sons arrive on my doorstep - the three sons physically holding down their mother whom they have signed out of Carrington Hospital two days earlier. She is labelled as psychotic and violent. I tell the sons to let her go which they do with some hesitation. I speak to her and I'm informed that she is deaf. Problem: How do you get through to a person whose mind is disordered and whose ears are deaf: I resort to sign language, to which she responds. She follows me inside. In a prayerful attitude I cast around for ideas on how to get through to her. Both from my cultural and biblical background I recall the principle that there are no barriers to love. I summon my wife and prayer partner who duly arrives. I explain the situation. They kneel and I pray that divine love may be poured into them. They both begin to weep in their compassion for this woman. I direct them to embrace her, to let deep call unto deep, for their spirit to touch her spirit and restore it to health and bring order to the mind. Fifteen minutes later she is completely restored. A regular client to Carrington/Oakley returns there no more. She continues to be in good health eighteen years later.

Scenario 2

A woman arrives seeking relief through prayer for arthritis. Her hands are twisted and swollen at the joints. I pray silently and then say to her, "What happened to you at the age of eleven?" She immediately regresses and begins to whimper, crying out, "Mummy don't hit me. Mummy don't hit me". When she is calmed down, she relates how she walked into their barn and a farmhand grabbed and raped her. She informed her mother who up to that point in time had never laid hands on her. Her shocked reaction was to grab a stick and beat the victim instead of comforting her. Now over eighty, that little child within her was still uncomforted. At that point I laid hands on her and asked the Spirit of Christ to touch and comfort her as she recalled those long ago events. Two days later her arthritis was completely healed.

Scenario 3

This is one of many. A young Māori boy labelled schizophrenic is brought by his mother. He is a third generation product of urban Auckland. His links with his tribal background are severed, he speaks no Māori. He insists that his great grandfather both appears and speaks to him - a phenomenon that is regarded as not unusual in Māoridom. Asked what they talk about and it appears that the grandfather is teaching him his genealogies. Knowing his background, I ask him to recite what he has just learnt. He does so correctly on different lines and for about fifteen generations back. It is no figment of the imagination. I say mass for his ancestors and especially for the grandfather and put his spirit to rest. The grandfather no longer appears and a year later he has had no further trouble. He has been on drugs and I point out that this has opened up his personality to that dimension.

I have never been over-concerned about theories which deny the realm of the spirit or those psychological methods such as 'rebirthing'. There are quicker and better methods of treatment available through the application of spiritual principles. I am more concerned with results. In the 'rebirthing' technique I would ascribe the power of healing to acceptance and love rather than to the various techniques such as suckling in the regression situation. Suckling is simply a physical demonstration of love (agape).

Domination: Methods, Strategies, Assumptions

Domination by the colonialist majority which we contend, creates social disorder leading to mental/spiritual dis-ease for the minority which tangata whenua takes many varied forms. There are three basic steps to be discerned - Initial Pacification, Assimilation, Integration.

Pacification methods are outlined on page above.

Assimilation as a strategy sets out deliberately to destroy the culture of the tangata whenua. To quote Dr Ranginui Walker:

> *In 1867 an education of public schools was introduced ostensibly to provide the indigenous people access to metropolitan culture. Its hidden agenda was assimilation. Schools became the instrument to subvert indigenous culture and replace it with the new culture or metropolitan society. In 1900 over 90% of Māori school entrants spoke their mother tongue as their first language. But because teaching was conducted in English, progress was slow. Thereafter schools*

became an arena of culture conflict when a policy of language sup-
pression was introduced. Within six decades, the number of chil-
dren speaking Māori had dropped to 26%. (source uncited)

Another mechanism introduced in 1867 which emasculated the Māori politically was the Māori Representation Act which created four Māori seats in
parliament, in a house of 70 members, when on a population basis, they were
entitled to 20. Such a large minority would have been inimical to *Pākehā*
designs on Māori land. Assumptions of Assimilationists are:

- That the assimilation of minority groups into the dominant society is
  always a positive development. We would ask, 'For whom?' In
  1845, the Māori population stood at 109,500 but by 1900 it had
  fallen to 45,000. It certainly wasn't positive for the Māori.
- That there exists a consensus about what constitutes right and wrong/
  fairness. In a mono-ethnic/mono-cultural situation this assumption
  might apply. Even this is doubtful. A classic example is the case in
  recent times in which the majority voted for a particular party, only
  to find that their opponents gained the majority of seats.
- That those who disagree with the dominant majority are deviant,
  naive, dangerous.
- Minimises the significance of power and coercion in everyday life
  between the dominant majority and the subordinate minority. (This
  could apply in a society where all were saints.)
- That economic growth is desirable. (If this is true, I wonder why up
  to 16 years ago, Bank of New Zealand policy was 'No loans to Māoris?'
  Perhaps economic development wasn't important for them!)
- The mechanisms to distribute social goods are reasonably just. (I
  wonder why Māoris complain so much?)

The above assumptions are regarded as the givens of the situation into which
solutions must fit. This positivist ideology is seen as the basis for 'rational
planning and control.' This methodology has two basic weaknesses. In its
consensual aspect, it makes no allowance for other alternatives and allows the
world 'as it is' to remain unquestioned, thus confirming the status quo whether
it is right or wrong, just or unjust. Its very limited parameters have a very
inhibiting effect upon the solutions offered. This applies especially in the
courts where adjudication (in cases where the tangata whenua are involved)
are based upon the dominant majority's value system and no account is taken
of the value systems inherent in the culture of the tangata whenua.

Integration/Assimilationist Policies

As a result of Activist movement, the Waitangi Action Group, and other protest movements, together with publications such as Sinclair's *A History of New Zealand³*, the document 'Institutional Racism DSW Tamaki Makaurau', the dominant society has become increasingly aware of the unequal status of the tangata whenua. This has resulted in a shift in philosophical posture towards the tangata whenua. Whereas it was once wholly assimilationist, it is now integrationist. This is the third step. Political and bureaucratic rhetoric, however, has not matched concrete policy. Self-interest prevents real commitment to elevating the status of the tangata whenua. The ghost of assimilationism is as yet unexorcised.

At the 'Employment Promotion Conference' in May 1985, the various government agencies overtly or tacitly admitted that they had failed the tangata whenua. As a result of this admission, we strongly advocated that the only logical alternative was to put alternate Māori structures in place of the old. When the negative statistics affecting the Māori, and the massive funding poured into these negative areas for no real returns in terms of real alleviation and relief or positive development, all the groups representing different sectional interests agreed (one or two reluctantly) to support our case.

Our proposition was simple: That our just proportion of the national budget be fast-tracked down to the tribes, through the Māori Economic Development Commission acting as a post-office, to the applicant. When the question of accountability to government through some bona fide agency was raised, it was pointed out that those same agencies had been making mistakes on behalf of the Māori for over 140 years. The Māori wanted to make his own mistakes. The iwi/hapū/whānau structures were still operative and viable and would do the job better than existing government agencies. The whole scheme was later aborted, when a Board of Māori Affairs was appointed as the distributing agency. A new bureaucracy was set up; the other agencies could allocate what they deemed fitting by the drip-feed method and still retain effective control. Māori Affairs could be used as a convenient tool and mechanism for social control. And so the sad history of Māori Affairs continues.

Within the short span of time from May 1985 to the present, the hooks of apparatus for social control have flourished like weeds after a warm spring rain. They are:

- The cross-cultural education of Pākehā decision makers.
- Attempts to erode the primary rights of the tangata whenua by switching the ideology of biculturalism based upon the Treaty of Waitangi to a diluted multi-culturalism and by the age old ploy of 'divide and rule' ensure majority domination. On the basis of the Treaty of

Waitangi, the New Zealand Bill of Rights does nothing for the Māori.

-   The appointment of Māori Advisory officers to the various agencies, but denying them any decision-making powers. This allows the Pākehā decision-maker to utilise the Māori officer to produce policy which the decision-maker can either accept or reject on the basis of whether it enhances and entrenches his power more securely or not. At the same time, the Māori officer can be a useful scapegoat if things go wrong and there is a need for self-justification.

On a more personal note, I was asked to become a Chief Advisory Officer to a government agency. I replied that if I was good enough to advise on policy then I needed to be a decision-maker to ensure that those policies would be implemented in a responsible manner. Even the courtesy of a reply was not accorded me. No real commitment to the Māori was discernible.

-   The appointment of Māori PROs to sell the department in order to get the co-operation of the Māori people. The bribe of a high salary only results in the selling of the people down the river.
-   The invitation of Māoris of some standing within their own community to sit on selection panels for preparing a short list, especially where Māoris are concerned. The final selection is kept in the hands of the Pākehā. The need for setting up authentic Māori groups to service the needs of their people, provides the sole incentive for the majority of Māori in this category to accede to such requests. Using Māoris in these and other ways is a major principle in the integrationist game.
-   Some have recognised the inevitability of Māoris becoming decision-makers. If the surrender of power is inevitable, there is the alternative of ensuring the retention of a high income. The latest ploy is to enter the field of consultation. Māori expertise is employed to teach the Pākehā Māori ways. At present scales of remuneration, a consultant can drag down eighty dollars an hour.
-   A major 'hook' in the system is certification by the system. Again, Māoris are engaged, many of them uncertificated, to inject the Māori element into educational courses and give them some credibility so that the institution can certificate Māori to work in those areas in which they are already expert, competent. Thus social control by the Pākehā over the Māori is ensured.
-   A closely allied method is to establish a parallel Pākehā structure alongside an authentic Māori initiated and developed structure already operating efficiently so that the Pākehā counterpart can certificate the Māori.

A classic example of this is the setting up of a Pākehā Infant Training Department alongside a Kōhanga Reo course in the same institution, in order to certificate Māori teachers for their Kōhanga Reo, about which the Pākehā counterparts know very little in terms of content.

Is this a new form of cultural genocide? It is at least self-evident that all these various mechanisms of socio-political control can only inhibit authentic Māori initiatives.

Cross-Cultural Education is directed towards the people in power - the decision makers; and to recruits of the agencies, especially the social workers and Police.

- Tends to emphasise differences between Māori and Pākehā, in cultural and customary terms.
- Programs are atheoretical.
- No detailed attempts to describe and explain the historical processes of pacification and its contemporary economic and social consequences are offered.

No amount of cross-cultural education will overcome the problems of discrimination and racism under a monist system.

The Law

The code is an imposed system - that of the colonial power. It is based upon the customary law of the United Kingdom and adapted according to the changing value systems, always in favour of the dominant majority. No account is taken of customary Māori law, despite the explicit agreement to do so in the Treaty of Waitangi. The one sole example of its application was the recent decision handed down in the 'shell fish' case in Christchurch[4]. There is agitation and panic in the ranks of the law-makers and vested interests lest this precedent becomes the norm. If I am any judge of the situation, processes are already under way to counteract the threat.

Double standards prevail. There is one law for the Medes and another for the Persians. Only the law of the Pākehā custom is recognised, despite the fact that the system and its application - jury peer system - emerged out of the struggles of the common people against the monarchy for social and political justice. So the Māori must be ruled by Pākehā folk-lore and folk-law. The Māori who seeks justice and redress under Pākehā law must rely upon the blunt-instrument of that very same law which is embedded upon the very mechanisms designed for his legal control.

Rationalisations to justify the system and gloss over the pitiful over-involvement of Māori in crime are given. It uses the 'blame the victim' ideology of culture conflict/culture of poverty/ignorance of their right/alcoholism and other manufactured stereotypes.

It is a brilliant ideology for justifying a perverse form of social action designed to change not society, as one might expect, but society's victim.

The next step is to look sympathetically/patronisingly at those who have the problem, single them out and label them as a special group that is different from the population in general - that difference seen as itself, hampering and maladaptive. So the different ones are seen as less competent, less skilled, less knowing (ignorant?) - in short, less human.

In these ideologies, symptoms are confused with causes. The social/political/economic consequences of deprivation, facilitated by social control mechanisms of the state, are glossed over - perhaps because of the magnitude of social/political/legal redress which would have to occur to solve the problem. Once again panic is evident amongst vested interests at the proposal to give the Waitangi Tribunal, powers to address injustices dating back to 1840.

One of the results of one hundred and forty-odd years of assimilationist policies, apart from reneging on the Treaty, is the great official reluctance to give the Māori control over services involving social and legal agencies.

The limited powers once accorded to the tribal committees to deal with petty cases were withdrawn and the Māori Warden system which operates very effectively on a voluntary basis is denied any legal status or effective power. Their effectiveness depends solely upon their own 'mana' and that accorded them by their people.

In its modern form of integration, the former assimilationist ideology allows some limited form of indigenisation. There are no autonomous Māori Legal Aid agencies to provide support and legal aid to Māori clients. A compromise arrangement using Māori Court workers and advisers to present a Māori perspective, aid lawyers, and indigenise the interface between the courts and the Māori accused, are employed. However, neither the court worker nor the Māori adviser have any real power since they are not advocates but simply 'go betweens' with limited roles and scope.

In a court system based on the 'adversary' model, only by empowering Māori as advocates, establishing autonomous Māori Legal Aid schemes, can Māori have some hope of equalising the adversary in the court situation. Māori advocates need simply to know court protocol for the sake of orderly procedure and he would be able to present a convincing case on behalf of his client in a no-nonsense manner and with good commonsense, rather than with legal guile, or nicely calculated legal prescriptions and questionable interpretations of them.

Police Processes and Procedures
In a similar case to that submitted to government by the Race Relations Office in regard to police over-concentration upon Pacific Island over-stayers, so undue attention is paid to Māori youth. Sometimes provocation is deliberately orchestrated by police to elicit an emotionally-charged reaction, such as

offensive language, whereupon an arrest may be made.

Scenario 1
The 'J Team', which I have joined for my own research purposes, received an urgent call for help from a policeman in an Ōtara mall. Arriving there we find two policemen hemmed in by about three hundred Māori youth psyching themselves up to 'doing' the policemen in. The 'J Team' was convinced that they had come to deliberately provoke the youth of Ōtara to gain an arrest. The scheme had backfired and the police were in dire peril. They were out of their jurisdiction, they had come to provoke. The Māori sergeant of 'J Team' sent them off with a flea in their ear. Calm was restored and the kids dispersed.

Scenario 2
Two policemen standing. Two Māori youths walk by minding their own business. Policeman: "Hey you."
Youth stops, looks round, makes no comment, looks at mate, turns away.
"Hey you, come here. What's your name?" End of scenario.
There is considerable concern in our society about violence. The foregoing is a prime example of the way to provoke violence. How many would not feel irritated/resentful at such an approach? This is a confrontation approach. Even if it doesn't go beyond this point, it would simply confirm in their minds the rumours they have heard concerning police treatment of Māori.

Scenario 3
(This is one of over thirty case histories recorded by a YPTP co-ordinator, also in Probation work, dealing with youth, many of whom have been convicted for various petty crimes.)
    Chris K. is apprehended outside Freeman's Bay Community Centre during the lunch break by a group of five adults. My attention is drawn to the cluster of our youth taking unusual interest in the goings-on. One of them rushes in to ask me to come quickly. I arrive at the scene where Chris K. leans on a post holding a glue bag. I approach to hear one of the adults roar,
"What's your f.....n name?"
"Chris K."
"What's your f.....n name?"
I jump in - "Who in hell are you mate?"
I turn to Chris - "Are you sniffing glue?"
"No, that prick over there gave it to me."
"Don't swear here boy". Chimes in another.
Again I ask - "Who are you and where are you from?"

They turn out to be members of Youth Aid doing a survey with a University on glue sniffing. I then tell them to go and ask why they hadn't informed me of their project. I ring Mrs A.H. their boss, and ask her to report to my office. She arrives within twenty minutes apologising for the unseemly conduct of her team. She gives the lame excuse that they were new recruits.

End.

Though we may ask why and how things happened in this way, it is more germaine to point out that it should not have happened. It left a bad taste. It only served to confirm to these youths that they were the target for the White man's persecution. This incident sowed in them the seeds of anger/ bitterness and other negative emotions. Such emotions are an invitation to violence.

Too many youths are charged with minor offences which brings them into the system, locks them into it and they become victims to continued processing by the system to the point that they become dependant on the system to service their needs. They in turn serve the needs of the institution in generating funding to create jobs for the 'controller'. The system becomes parasitic by nature and turns to cannibalising its host. Perhaps symbiosis may be a more appropriate term since the host victim becomes dependant upon its parasitic neighbour in order to survive.

Application

I have ranged over a wide field analysing the basic realities from which both Māori and Pākehā are coming; the basic convictions and motives which drive the dominant culture and the base from which it proceeds. We have compared the differing value systems, studied methods and mechanisms of socio-political control imposed by the dominant society. I have challenged assumptions and the approach of the dominant society to life and being. I have not dotted all the 'i's' nor crossed all the 't's'. We can do that for ourselves, and draw many conclusions that are logical consequences arising from the various statements and specific examples quoted.

I have been deliberately provocative in places and necessarily, in my view, quite blunt. The situation of the Māori whose escalating statistics in all negative areas of crime, health, education, employment, etc, point to a massive disorder in their ranks, and must compel us towards affirmative action programs to rectify the situation.

Conclusion

The problem of race relations, of conflict, of over-involvement takes courage to understand and courage to implement positive changes. This will entail sacrifice, especially in the area of power-sharing. It will mean a commitment to the cause of Māori emancipation. Only so will the day of confrontation be forever put off.

Endnotes

[1] Professor Ranginui Walker of the University of Auckland. Personal correspondence. This material is drawn from an undated paper. by Professor Walker.

[2] For a discussion on the work of the New Physicists, see *The Tao of Physics* by Fritjof Capra (Shambhala, Boston 2000) and *The Dancing Wu Li Masters* by Gary Zukav (Bantam Books 1980)

[3] Keith Sinclair, *A History of New Zealand.* Penguin, Auckland 1988

——RANGATIRATANGA ME TE KĀWANATANGA——

Introduction

'How do you legislate for spiritual values?' This was the question posed by the Government to the Royal Commission on Social Policy in February of 1987. This question was redirected to a Māori group of elders in Auckland for them to address. After some discussion, it was conceded that spiritual and cultural values are inseparable since the spiritual life of a people develops within the cultural context of a community of Believers. I suggest, that at heart this is the same basic question that we have been convened to address. The emphasis placed by Government on the Treaty of Waitangi and the directives issued to various Government Departments to give due regard to the principles of the Treaty in giving effect to their statutory responsibilities and obligations provide the occasion for our hui.

Since the enactment of the Treaty of Waitangi Tribunal Act 1975, the influence of the Treaty has become nationally ubiquitous and now impinges and impacts upon the life of all New Zealanders. Explicit legislative provisions to various Acts and Bills make specific mention of obligations and rights under the Treaty. They comprise the Fisheries Act 1983, Treaty of Waitangi Amendment Act 1985, Environment Act 1986, Conservation Act 1987, Māori Language Act 1987, State Owned Enterprises Act 1987, and the Māori Affairs and SOE Bills.

Whilst the directives to those bodies listed above have been explicit enough, there is one particularly important area in which Government has been remiss and that is in the area of local and regional bodies and agencies. Constitutionally, the local and regional bodies are created by statute but operate under and within the confines of their relevant Acts in which no mention of the Treaty is made. These Acts do not require these bodies to implement the provisions of the Treaty. Now, if the right to govern stems from the Treaty, the guarantees incumbent upon Government are as firmly entrenched. In my view it is a breach of the Treaty to establish local and regional government in a form inconsistent with or which does not give effect to the Treaty.

I believe that this is one of the concerns that the Māori Group must address at this hui for until this matter is dealt with, then much of the objectives and aims of this hui could be aborted. So long as the Crown confers an inconsistent jurisdiction on others, so long will Government Departments and Māori Authorities be involved in unnecessary disputes and wrangles, with those bodies.

The Māori Reality
The reality of the plight of Māori people as the most deprived ethnic group notwithstanding their status as tangata-whenua, and as equal partners under the Treaty has been spelt out often enough. This paper is predicated on the thesis that:

1. the emphasis on the Treaty of Waitangi, the climate of goodwill and genuine concern by the vast majority to accord to every citizen of this nation social, justice, equity and security is auspicious for affirmative political and social action; and

2. the continued and persistent deprivation/oppression/intrusion/imposition/manipulation and exploitation of tangata whenua by the dominant society/culture/government poses a serious threat to the self-esteem humanity/dignity of tangata whenua which lead to serious disorders social/cultural/organic/mental/spiritual.

Social ills and disorders are but symptoms of mental/spiritual dis-ease of which tangata whenua is the major victim/client, as demonstrated by the high incidence and the gross over-involvement of the Māori in the negative areas of social ills and disorders as demonstrated by the horrific negative statistics across the whole social/national spectrum. But the recognition that problems exist for tangata whenua, one of the basic reasons for which we are gathered, does not guarantee that either viable or legitimate solutions will be implemented by Government/Government Departments/bureaucrats in ensuring that Māoridom enjoys its just rights.

Let me therefore suggest to the Māori Group that we are here not simply to provide 'cross-cultural education' or 'Māori Perspectives' to bureaucrats; for that only authorises and legitimises their status, role and function thereby reinforcing their power; nor are we simply a 'Māori Consultative Body', for to accept that perception is to deny to ourselves as tangata whenua the status of 'equal partners' and our mana and 'rangatiratanga' under the terms and guarantees of the Treaty. We are more than that. We are a 'Māori Task Force' with a Mission. Our objectives and aims (and I include here our Pākehā confreres), must be to:

1.   uphold by whatever means, the principles of the Treaty on behalf of tangata whenua in order to restore to them the dignity/self-esteem/mana so long denied them, that they might pursue without let or hindrance the development of their highest and best potentialities.

2.   elicit and secure from Government/chief executives/senior-management a sincere commitment to actively protect Māori interests in the utilisation and management of this country's resources, together with the right of the Māori to possess what is theirs and to control and manage them in accordance with their preferences and perceptions under the principle of rangatiratanga.

3.   address the question of how tangata whenua can take power in 'the unqualified exercise of their tino rangatiratanga under the guarantees of the Treaty.'

The Approach

I do not anticipate that we will receive immediate or whole-hearted support for what is proposed from those with vested interests. But we can prick the Government's conscience as we show how, up to the present, Government has not exercised its powers of government either reasonably or in good faith. To this end our approach will be based upon:

1.   Philosophy - to compare Western and Māori worldviews; ethics as the basis of value judgements; and political philosophy with a view to examining the objective ends or values which underlie the purpose of political action.

2.   Colonialist Policies - to provide a legal framework within which the relationship between the Crown and tangata whenua can be worked out. Colonisation provided the basis for the 'minoritisation of indigenous issues.'

3.   Treaty of Waitangi Issues

4.   Commitment to Partnership

On the whole, we will be asking basic questions, challenging assumptions and providing new goals. By this means we hope that we all might fulfill the ideals of the general teaching of the great tradition of philosophy that, 'If we live as we ought, we shall know things as they are, and that if we see things as they are, our vision will help us to live as we ought. (Source uncited.)'

Philosophy

A man's philosophy is the sum of his beliefs; the assumptions upon which he habitually acts. They comprise those views about the world by which he guides his actions. Whilst the expressed philosophy of a given group or individual may not always correspond to that evident in its practice, ideas have a way of working themselves out in conduct in the long run. As we think we live. And as Chesterton remarked, '...the most practical and important theory about a man is his view of the universe' - his philosophy. Philosophy is significant for the whole of society for it provides a frame of reference, and a world outlook which gives meaning to life, sets standards of conduct, and forms the basis of political convictions. In other words, provides values.

To answer these fundamental questions, Philosophy asks three separate but connected questions:

-       what is the nature of reality?
-       what is the nature of right and wrong?
-       what are the grounds of valid belief?

The first is concerned with the ultimate nature of reality - things as they really are. The second is bound up with ethics; and the third, with the question 'How do we know?'

Western Scientific View of Ultimate Reality

a.   *Nineteenth Century View* - the Universe is composed of indestructible atoms of solid matter existing in infinite space and absolute time.
       - it conforms to strict mechanical laws operating in an absolutely predictable manner.
       - since space is infinite and time absolute, the universe is a closed system, nothing can impinge upon it from without or disturb its regularity. The whole of reality is confined within its borders.

b.   *Methdology of Traditional Science*
    - *Observation* - you observe something happening, you seek its cause.
    - *Hypothesis* - you come up with a tenative solution
    - *Experiment* - you put your thesis to the test by experimentation ideally under controlled conditions.

- Result - If your results bear out the original hypothesis, you have a theory. If after exhaustive testing you obtain the same results under all conditions at all times, you may have a general law.

c.   *The New Physicists -* By the turn of the century the validity of the mechanistic view and its whole philosophical base was being seriously questioned. What about those things beyond the range of human observation, in the realm of the microcosm and macrocosm? Can we assume that the laws that apply there are the same as those which obtain in the world of sense-perception? There are certain intractable factors that refuse to fit into the old framework. Further difficulties arose when a new breed of physicists propounded new theories at variance with accepted ideas - 1900, Max Planck - Quantum Theory; 1905, Einstein - with Relativity; 1927, Heisenberg - Uncertainty Principle.

They ask us to think of a Space/Time continuum in which space and time are relative to each other and cannot be understood apart form each other. According to this concept, the universe is finite in extent, relative in time, and in it there is no absolute rest/size/motion/ simultaneity.

Matter can no longer be conceived in terms of solid atoms but rather as a complex series of rhythmical patterns of energy. Under these conditions, the atom obviously needs only a minimal space and time in which to exist. In other words, it is *process*. If it is process rather than inert matter, it is more akin to life mind/spirit which are obviously processes. If true, then the world of sense-perception is unlikely to be ultimate reality.

d.   *Worlds -* The New Physicists ask us to conceive of three worlds - Sense Perception, The Real World and The World of Symbol.

- The World of Sense Perception is the physical world around us as perceived by the senses.

- The Real World - though we cannot prove its existence by logical argument, we are compelled to assume its existence behind that of the world of sense-perception. This world is independent of us and cannot be apprehended by direct means. We grasp it by speculative means. Suffice to say that by means of this new approach, many technological developments have taken place and an atom bomb produced. That is more powerful evidence than any logical argument.

- The World of Symbol is a deliberate creation of the mind and refers indirectly to a perceived reality. The human mind creates maps/ model/formulae as a means of grasping/understanding/ representing/ reconciling both the worlds of the senses and the real world postulated by the New Physicists.

e.   *Māori View* - The three-world view of the New Physicists, with its idea of a real world behind the world of sense-perception, consisting of a series of processes and complex patterns of energy, coincides with the Māori view. The Māori, however, goes beyond this schema and asks us to conceive of different levels of processes which together comprise the world of spirit which is ultimate reality. The world of sense-perception including all life is part of this process. All existent being derives from a common centre; everything depends for its existence, whether in this world or in that behind it, upon *mauri* (life-force) which originates in *Io-taketake* (Io the First Cause). Io, whose mauri is primary and whose mauri both unifies all things and at the same time bestows them with unique qualities, providing for unity in diversity. Man is therefore an integral part both of the natural and spiritual order, for mauri animates all things. From this basic conviction derives the holistic approach of the Māori to all life.

f.   *The World of Symbol* - Māori developed his sets of symbols in the form of a genealogical tree to portray the process by which the world of sense perception came into being (see Appendix Three). The series reads thus:

-    Io, the Creator and First Cause, begat:
-    *Te Korekore, Te Kōwhao, Te Pō* (Void, Abyss, Nights), The Realm of Potential Being, which begat:
-    *Te Pū* etc. Foundation Principle of all things
-    The seeking, pursuit, burgeoning, increase, elemental energy; i.e. The realm of energy and processes, which begat:
-    Latent memory, deep mind, emerging consciousness, sound, the Realm of the Mind which begat:
-    Word and Wisdom. Into that total milieu was infused:
-    The Breath of the Spirit and of life - the realm of Mauri. Then was begotten light/shape/form; begetting in turn:
-    Time and Space. Into this framework of the Space/Time continuum was born:
-    Rangi and Papa - Sky Father and Mother Earth - the world of sense-perception.

g.   *Humanistic Philosophies* - The view of ultimate reality held by the New Physicists is fast becoming the accepted modern view. It still has some way to go before it percolates down to the masses. This view which is closely paralleled by the Māori View, is being hampered in its acceptance by the redundant Humanistic Philosophies by which many westerners still guide their actions. These philosophies are still based solidly upon the traditional scientific method and pragmatic approach. Their ideas may be summed up as:

111

- *Evolution* - a movement from lower to higher forms. Based upon the theory of Natural Selection, it purports to explain automatic and natural processes of change on the basis of 'the survival of the fittest'. It is a 'this world' only philosophy.
- All high manifestations of human life - art, religion etc - are but phantasmagorias in the human brain. Yet traditional philosophy attributes the bases of values to this faculty in man.
- Sigmund Freud - The higher manifestations (value base) are but the dark stirrings of the subconscious mind resulting from the unfulfilled incest wishes of childhood.
- Positivism - Valid knowledge is obtainable only through the scientific method. No knowledge is genuine unless based upon observable facts. The New Physicists have exploded this theory.

Some Basic Conclusions

1. Science and technology produce 'Know-How' but it is nothing without 'Know-Why'. 'Know-How' is a means without an end, a mere potentiality. The real problem is to turn 'Know-How' into 'Know-Why' - the potential into being (reality) in order to achieve authentic existence. This process is only possible if we can visualise and understand the *meaning and purpose* of life.

2. Western civilisation is in a state of permanent crisis because they insist on clinging to obviously outmoded redundant philosophies, and elevate 'Know-How' into primacy. It is foolhardy to put power into the hands of people unless they know what to do with it. The various tohunga - scientists - made this mistake when they put the knowledge of the atom bomb into the hands of the military and politicians.

3. The transmission of values is the major task of education. Unless it is integrated part of the mental make-up, education cannot help us to pick our way through life - to choose between different options. Values are more than mere formulae or dogma. They are instruments by which we view, interpret and make sense of the world.

4. We have seen that science cannot answer the question of the why of life. Neither can education help us so long as it ignores metaphysics - our fundamental convictions about life. Man is looking for life abundant - (the field of ethics) - and it is not true as Ortega thought that 'knowledge is sorrow.' It is poisonous error that brings unlimited sorrow, the failure to keep alive one's fundamental convictions. Owing to faults in metaphysical analysis, and deliberately orchestrated propaganda to the contrary by the media, the general populace is confused as to what those convictions were.

5. All subjects no matter how specialised must be connected to a centre. This centre is constituted of our most basic convictions - ideas that transcend the world of sense-perception. This does not mean that they are purely subjective, or relative, or even mere convention. But they must approximate reality whether in this world of sense-perception or the real world behind that. Such ideas without this approximation inevitably lead to disaster. A truly educated person is not one who knows something about everything, or everything about something but one who is truly in touch with his centre. He will be in no doubt about his basic convictions, about his view on the meaning and purpose of life, and his own life will exhibit a sureness of touch that stems from inner clarity. The centre is where he must create for himself an orderly system of ideas about himself and the world, in order to regulate the direction of his life.

6. If he has faced up to the ultimate questions of life, his own centre no longer remains in a vacuum which ingests any new idea that seeps into it. Those ideas are likely to be a denial of the meaning and purpose of life which leads to total despair and meaninglessness. Fortunately the heart is often more intelligent than the head. So he is saved from confusion but lands in confusion. Only by fronting up to the question of his fundamental convictions will he create order where there is disorder.

7. What I am really saying is that, in the west, metaphysics and philosophy seem to have lost their way. There is today a plethora of Modern Philosophies mostly 'this worldly'; mostly spurious and therefore confused; lacking wairua; lacking a challenge to seek out the 'why' of life. There is no authentic vision and 'without a vision, the people die.'

New Physics and the Māori Worldviews

A brief reflection on these two views will reveal some remarkable parallels - the major one being the idea of 'a world or worlds' beyond this familiar world. It is, however, when we turn to the conclusions arrived at by these tohunga travelling along different paths that the parallels become even more remarkable. It is true that the New Physicists do not postulate 'a world or worlds of the spirit', but they do not deny the possibility. For them, the World of Processes - of rhythmic patterns of energy - is the only world so far discovered behind that of sense-perception. But because the universe is not a 'closed' system the existence of other worlds cannot be discounted. For the Māori tohunga, there are worlds within worlds.

-   The framework (see Appendix Three) in which the Process occurs is comprised of primeval time and space. *Time* is denoted by the 'Nights' (Pō) and *Space* by the 'Voids' (Korekore), and Abyss (Kōwhao). This is the 'Seed-Bed' of Creation. It is out of this milieu that all things evolve through the epochs and aeons of nights to emerge into the realm of Day (Ao) the realm of Created Being. These epochs or stages of evolution are clearly demarcated.

- The Root Foundations from which all find their being.
- The World or Epoch of Pure Energy
- The Epoch of Emerging consciousness culminating in Wisdom and the Word - the Agent of Articulation which calls the potential into being.
- The Epoch of the 'Wind of Life and Spirit'
- The Dawn Light out of which emerges 'Space and Form'
- The 'Space-Time' Continuum which provide the framework or Cradle into which Rangi and Papa - (the World of Sense Perception) - is born and finds its setting.

In this schema - (sets of symbols?) - we note:

1. That Ultimate Reality - (First Cause) - is Spirit (Io-taketake)
2. That a similar conclusion regarding the World of Energy or Processes as postulated by the Māori is endorsed by the New Physicists .
3. That the Space-Time continuum as the framework for the Universe is again endorsed.
4. That the general evolutionary process is endorsed by the Biblical Story of Creation.
5. That the Whakapapa (Genealogy) of Creation are symbols which provide the maps and models of these worlds by which they are apprehended. However, for the Māori, these worlds are apprehended not by the 'speculative means' of the Physicists, but by the spirit of the seer whose higher-consciousness is developed to the point where he apprehends that world with his spiritual eyes.

Retrospect
The paths traced by philosophers regarding the given world converge at one major point, namely, that the World consists of many individual things extended in space to a reality which is a single whole or unity expressing itself in the infinite variety of the familiar world. Plato conceived of a reality as a system of immaterial forms. Māori would heartily endorse this conception; and, in so far as it asserts that when we are looking for an example of reality we are closest to the mark when we equate it with what the modern world calls 'values'. The highest forms of value as conceived by Plato's model are truth, beauty and goodness.

Ethics

1. The common-sense attitude to the familiar world only recognises the things we see, touch, taste, smell, hear as true reality.
2. The equivalent common-sense attitude to human conduct denies any-thing in the mental realm as real other than our desires, impulses, aspira-tions and thought which make up the stream of our consciousness. It denies therefore that there can be any motive to action other than the pull of our desires, wishes and impulses.
3. This common-sense attitude to conduct meets the fact of *moral obligation* in the familiar opposition of, "I want to do this but I 'ought' to do that."

Like the common-sense view of metaphysics so the common-sense attitude to conduct denies the existence of universal values as existing in their *own* right and which human consciousness recognises as *ends* of human conduct and the goals of human aspiration as ideals. Just as the common-sense attitude to metaphysics reduces the familiar world to the province of science, so in ethics the common-sense attitude reduces the human soul to the province of psy-chology. If the latter were true then science and psychology would, extended sufficiently in scope, tell us all that may be known about the universe for according to this view no realms or orders of being exist outside their pur-view. Most ethical philosophers subscribe, however, to the view that an order of being other than the psychologists world of thoughts, desires and emotions must be postulated.

The Subjectivist would deny this latter and therefore reject the notion of a moral order which gives meaning and significance to ethical judgements. But the Objectivist protests this stance by pointing out that there is a general consensus amongst almost all men regarding certain general ethical principles e.g. that kindness is better than cruelty, honesty than deceit, telling the truth better than hypocrisy. This is reinforced by the ethical precepts of all the great religions tending to converge in proportion as they embody developed *spir-itual* experience. We may summarise the main arguments for 'Ethics as being the revelation of Values' as:

1. That there is something unique about man's moral consciousness.
2. To say that 'this is right and ought to be done' is to give expression to a unique experience and to report a unique fact about the universe.
3. Ethical attributes do belong objectively and in their own right to the characters of human beings, to the courses of conduct upon which they embark, to *social institutions* and to *codes of law.*
4. That the characteristic actions, institutions, codes and so on which are met with in the familiar world are recognised as good and right be cause they possess a moral quality derived from an order of reality beyond the familiar world. There is another order of reality which is immaterial and which contains values.

115

Political Philosophy

The purpose of ethics according to traditional philosophy was to prescribe the nature of the good life for individuals. The purpose of politics is to prescribe the nature of the good life for communities. Ethics and politics therefore interlock because:

1. the good life for communities is desirable insofar as it is a condition of and the means to the living of good lives by the individual citizens.

2. the good life for man is the good life for man the citizen and it can be lived only in co-operation with others in society.

3. It is the business of wise government to lay down good laws to enable members of the community to live the good life and to develop and provide the environment in which man might fulfill his highest potentialities.

In this sense politics is the supreme art since it prescribes the nature of well-being for the community as a whole. The various ends that governments may pursue are:

1. *Power* - This is the ability to impose your will upon other human beings by inflicting pain through force if they refuse to submit to it. Power has many forms - the power of money, of place, of birth, and blood and of learning; and above all, the power of superior force. This is the reality of colonialist expansionist policies embarked upon a career of conquest. They demand that they rule a territory, to be in a position to impose their wills upon indigenous peoples. They say that power may be justifiably exercised against other communities who are wicked and ought to be punished, or because they are underdeveloped and ought to be protected/assimilated/civilised. But belief or rationalisations in the wickedness of whole peoples cannot be sustained. The assumption that assimilation by the dominant majority of tangata whenua into its orbit is certainly not the experience of the victims. The implied conclusion that desire for power leads to self-deception with regards to motives is admirably summed up by Lord Acton's terrible verdict upon human history - 'all power corrupts and absolute power corrupts absolutely'.

2. *Prestige as An End* - Prestige is bound up with military greatness. But military power depends upon efficiency in the art of slaughter. This puts a particular state in the position of being able to impose its will upon another state. This is the power of the bully to impose its will on the weaker ones unless they submit. It is the power of blackmail. Now, states which possess military power are given to aggression yet history shows that aggressive militarism has sooner or later ruined the state that practises it. Hence, military prestige is not a good in itself.

3. *Wealth as an End* - Men value wealth for what it can buy. We also want it because it enhances our status in the eyes of others. Or else we may value money for the power money gives us over others. Insofar as money is

good, it is good as a means to an end. But the possessing of money and the power of money is not in itself good. Now power, prestige and wealth are not entitled to be regarded as the rightful ends of human endeavour. When they are good, they are good as a means to an end which lie beyond them.

Summary

Ends professed to be pursued by statesmen may be summarised by the four freedoms of the Atlantic Charter (source uncited) - freedom from fear/want of expression and of worship. Of these ends *perhaps* the three most high-lighted are Social Justice, Liberty and Education.

> *Social Justice* - Includes freedom from want; it includes a fairer distri-bution of the community's wealth and the extending to every citizen of the right to make the most of himself and his talents in the interest of his own self-development or that of the community. Freedom from want is a comprehensive phrase covering all we mean by economic goods - a fair wage, secure job, social security, health services, etc. These things do not constitute 'a good' in themselves, but may be valued as a means - to other things. In their absence we cannot enjoy the 'good' life.

Again, Social Justice covers the term 'Equality'. The doctrine of Equality asserts, I believe:

1.   That all men are equally important in the sight of God, for they are his creatures and children.
2.   All men are equally important to themselves.
3.   Effect can be given by the state to 1 and 2 by extending to all its citizens an equal opportunity of developing themselves. Equal-ity then is not a good in itself but a means to something else e.g. self-development and self-realisation.

Liberty and Education - The Picot Report has spelt out new directions for education so these two need not detain us for long. Liberty is a means to an efficient and freely acting body, mind, and spirit. It is freedom to think some-thing, plan, devise, organise, acquire, pursue something and upon the quality of these 'somethings' depends the value of the liberty which we think, plan, devise, acquire, organise, pursue. It is how we use it. We may use our freely acting bodies and minds to beat our wives, bash others on the head or rescue a child from drowning, or report lies about others. Similarly with education. An educated mind is more effective than an uneducated one, but effective for what ends? Educated men have done more harm in the world than the uneducated.

117

The State is made for man, and not Man for the State. Its function is to establish those conditions of order, law, security, and justice in which alone the individual can live the good life, develop his personality and realise his potentialities.

Every individual should have a voice in determining the nature of the society in which he lives. In the New Zealand situation the Māori as *tangata whenua* and under the guarantees of the Treaty of Waitangi must be accorded this basic right.

Every individual has certain rights - liberty of action, thought, speech; and of freedom from want, fear, oppression, poverty.

The individual should not be arrested save for offences prescribed by the law of the land. If arrested, he should not be held in prison without trial, and his trial should be by an independent judiciary.

Whilst the emphasis here is on the individual, he must be seen within the context of the whanau unit. For 'individual', therefore, read 'whānau'.

Modern Western Values and Māori

Modern western man has fallen into the trap of regarding values as tangible goods. The secular and spiritual are disconnected and this disconnection is linked to the capitalistic mode of production. Capitalism expropriates and commodifies the land, its resources and people. All have a price in the market place. Hence, once recognised values are sacrificed to the god of mammon. This dysfunction has not occurred in Māoridom. They think of themselves as holding a special relationship to Mother Earth and her resources.

Man is an integral part of the natural order, recipients of her bounty rather than controllers, exploiters and destroyers. For Māoridom then, primary values are generosity/caring/sharing/hospitality/service fulfilling one's social obligations. Translated into political action, the values here fulfill what we have been talking about in terms of traditional ethical and political philosophy.

PROGNOSIS FOR THE
SOCIO-ECONOMIC FUTURE OF MĀORIDOM

He Mihi

Ko te mihi tuatahi, ki a Ihowa-o-ngā-mano,
Ki te Kaihanga o Rangi e tū nei, o Papa e takoto nei
o ngā mea ngaro o te Ao Wairua,
o Te Korekore, me ngā Pō,
o ngā mea i whakatinanatia ki Te Ao-tū-roa.

Kia hora tōna marino ki te marae i waho
tōna rangimārie ki tēnei huihuitanga.
Kia whakapāoho iho tōna wairua
Ki runga ki tēnei minenga;
kia whakamanuhiritia te wairua-o-te-mohio,
taua wairua i tukua ki a Kīngi Horomona,
Kia tika ai tāna whiriwhiri i ngā take i horahia
Ki tōna aroaro, i runga i te tapu, i te pono.

Ko te mihi tuarua,
E Koro mā, e Kui mā, e te whānau,
nau mai, e waha i taku tua,
I te Kōmihana o te Karauna mō ngā Kaupapa

119

Toko-i-te-ora, Toko-i-te-Rawa
kua eke mai nei, kia ai tāku ki ake.

Tuia te Rangi e tū nei,
Tuia te Papa e takoto nei,
Tuia rātou kua riro,
I Te Ara-whānui-o-Tāne,
I te Muriwaihou, o te Pō-tiwha,
I te Pō e okioki ai te moe.
He maimai aroha ki a rātou,
He maioha ki a koutou kua eke mai nei,
Tēnā koutou, tēnā koutou, tēnā koutou.

Nā, ko ēnei kupu kei runga i te mata
o te whenua e takoto ana,
Kia tiria iho, mahu ākuanei, mahu āpōpō
i raro i te kupu mana i herea e te Karaiti,
e te tama a te Atua - 'Ko tāu e here ai i te whenua,
ka herea mai i te rangi.'

Nā, ko ēnei kupu ka horahia nei ki te aroaro o te Kōmihana;
kia poua, kia tiria, kia rurukutia i raro i te mana,
i te tokomauri tapu o Ihu,
tapu nui, tapu roa, tapu whakahirahira.
Ko te tokomauri tapu tēnei i poua,
te tokomauri o te ripeka o Kawari,
ki a Papa-tua-nuku e takoto nei,
taiāwhiao ki te Ao Whānui.

Ka eke, eke panuku,
te ohaaki o ngā mātua,
'Toi te kupu, Toi te Mana, Toi te Whenua.'

To the members of the Royal Commission on Social Policy, we, the tribes of
Te Aupōuri, Ngāti Kahu and Te Rarawa resident of the 'Tail of the Fish of
Māui', we welcome you - Nau mai, haere mai, tēnā koutou.

Introduction

We are keenly aware that you have been commissioned to perform a task that
is both onerous and fraught with many difficulties and hidden pitfalls. Your
task is onerous and extremely important because of the prevailing socio-economic conditions and climate. Because there is manifest uneasiness regarding

the unforeseeable consequences of present socio-economic policy changes and a vague disquiet that theory may not match the concrete realities and expectations for the future, you have been asked to determine those principles which Government may apply to all policy in order to achieve a more just society.

Again, accepting our limitations as human beings without the gift of omniscience and lacking the ability to forecast the future or to anticipate what social forces and changes, what market and other economic forces might scuttle the best theories, how may we determine what changes are necessary or desirable in existing policies, institutions, administration or systems to secure a fairer, more humanitarian, consistent and efficient socio-economic policy appropriate to the changed and changing requirements of New Zealand Society?

I suspect that Government realises that it has a 'tiger by the tail', or maybe its not a tiger at all but the 'Prince of the World' disguised as such. Whatever it may be, Government is manifestly pleading for a life-line, and looking to this commission and other consultative bodies to provide that life-line. In my view, this Commission ranks amongst 'the top ten' of Commissions ever set up in the history of this country. Your recommendations could determine for good or ill the quality of life that this nation may either enjoy or suffer for the next half-century or more[1].

My prayer for this Commission is that God, who alone is omniscient, might grant you the spirit of wisdom that He granted to King Solomon to enable him to order the affairs of his nation. And then, too, I pray that He will grant you the spirit of humility through which alone clarity of vision is vouchsafed, that what you produce from this Commission may be authentic and profitable, in social as well as economical terms, for this country. To conclude this introduction, different groups will have presented and will present submissions from their particular perspectives. I will be proceeding from a Māori perspective. Whilst passion may intrude at times, I believe that I am disciplined enough to be quite objective in these submissions that I now present.

Socio-Economic Policy Changes

No one viewing the sweeping policy changes introduced by the Government over the last four years can doubt that those changes will have far-reaching implications and effects on this nation. Their impact is such that the socio-cultural fabric of New Zealand is being radically altered. Emerging trends already demonstrate that:

- The rich are getting richer.
- That more millionaires have been created over the last four years than any other period of New Zealand history.
- The whole basis of the New Zealand economy has changed

and it is no longer linked to basic products but is based upon a symbol economy operated on the basis of paper transactions.

- A decline in Production and Manufacturing and the Rural sectors with a corresponding rise in Investment and Development Companies.

- Class distinctions based on wealth as opposed to poverty are social realities.

- An estimated 40% of the population now live below the breadline.

These changes pose disturbing questions. How will the Nation adjust to and cope with these changes? How can Government hope to reverse negative trends for the majority population which have moved beyond the point of no return without creating even worse disruptions to society? Given that the Māori is at the bottom of the heap, what further negative impositions will he have to endure in a racist society? This paper sets out to present past and present effects of Government policies upon Māoridom and in the light of that experience predict the likely impact of present policy changes upon Māoridom. The prognosis for Māoridom is very grim and the Commission is urged to devote special attention to Māori needs in terms of its directive of ensuring a more just society.

Backdrop

Our approach to these questions already posed must ensure that theory is balanced and endorsed by a historical appraisal of past realities which particular ideologies have effected, and face the present reality from which various sectors of the Community are coming, i.e., what their actual conditions are. For this we turn to present policies by contrasting them with past Labour Party Policies.

First Labour Government - (1938)

Labour first took office in 1938. New Zealand was suffering from a depression. The majority of the population was poverty stricken, suffering from malnutrition, ill health, lack of housing, depressed mentally and spiritually. Government was faced with the option of trying to turn the economy around or instituting a socialist policy to care for the underprivileged and ensure a fairer distribution of the national resource and to provide equality of opportunity in the labour market, in the field of education, and access to health services. In other words, the Government could emphasise the economic or the social aspect. In the event, it chose to emphasise social policy as its priority and provide Social Security.

To achieve their goals the then Government imposed economic controls based in an indirect sense upon ethical considerations of social justice and equity. They proceeded to nationalise certain institutions in order to provide welfare services rather than proceeding from the base of a profit motive. To stimulate the economy, Government introduced various forms of protectionism by way of subsidies, rebates, various forms of tax-exemptions for the Production, Manufacturing and Rural sectors. For the Rural Sector, that is the Primary Producers, the Government came up with the concept of the 'Guaranteed Price', a mechanism whereby farmers would not be subject to the vagaries of fluctuating prices. This would allow them to plan their operations on the realistic basis of their projected income.

This policy was implemented by the setting up of various Boards - Dairy Board, Wool Board, Apple and Pear Marketing Board etc. - to structure, organise, administer and co-ordinate the operations of the various primary producers. Thus, whilst Social Policy was primary, the economic aspects were not neglected. The success of those policies enabled the nation to provide one of the highest standards of living in the world, education for all of a standard that was the envy of other nations, health services that were lauded and imitated where possible by other countries, full employment, and a well-ordered society.

Some argue that the success of those policies can be attributed to an upward turn in the world economy together with the outbreak of World War II in which New Zealand came into its own as a primary producer of foodstuffs for her allies. More positively, the War demonstrated that in a crisis situation, given commitment and determination, together with unity of purpose, peoples and nations can work together to overcome crises and achieve positive results.

Present Government Policies
On coming to power, the present Labour Government faced conditions almost identical with those prevailing at the time of the First Labour Government, conditions which had developed in the period from 1974-1984. They were faced with:

- A massive external debt
- Inflation spiralling beyond control
- A depressed New Zealand dollar
- Imports exceeding exports and creating balance of payment problems
- The problems of servicing the external debt and the internal Social Welfare services now beyond the power of the economy to sustain
- A social order which, because of the negative economic con-

ditions created in its train, which gave rise to negative social conditions of unemployment/rising crime rates/educational under-achievement/mental, spiritual and organic ill health/ general social disruption.

In all this the Māori was the most affected, the major casualty at the bottom of the heap.

Options

The options facing Government were the same as those facing the First Labour Government. Should they emphasise economic policy over social policy? Or emphasise social policy over economic policy? In the event the present Government decided to opt for an economic policy, now known as 'Rogernomics'.[2] Now, previous governments had followed a policy of government regulation of the economy. Protectionism prevailed to safeguard the Rural Sector primarily and also the manufacturers to a lesser extent. The economy had been firmly linked to primary production and manufacturing.

Economic versus Social Approach

As an accountant, Roger Douglas, of 'Rogernomics' notoriety, set the economic course under the capitalistic theory that economic efficiency can only be achieved under self-regulating market price mechanisms owned and managed by private enterprise. In other words, demand will regulate supply, and in the market system, prices will adjust according to this supply-demand criterion. That is, prices will level out realistically when quantity demanded just equals quantity supplied.

Market prices are a means of rationing supply according to consumer demand. It restricts consumption either to those who need or place a high value on that product, or simply to those who can afford it. The latter applies particularly to luxury lines as opposed to products which meet basic needs. By adopting 'Rogernomics' the Labour Government did a 180 degree ideological turn. It now became openly capitalistic in its stance. As the State Owned Enterprises Act outlines in Part I - Principles, 'The principal objective of every State Enterprise, which is to operate as a *successful business*, and, to this end, to be as *profitable* and *efficient* as comparable *privately owned businesses*, to be a good employer and have a sense of social responsibility.' (My emphasis) We may note two things under this SOE directive:

- The emphasis upon the profit motive, and private as opposed to public ownership and management.
- Attempts at window-dressing by tacking on the clause, 'have a sense of social responsibility'.

Historically, private enterprise has always had a poor record in the field of social responsibility.

Economic Deregulation

The economic approach outlined below demonstrates the reality from which 'Rogernomics' is coming. Rejecting its former socialistic policy, the government took the lid off the economic pot, stoked up the fires and allowed it to boil over. It did this by:

- Deregulating the economy through the withdrawal of controls and 'freeing up the market'.
- It withdrew its protectionist policies and withdrew subsidies especially to the rural sector.
- It floated the dollar
- Introduced GST
- Promoted a 'User Pays' philosophy
- Promoted Private Enterprise and the support of Multinational, Development and Investment Corporations.

Economic and Social Impact
Symbol Economy

The major impact of such changes, whilst not yet fully evident, may be monitored and assessed on the basis of emergent trends. The first and greatest impact is the change in the whole economic base of this nation which has begun to change the whole social fabric of the nation. The economy is no longer linked to the primary products of the nation. We now have a 'symbol economy' based upon paper transactions and linked into the international market and economy. This makes the New Zealand economy vulnerable to international market forces. Symbols have two major characteristics. They are an indirect reference to some other reality. Secondly, they are a deliberate creation of the human mind. In contrast to scientific method based on direct observation, the world that symbolic representation portrays, (in this case the economic world), is apprehended by speculative means. So speculators try to anticipate and predict market trends, and on that basis, invest their capital in order to gain profits. Hence the saying, 'money makes money'. On the other hand, you can 'lose your shirt too'.

We are not sure as to what reality our new economic symbols refer to, except perhaps that paper money possesses tenuous links to a supposed gold standard whose value fluctuates and is subject to the same weaknesses as paper or symbolic money. The term 'gold-standard' is a misnomer since it does not really set any standards but is subject to change. These fluctuations or changes occur simply because the symbols are not attached to those primary realities which are based on the natural resources which supply our basic needs for food, shelter, clothing and our psychological and spiritual needs. In other words, fluctuations occur because the symbols are based on other symbols both of which are deliberate creations of the human mind. Thus a symbol economy based upon monetary symbols and not on primary products are two steps removed from reality.

Emerging Trends
1. The rise and dominance of Investment and Development Corporations over the Production and Manufacturing Corporations. Over the post-war-years, production and manufacturing companies have had an exclusive dominance in the top ten most profitable companies, with Forest Products and Watties at the top. Last year, 1986, the two categories were evenly balanced with five each, Forest Products maintaining its position at the head. This year, Brierley's, Equiticorp, Carter-Holt-Harvey hit the top in that order whilst Forest Products dropped to fifth, and Watties to seventeenth.
2. The economy, linked as it is to the International Economy, is subject to International Market forces and fluctuations reflected by the stock market. It was inevitable that the 'bullishness of the stock market', which was obviously an unrealistic state of affairs when the various countries almost without exception were in debt, should crash so resoundingly.
3. There is a widening gap between the rich and the poor. More millionaires have been created under 'Rogernomics' than in any other time in the whole history of New Zealand. This development has seen the growth of class distinctions which must inevitably lead to class conflict and Employer-Labour conflict. Inevitably too, race conflict will heighten as Māori become more deprived, and a larger Pākehā section join the ranks of the poor and compete for the few jobs available.
4. With the Governments' emphasis on profitability and cost-effectiveness those State Owned Enterprises that have been corporatised will centralise their operations by phasing out many of their branch operations. The Post Office has already begun this process.
5. Other cost-cutting devices will be achieved by cutting labour costs through the introduction of high-technology.

Together then, four and five will mean massive redundancies and escalating unemployment which in turn will escalate welfare service costs. I predicted in mid-August that our unemployment figures would top the ninety thousand before the end of September. That event occurred a week before the date predicted. With further centralisation of Post Office services and a predicted twelve hundred branches being phased out together with other corporations following suit both in the private and public sectors, plus the school leavers joining the labour force, I would estimate that unemployment figures will reach 120,000 by the end of January, and about 150,000 by the end of the first quarter 1988.

State Owned Enterprises (SOEs) and Devolution

To compound problems, the Government has introduced new policies regarding State Owned Enterprises. Certain SOEs have been corporatised and others devolved. Corporatisation and devolution are essentially the same thing occurring at different ends of the economic spectrum. Consistent with his basic business approach of making profits on the one hand and cutting costs on the other, the Minister of Finance has split the SOEs into two categories - those that can be converted into profitable business enterprises and those that fall into the Welfare Services Category.

From here, the process is simple. All those SOEs that can become profitable business enterprises have been devolved into the hands of an elite minority drawn from successful private enterprise management. Those SOEs delivering services to the community, eg Social Welfare, Labour Department, Māori Affairs which depend on Government funding for their operations are in the process of being devolved to the community to help operate partially, and others, I fear totally. By the devolution and handing over of the profitable enterprises and national assets of land, forestry, etc, to the private sector, the Government has placed the wealth of the nation into the hands of the few.

In terms of SOEs, the non-profitable SOEs, as a cost-cutting measure, have been handed over to the community. The rich under this system get the cake, the poor get the crumbs. These are crumbs for which the various groups within the community have to compete for like dogs over a bone. It is obvious that the government hopes that by involving the community in the capacity of voluntary welfare workers, labour, administration and delivery costs will be lowered. Then again such measures could mean the possibility of staff cuts and therefore lower staff costs.

Māori Affairs

Various purely service enterprises have already begun the devolution process. Social Welfare has begun to set up District Executive and Institutional Management Committees which will help to initiate policies and community projects based on local needs, prepare budgets for local welfare projects, allocate funding and monitor those projects, monitor the local office and ensure best delivery of services. The Labour Department has devolved much of its employment work schemes to the community under the 'ACCESS' Schemes. Then there are the 'COGS' Committees involved in schemes on behalf of the community. This is partial devolvement.

However, the Māori Affairs Department seems to be a different case. Under dressed-up rhetoric such as 'Tuku Rangatiratanga' and the deliberate misrepresentation of what the Māori group asked for at the Employment Promotion Conference, the Minister of Māori Affairs and the Secretary are saying that Māori have asked for devolution. A perusal of the proceedings of 'Hui Taumata' and those of the Māori Group of the Employment Promotion Conference will show that devolution was not a policy advocated by the Māori Section. I presented the Māori Submissions at the Employment Promotion Conference. Those submissions received the endorsement of all the groups present such as the Federation of Labour, the Employers Federation, the Local Bodies, the Churches, the Education-Training groups.

There were two major and several minor principles which I submitted on behalf of the Māori Section.

1. That the just proportion of the National income due to Māoridom and calculated on a pro rata basis be given over and re-targeted to meet Māori needs.

2. That the amount identified as negative funding being poured down the drain by government on behalf of its Māori clients without achieving any results be handed over to Māoridom together with the appropriate plant, eg school buildings, offices, etc to be managed by Māori boards and authorities.

Devolution of Māori Affairs as proposed by government has, as its hidden agenda, the dismantling of that particular department. The Labour Policy conference has realised the dangers of devolution and have voted for a policy of continuing government oversight over the Welfare division of SOEs.

The role of the Department of Māori Affairs is so important that it deserves a paper on its own and shall be presented elsewhere. Devolution is not the answer but the development of an alternate system.

The Treaty of Waitangi
Interpretation
Following Capt. James Cook's visit to New Zealand in 1769, culture contact steadily increased to the point where the need to regulate and define the relationships and rights of the *tangata whenua* and the *manuhiri* - indigenous and immigrant peoples - culminated in the signing of the Treaty of Waitangi between Captain Hobson, as agent of the British Queen, and the Māori chiefs. Its intention and motivation was, as the preamble specifies, based upon the principle of bicultural development and partnership. Those principles are quite clear, however, we interpret individual words.

Article 1: The Māori chiefs granted sovereignty under this article, to the Queen. The words 'sovereignty' and 'rangatiratanga', the Māori equivalent, were twisted and given an interpretation, especially by the courts, to mean 'a grant of ownership' when in fact it means nothing of the sort. The Queen has now sovereignty over all the countries of the Commonwealth who recognise her as head. As such she owns little or no lands in any of these countries, nor has she any rights of ownership solely by virtue of the fact that she is sovereign. Sovereignty has a meaning of chieftainship rather than anything to do with the rights of ownership of land. Thus the Māori version and view of the underlying principles of the Treaty is correct if one looks at it from the point of view of the correct use of English. Furthermore, *rangatiratanga*, as a function of the office of a chief simply means in the Māori view 'oversight or headship'. There is therefore no contradiction in English of saying that the Māori chiefs ceded sovereignty of their lands to the Queen, and the Māori understanding of rangatiratanga as oversight, - which had nothing to do with the ownership of land. The principle is the same as that which recognises the Queen as Head of the Church of England.

Article 2: The next basic principle, which reinforces the argument that 'sovereignty' does not mean 'ownership', was that the Māori was promised the 'full, exclusive and undisturbed possession (ownership) of their lands, estates, forests, fisheries and other possessions which they collectively or individually *owned* so long as they wished to do so.' (my emphasis) This was subject to a proviso that if they wished to sell, then the Crown has the first right of purchase. The Amendment to the Treaty of Waitangi Act 1975, is an admission that the Māori interpretation of the principles of the Treaty are correct. Also, we should note the inclusion within the State Owned Enterprises Act 1985 of the principle that 'due regard must be given to the principles of the Treaty of Waitangi.'

Recommendations

Since it is implicit within those principles that the intent was to enter into 'bicultural development and partnership', the Royal Commission, in fulfilling its directive to determine the principles which Government may apply to all social policy in order to achieve a more just society, can only do that by ensuring that the foundations upon which New Zealand society was originally founded are firmly established. The Royal Commission is therefore urged strongly to advocate:

- That the Treaty of Waitangi be entrenched in Law. A Bill of Rights for Māori would be superfluous should this be done.

- That the Commission support the principle of granting judicial powers to the Waitangi Tribunal, rather than the present
recommendatory powers.

These two recommendations are mutually interdependent. The first would guarantee that future injustices and inequities would no longer be perpetrated under institutional racist policies, and the second would give the Māori some hope of redress for past injustices from which they presently suffer and will continue to suffer.

Colonialist Policies

Within the decade of the signing of the Treaty of Waitangi, the now numerically superior Pākehā began to impose its colonialist policies. Wherever colonialist policies have been imposed across the world, its methods of operation and pattern of imposition are clearly distinguishable and highly predictable. Its aims and objectives are implemented according to the following successive stages:

1. *Pacification,* by Treaty/ Military/Paramilitary/Legislative means
2. *Dispossession,* by appropriation of lands and resources
3. *Disenfranchisement*
4. *Deculturation,* by cultural genocide under assimilationist policies
5. *Assimilation,* the assimilation and conditioning of the minority *tangata whenua* to integrate them into the dominant majority culture on the arrogant assumption that assimilation is always a positive step.

Application of Colonialist Policies

Taranaki is a prime example of how these various processes were applied. By the 1860s Taranaki was under intensive cultivation. The tribes were shipping considerable agricultural produce to Sydney markets. Land hungry settlers viewed these initiatives by tangata whenua with envy. They agitated the Government to appropriate Taranaki lands. Agents were despatched to Taranaki to foment trouble. Using the Māori principle of tribal ownership of land, they drove a wedge to divide the whānau into factions. They obtained signatures from one or two individuals for the sale of land. This ploy had the desired effect. Meanwhile a gunboat was stationed outside Waitara river mouth waiting for the balloon to go up. When hostilities broke out, agents began to lease out land to settlers without the consent of owners. These were 99 year 'Glasgow' leases giving the lessee the right of renewal in perpetuity. The deliberately orchestrated land wars of the 1860s was the means by which millions of acres of Māori land were alienated.

Whereas, at the signing of the Treaty of Waitangi the Māori owned 66.5 million acres, now they have control of only about 11.5 million acres.

Passive resistance was initiated by the Taranaki chiefs Te Whiti-o-Rongomai and Tohu Kākahi. The constabulary was sent in to suppress the movement. So has it always been with the rise of charismatic leaders trying to turn the situation of the indigenous tangata whenua around. Here as overseas with Te Rauparaha, Te Kooti, Tamehana, the King Movement here in New Zealand and others overseas Africa, India, North American and so on. Both the military and para-military forces are employed to suppress any such movement. So it is with South Africa today and leaders such as Nelson Mandela.

Legislative Means
After the war in Taranaki the Liberal Government then in power, admitted its duplicity. It called the Taranaki tribes together and proposed that the leases be allowed to stand. The Taranaki tribes unanimously rejected the proposal. The Government thereupon hastily passed legislation giving the Māori Trustee, who was a Pākehā, powers to confirm the previous leases and to negotiate new leases without the consent of the owners. Thus Taranaki lands were alienated. One hundred years later, Taranaki tribes were receiving sixpence per acre. No rental adjustments had been made. Many of the descendants of those original leases have sub-let those same lands and luxuriate in leisure upon the income derived from sub-letting whilst the real owners live below the bread-line. These and many other iniquitous laws aimed at the appropriation of Māori lands and resources have a prominent place in this nation's legislation.

Disenfranchisement
Much legislation concerning the tangata whenua was passed in a period when Māori were not even represented in Parliament. Due to pressure from the Colonial Office the New Zealand Government decided to grant the tangata whenua the franchise. By the 1867 Māori Representation Act, Māori were allowed a token 4 seats in a Parliament of 70, where, on a population basis they should have received 20 seats. But such a large minority would have been inimical to Pākehā designs on Māori land. This inequity and injustice still prevails.

- On a population basis, they should have about eight.
- If the enrolment figures were justly compiled and managed the Māori on a population basis should have at least eleven.

Whereas Māori were automatically placed on the Māori Roll at birth and given the option of transferring to the General Roll at voting age if they so chose. In recent years, the rules were changed. The reasons seem obvious and so do not need to be spelled out explicitly. On birth, the Māori child is transferred to the Pākehā or General Roll and can transfer back to the Māori Roll at voting age. The inequity of the system by which mechanisms of social and political control are put into place to deny the Māori political power must be obvious to members of the Commission.

Cultural Genocide

By the 1867 Education Act, compulsory education was introduced for Māori. Its hidden agenda was assimilation. But because teaching was conducted in English the process of assimilation was slow. To speed up the process, a policy of language suppression was deliberately introduced making the school grounds a place of culture conflict. By suppressing the language, Māori culture would be eroded and assimilation ensured. Whereas in 1900, 92% of Māori school entrants spoke their mother tongue as their first language, by 1960, that percentage had dropped to 24%. We have no present figures for today's situation[3]. My own estimate is that the figure would be in the region of minus 10%.

Now, if language is the major means of transmitting culture from one generation to another, then in the six decades from 1900-1960 Māori culture would have eroded or destroyed to the order of 70%. Initiatives such as 'Kōhanga Reo' and other 'Tū Tangata' programmes is a Māori response to the situation - an attempt to retrieve and recover the elements of their culture. This type of response is not confined to Māoridom. Similar initiatives by tangata whenua operate in Wales, Scotland, Ireland, Hawai'i, the Indians of North America and elsewhere. Only by the recovery of their culture can these people recover their identity, self-esteem and dignity.

To achieve these desired ends it only seems fair that the perpetrators of cultural genocide upon the Māori should help now in the means of recovering their culture by:

- Providing an alternate education system for Māoridom in which language, cultural perspectives, values, beliefs and norms together with standard educational curricula subjects can be taught;
- Setting up Māori Education Boards to manage and administer such a system;
- Providing the funding, plant, facilities, etc, necessary to support the system.

In social terms, the returns to the nation would far outweigh the costs. It is a social principle that when identity, self-esteem and dignity are restored then crime, violence, sexual abuse, mental and inorganic ill-health and other negative social conditions are arrested and reversed. In economic terms the sav-

ings would be enormous; in social terms the quality of life would be so en-
hanced that psychological security, confidence and peace to the nation would
be restored.

Assimilationist Policies

Assimilation proceeds on the assumption that the integration and assimilation of the minority tangata whenua into the dominant majority culture is
always a positive step. Such a social philosophy is itself based upon a further
value judgement that the dominant culture is superior to the minority culture. Like other value judgements founded on a comparative basis, such judgements being personal to a particular community, their validity is doubtful.
Values are based on particular preferences and free choice. Whilst culture is
the most powerful mental imprinting process in society, freedom of choice is
an integral part within that process. Departure from the norm is always a
possibility for the individual.

Such individuals are termed by the establishment as radical, eccentric,
ignorant, criminal. In a culture contact situation, the dominant majority apply
such labels to the oppressed minority to justify their oppressive assimilationist
policies. It is the 'blame the victim' ideology used consciously or uncon-
sciously to cover a multitude of sins. In plain terms, assimilationist policies
are racist. From the Māori point of view, such policies are not positive but
extremely negative for them.

The Māori Reality

Assimilationist policies, the basis of Government legislation and socio-political
mechanisms of control concerning Māoridom have resulted for them in:
- The massive development of underdevelopment.
- The almost total loss of their lands and resources.
- Created social conditions which have resulted for Māoridom
  in the high incidence and excessive over-involvement in the
  negative areas of crime, violence, ill-health, unemployment,
  etc.

It is our contention that there is a direct link between economic deprivation,
oppression, dispossession, manipulation, intrusion and other racist impositions; and the development and escalation of social ills within Māoridom.
This link has long been recognised by sociologists. The reality for Māoridom
is:

i.   That having lost his lands, estates, forestries, fisheries and other 'taonga'
        he has been pushed to the extreme lower end of the economic spec-
        trum. He has no resources whereby he might build an economic base
        for himself. Despite political rhetoric about democratic principles, the

       Māori can understand and sympathise with the Fijian 'tangata whenua', in their move towards self-determination;

ii.   That his last remaining resource; namely, his labour, is no longer a viable option. The introduction of high tech/the streamlining of business operations/cost-cutting methods/the centralisation of corporation and company operations with the phasing out of unprofitable branches, eg, Post Offices, thereby creating redundancy, has put pressure upon the labour market and attempts to provide employment;

iii.   That the education system orientated as it is towards servicing the white, male middle class sector has failed miserably to provide the necessary skills by which Māoridom can cope with the modern economic demands for management and administration skills, for high-tech skills, - for coping with a 'Symbol Economy'.

iv   That in a receding job market where once he was at least in the category of 'the hewers of wood and drawers of water', that category is now denied him because of the influx of Pākehā under 'Rogernomics' policies into that lower economic strata pushing the Māori further out into the new category of 'dependency'. He must now rely upon Government charity to survive. Even here, there is cause for concern. Under a 'User Pays' system how can Māori pay for health and other welfare services?

v   Recently, I joined the Cultural Development Unit teams setting up District Executive Committees for the Department of Social Welfare. The districts covered were North Auckland, Auckland, Taranaki, Hawkes Bay, Upper Wairarapa. The work involved talking to and briefing office staff, community groups and Māori communities. On the basis of talks with the various sectors together with Department of Social Welfare Directors and management, with Māori leaders, together with a study of the percentages of client groups serviced at the local level by Department of Social Welfare, my estimate of Māori living below the bread-line is in the region of 75-80%. Some offices informed me that the Māori client group they serviced was as high as 85%.

Reliable sources inform me that in the Ruatōria district on the East Coast, the average family income is $84.00 per week. This rate I believe would be obtained in many isolated communities of North Auckland. I believe that the Royal Commission Research unit should do some practical research in these areas, and I would offer my services in this field in North Auckland. Such a project would give a truer picture of actual conditions prevailing in Māoridom than a whole host of theories and slanted government statistics.

    It is further suggested that such research be conducted by Māori Research Teams whose members come from that region. In the law-courts Māori are not simply disadvantaged but find it extremely difficult to gain redress for wrongs suffered. Since Pākehā law is based upon the value systems of Pākehā culture and derives from the Westminster model, no account is taken of the value systems inherent in Māori culture. The laws are enacted by Pākehā and executed by Pākehā and therefore weighted heavily against the Māori. In order to get justice and obtain redress, Māori have to appeal to the blunt instrument of that very same law that opposes and/or ignores his values and therefore his rights. This, of course, transgresses one of the major principles of the Treaty of Waitangi which accorded Māori 'the rights of British subjects'.

Recommendations

It is recommended that the Royal Commission on Social Policy should present the following submissions to Government to:

- Secure the principles of the Treaty of Waitangi by entrenchment in law;
- Secure judicial powers for the Waitangi Tribunal;
- Cease any further alienation of Māori lands and resources, especially under corporatisation deals;
- Find ways to restore lands alienated under 'Glasgow' Perpetual leases - West Coast leases, Palmerston North, Wellington, Nelson Tenths, etc;
- Institute alternate systems of Māori Institutions in Education, Justice; and Service Institutions in Health, Māori Affairs, Employment Training, etc;
- Change the role and functions of Māori Affairs so that it can act as an interface between Māoridom and Government along the lines of the 'Bureau of Indian Affairs' in Canada. In this regard, that a 'hold' be put on plans for the devolution of Māori Affairs until extensive consultation with Māoridom is completed;
- Commit Treasury to granting the just proportion of the National income due to Māoridom to finance these 'Alternate Systems';
- To retarget the 'Negative Funding' being poured down the drain by Pākehā bureaucrats without any positive results, towards the development of initiatives managed and controlled by authentic Māori authorities;
- Commit itself to the principle of a just political Māori representation in parliament;
- Register Māori at birth upon the Māori rather than the General Roll;

135

- Ensure that Ministerial Policy Committees have a fair Māori representation on those bodies.

(NB: Perhaps the Commission might begin by co-opting more Māori onto the Commission to aid Dr Mason Durie[4] in the massive task that he faces on behalf of Māoridom).

Conclusion

Time constraints prevent us from giving consideration to other aspects of the Māori situation. There remains other areas of concern which I hope to address at a later date, eg. Māori Affairs Devolution. In conclusion, let me wish the Commission well in their deliberations praying that the Commission will give special consideration to the Māori dimension of Social Policy.

Takapau tūranga maomao,
Kei hea te tō i rangona nei?
Ko te hiki o te wae, ko te hiki whakamua,
Ko te hiki o te wae, ko te hoki whakamuri.
Kia mau, kia ū, tū mai te uru.
Ngā tai mimihi, ngā wai marama
I runga o Hūnoke.

Kia ora mai.

Endnotes

[1] In fact, the Royal Commission on Social Policy enjoyed limited success in influencing key decisions in the Government policy environment of the late 1980s and early 1990s.

[2] The brand of economic theory and practice entitled 'Rogernomics', which was to have wide and sweeping influence over almost all sectors of New Zealand society, was introduced by the fourth Labour Government in the period from 1984 to 1990. It was named after Sir Roger Douglas, the Minister of Finance in that period.

[3] Research on the state of the Māori language has been conducted in recent times. For example, the Māori Language Commission - Te Taura Whiri-i-te-reo-Māori - is conducting ongoing research.

[4] Professor Mason Durie of Ngāti Rangitāne, Ngāti Kauwhata, Ngāti Raukawa. Now Pro-Vice Chancellor (Māori), at Massey University, Palmerston North.

'TE ARA HOU FORMULA'
The Principle of Evolution not Devolution for the Department of Māori Affairs

Introduction

This paper is submitted to the Royal Commission on Social Policy to fulfil the commitment made at Maimaru[1] (12.11.87) to present a further paper in the context of the paper 'Prognosis for the future of Māoridom' regarding the reorganisation of Māori Affairs. Copies will be sent to:

> Minister of Māori Affairs
> Department of Māori Affairs
> Cabinet Ad Hoc Committee on Māori Development
> Hon. Stan Rodger
> The New Zealand Māori Council

It is entitled 'Te Ara Hou Formula' and is based on the positive principle of 'Evolution rather than Devolution'. It envisages a process of evolution - a gradual transition by stages instead of devolution with indecent haste which in some quarters is given a time-span of one year. Inordinate haste is a recipe for confusion - a programme for failure. Relevant issues must be first addressed, Government concerns met, Māori aspirations articulated, authentic goals set, organisational structures and mechanisms determined, to ensure success. Each area must be scrutinised and their likely impact on Māoridom in the long term given the full attention they deserve.

137

Scope of Paper

This paper sets out to:

- Present the evolving process by which we believe the ultimate goals of Māoridom and of Government may be satisfactorily achieved;
- Outline the specific goals to be aimed at and achieved as the minimum prerequisites necessary for transition from one stage to the next;
- The nature of the completed stage which will see the final structure emerging and functioning efficiently.

Advantages of Evolution

The schema developed to effect the objectives aimed at and the method of implementation by transition will:

- Allow for adjustments and corrections - for ironing out the bugs in terms of Māori and Government aspirations can be made according to the dictates of general or local requirements, conditions, situations and identified needs;
- Help avoid patchwork solutions, band-aid dressings should the process go beyond the point of no return and movement loses impetus and becomes petrified into monument when change becomes either extremely difficult or impossible.

Concerns

Unless success is assured at first try, the whole process could be fraught with danger. For if the real issues of Māoridom, as the most deprived and underprivileged sector of society, are not addressed sensitively and successfully resolved, the escalating volatility in race relations could cause a spark to trigger an explosion. Māori grievances, resentments and hurts run deep. One hundred and fifty years of injustice/exploitation/racist impositions and/or deprivation/powerlessness and negative mechanisms of socio-economic controls imposed upon them have driven them to the brink of desperation. Their continued perpetuation can have but one end; namely, violent reaction and retaliation.

Only a successful evolution, re-orientation and restructuring of the Māori Affairs Department can guarantee conflict resolution as Māoridom at last looks favourably at Māori Affairs as the last hope for bi-cultural development and partnership, in accordance with the spirit of the Treaty of Waitangi. Despite the polarisation and hardening of Māori-Pākehā attitudes, deliberately orchestrated by extremists of the Right and Left, an abundance of goodwill exists within the broad mainstream. To this end, that genuine partnership, racial conciliation, and justice and equity may prevail, this paper is presented.

Party Positions
General Majority
Move towards genuine bicultural development and partnership in the spirit of the Treaty of Waitangi and as articulated by Captain Hobson.

Māoridom
- To achieve equity, Māoridom develop own alternate systems based on their cultural values
- To move towards 'self-determination'
- To become an 'active and resourceful partner' in the spirit of the Treaty of Waitangi as envisaged by their ancestors in 1840.

Government
To implement the successful and progressive transfer of programmes and associated resources to Māori people in order to achieve self-determination.

Māori Affairs
- To fulfil Government directives according to the principle of 'Tuku Rangatiratanga'
- To help Māoridom adapt to the environment.

Intentions and Goals
Government
1. Is seeking a mechanism to provide for people involvement through their authorities in policy development and advocacy for resources and allows for the design and implementation of programmes to meet needs at local levels, within the broad parameters of Government policies. To achieve these ends, Māori Affairs is directed to:
   a. Focus on transfer of existing programmes to Māoridom.
   b. To develop a suitable model for devolution.
2. Examine all other publicly-funded programmes under other departments and develop and implement strategies for their transfer. Identify those issues which impact on other departments and issues.
3. This transfer of programmes and associated resources will eventually enable Māoridom to achieve *rangatiratanga* - self-determination.
4. To identify and establish authentic Māori authorities to serve the people, and develop a structure by which this transition may proceed along a carefully planned path through disciplined and manageable stages.
5. To ensure that output matches Government input. The Government will not wish to finalise arrangements unless it is satisfied that the respon-

sibilities and resources can be efficiently managed.

6. The Government regards as important, the principles of Consultation and flax-roots driven approach to devolution.

7. In order to be successful, Government recognises the principle that Devolution must not be imposed.

8. The Government retains ultimate responsibility in relation to welfare and the development of people and expenditure of public funds.

Māori Affairs

1. The Māori Affairs Department has been deluged with many suggestions and plans. Most of those I have sighted, especially those produced by the bureaucrats, are elitist in thinking and I sincerely believe that they will not work. Of those sighted, I believe that the basic principles laid down by Mr K Hui, Director of Māori Affairs, Auckland are the soundest.

2. I have not as yet sighted any structure that I would judge as being either workable, or capable of fulfilling the requirements laid down by Government. I believe that they generally lack any in-depth Māori thinking but are conditioned by 'Pākehā and Bureaucratic systems' thinking. In attempts to meet Government requirements in what is perceived as those ways most pleasing to Government and therefore most acceptable; the authors have fallen foul of the Government directive that devolution must not be imposed.

3. Government recognises that consultation and 'a flax-roots' drive approach to devolution offers the only real hope for success. The Department and other bodies are therefore urged to 'think flax-roots' - 'think Māori'.

Analysis of Māori Affairs stance

In the paper - 'Role of Department of Māori Affairs: Reform and principles of Organisation' it is admitted that:

- The Department has failed the Māori people
- Attributes that failure to past paternalistic methods of 'directing from the top'
- Maintains the key to the success of such a method depends upon the obedience of the staff officers

We concur with the 'failure' part but cannot concur with the reasons. We believe that failure has been due to:

-       The Department, too often, being used as a tool and mechanism to implement hidden agendas

-       That 'paternalism' should read imposition from the top. Imposition always creates resistance from below, a factor that Government has

belatedly recognised
- Māoridom sees staff failure as not so much due to disobedience but rather to slavish obedience to the demands of the system and not truly servicing the needs of the client;
- The other reasons are lack of consultation, and imposition of policies from the centre whilst local needs are ignored

Goal

The broad aim of the Department is 'to take active steps to enable the Māori to adapt effectively to a rapidly changing environment.' The basic method proposed is education, retaining, and experimentation (innovative behaviour) as the key to 'adaption'. 'Adaption' must never be confused, as it so often is, with 'assimilation'. The primary method of achieving the various goals places the emphasis heavily upon education - retraining. Cursory attention is paid to Māori values, attitudes, norms and beliefs. A basic tenet in educational theory is that a good teacher proceeds from 'the Known to the Unknown.' One of the major failures of the New Zealand educational system is to overlook this very principle where Māori pupils are concerned. As a result the Māori pupil starting from a different value and attitudinal base had difficulty in making a connection with the Pākehā middle-class base. Since culture is the most powerful mental and emotional imprinting process in Society, most Māori students will resist acceptance of and commitment to other value bases. Most behavioural problems may be traced to this innate resistance to change which is seen as threatening.

General Comments

Dependency is attributed to Government paternalism. I believe on the contrary that dependency is the result of institutionalised racism and deprivation. Mental dependency is the consequence of a loss of identity, self-esteem and dignity which in turn leads the victim to accept those stereotypes which the dominant majority imposes. The linear progression is dependency - disintegration of pride - dependency. Continuing deprivation, unemployment, poverty, lack of resources lock them into the dependency syndrome. Accept the benefit or starve. Where children are concerned there is but one option. About 70-75 per cent of Māoridom is living below the breadline. The average family income in the Ruatória area, Te Tai Rāwhiti, averages $84.00 per Māori family per week. Dependency cannot be overcome by rhetoric. Social ills cannot be cured by education but by the provision of the appropriate resources - funding, people, plant. Only then can training and education initiatives become fully effective. This will be outlined later.

Māori Trustee: Functions, Roles, Powers

The Māori sees the Office of the Trustee as that arm of the Māori Affairs that Government has used as the major tool and mechanism for Māori deprivation. Its link with the Māori Land Court has granted that office absolute powers to do with Māori lands whatever it wished. A glaring example of the misuse of power is the leasing of the Taranaki Lands by the Māori Trustee to Pākehā under Glasgow Leases with right of perpetual renewal.

The Māori Trustee holds an ambivalent role as an officer of different departments holding different briefs. He is an officer of:

1. The Māori Trust Office
2. The Māori Land Court
3. The Department of Māori Affairs
4. He is also the Corporation Manager of the Māori Land Court

The Māori Trust Office

As an officer of the Māori Trust Office - which is a Government Department, he is its agent for carrying out Government policy and serving its interests.

Māori Land Court

The Trustee is an officer of the Māori Land Court - an arm of the Court of New Zealand dealing with Māori Land matters and various other Māori resources. As Māori Trustee he is charged with The stewardship of all Māori lands and is answerable and accountable to the Court alone. As the Corporation Manager of the Māori Land Court, the Trustee may negotiate and contract legally binding agreements in lease, trust and other business arrangements without reference to or the consent of owners and beneficiaries. In contrast to other legal counsel and trustees under General Trust, Corporation or Company Laws the Māori Trustee is exempt from the principle of accountability to the beneficiaries.

In his capacity as Corporation Manager, the Māori Trustee has littered both the Māori Land Court and Māori Affairs Land and Legal Sections with Land and Trust deeds, Business Agreements and contracts either alienating and/or tying down Māori lands, resources and rents accruing there from. These contract arrangements are secured by the Judge of the Māori Land Court endorsing the Trustee's recommendations as 'Court Orders'. As such, Court Orders appear to be completely contained. The contract arrangement is effectively a Court Order which excludes the necessity for involving or engaging Māori owners, beneficiaries or shareholders for reasons of expediency.

This 'Mickey Mouse' process takes audit control and audit review of Māori Trustee activities away from Public Scrutiny. The question remains:

what is Government's ulterior motive for exempting the Māori Trustee from the due processes, the requirements for accountability demanded by law from others? Is it because it is in reality the Crown through the Māori Trustee who is evading the principle of accountability.

This evasion is further reinforced by the role of the Minister of Māori Affairs as Public Spokesperson on behalf of the Māori Trustee in his various roles and functions. The Minister is answerable to public opinion only by questions in the House of Parliament. By these various means the Māori Trustee has been protected by the Court. In many instances the Māori Land Court Judge has prevented critical cross-examination of the Māori Trustee's activities. This has been a major source of Māori grievance.

Sometimes adversarial methods help to clarify positional interests (i.e., who is doing what to whom?) In these situations, the Māori people's attendance as a group with a general grievance does not help to identify the focus of their general grievance. The oppressor hides within the protocols of judicial decorum. The Māori Trustee has been a major corporation negotiator in the contracting and leasing out of Māori lands to Pākehā interests. In afforestation and other matters now subject to SOE activities.

The multiple role of the Trustee can be said to have been instrumental in the accelerated loss and alienation of Māori lands. It is ironical that Government insists on Māori accountability when it has by legal means avoided and evaded accountability to Māoridom for 150 years. Whilst protesting the principle of 'one law for all' to avoid double standards, Government in self-interest changes the rules to suit its own ends and enacts one law for the Pākehā and another for the Māori. Now that the Māori Trust Office has fulfilled its purpose of appropriating to Government nearly all the lands and resources of Māoridom and other mechanisms such as the SOE Act are now in place to effect the final 'coup de grace' to Māori lands and resources the Office of the Māori Trustee has become redundant, together with that of the Māori Land Court.

In the past, this was the arm of Māori Affairs that paid its own way and that of the Department of Māori Affairs generally by netting for Government countless billions of dollars in lands, resources and other assents. Now that it has served its purpose and the general operational costs of the Department of Māori Affairs is no longer profitable, one wonders whether devolution as proposed is not the beginning of a process whose end is abandonment. Before that event occurs, the Māori Trust Office and Māori Land Court should begin to get its house in order, begin stock-taking with a view to handing back control to Māori owners and beneficiaries.

143

Te Ara Hou - Evolution not Devolution
He Timatanga
He Pepeha

Tērā te uira te wāhi rua i runga o Pōneke.
I te whare miere, whare pou i te ture, pou i te tinihanga.
Ehara ia nei ko te tohu o te mate
Kia miere ko Ngāti Māori, uri tangata
Whare wāwāhi i te wairua o Te Tiriti
Kawenata tapu i herea e ngā mātua
Ki te remu o te kahu o Wikitoria.

Hua hoki rātou ka maringi mai,
Ko te waiū, ka tureture ko te miere
I puakina e te pukapuka a ngā Mihinare.
Waihoki te hua, he takahi mana, he huti pouwhenua.
Topea ana e Heke te haki a te Kuini
Rukuhia e Kawiti te Atua o te pō
Maea ake ki uta, he toto te kai.
Riro ana Ngā Puhi ki ngā niho o Tū.

Titiro whakarunga ki Ōrākau ko Rewi Maniapoto
Ki te maunga hauhunga, ko Tītokowaru.
Ki a Te Whiti-o-Rongomai, Tohu Kākahi, ngā tāroi o te riri
Kei Ngāti Toa ko Te Rauparaha,
Kei Tūhoe-pōtiki ko Te Kooti Arikirangi,
Ēnei rārangi tāngata, i whēke ai,
Kia 'Toi te Kupu, Toi te Mana, Toi te Whenua.'

Te whenua kua mahea, te iwi kua ngaro,
Ngā pou-toko-manawa o ngā whare maire,
Tūpou ko ngā rau titapu, i hoaina ai ki taku tikitiki
Te hou o te kotuku, o te toroa māpuna
Te rau o te huia – tohu amorangi, tohu rangatira.

He aha tēnei kupu e wawara mai nei,
'Te tuku rangatiratanga' a Te Kāwanatanga?
E kore, kore rawa taku mate, e ea i te moni.
Mā ngā toto anake rā o taku Ariki,
E hoko kia ea.
Ngā mate o te iwi, o te ao,
Waiho atu ki ngā ara tawhito i poua ai,
Te ara mai o te mana – Mana Atua, Mana Tupuna, Mana Whenua

E tū e te Tari Māori, ki te wehenga o ngā ora,
Tirohia atu ngā ara tawhito o namata.
Uia ki te wāhi ngaro, "Kei hea tō wāhi pai?"
Haere rā reira ka kitea rā e koe,
Te tānga manawa mō te iwi – mō te rahi, mō te iti

Hoea tō waka kia mārō te haere
Wāhia te moana waiwai o te Ao Pākehā
Papaki te tai ki te papa rape nui o te waka
Takiri tū ki te pae o Rēhua

Kia mai e tauiwi kāhore ōu toa.
Kao! He toa anō tōu!
He uru mataku te uru o te hoe
He kakau whakawhana.
Wāhia te ara o Tāwhiri-mātea
Ki te whare o Māui-tikitiki-a-Taranga,
E takoto mai nei. Kia eke, eke panuku.
Pūtātara! Pūtātara! Ki Te Wheiao, ki Te Ao Mārama.[2]

Organisational Structure
Introduction
Accepting at face value the stated stance of Government and the directives by the Hon. Stan Rodger, and in the hopes that political rhetoric will match concrete policy, we present the following Organisational Structure that we are confident will fulfil:

-    The demands of Māoridom for self-determination – 'mana motuhake' in the best sense of that term; *viz a viz*, the restoration of one's due rights.
-    The stated requirements and aims of Government regarding the devolution of Māori Affairs.
-    The goals of all parties as a movement toward bi-cultural development and partnership in terms of the Spirit of the Treaty of Waitangi.

The structure is therefore called 'Rārangi Tūtahi-Partnership Structure'. It means, 'The Means by which we stand together'.

Organisational Goals
The structure outlined above will, we believe:

Structural Framework

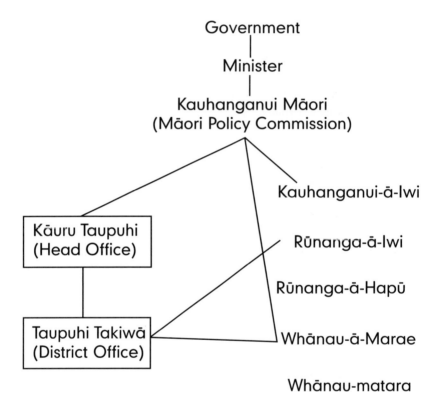

Government

Minister

Kauhanganui Māori
(Māori Policy Commission)

Kauhanganui-ā-Iwi

Kāuru Taupuhi
(Head Office)

Rūnanga-ā-Iwi

Rūnanga-ā-Hapū

Taupuhi Takiwā
(District Office)

Whānau-ā-Marae

Whānau-matara

- Provide the mechanism whereby the requirements and aspirations of all parties will be realised
- Provide the means by which policies may be developed at national and local levels in order to design and implement programmes to meet needs at the local level.
- Provide the means by which two-way communication from top to bottom may be effected to ensure that the 'flax-roots' are not isolated from the stem, leaves and 'the Crown'.
- It distinguishes between 'Traditional' and 'Executive' Leadership and defines the legitimate Māori authorities with whom Government may negotiate and thereby avoid conflict and confusion.
- Provides the mechanisms for accountability upwards, downwards and laterally.
- Mechanisms for drawing up budgets and determining funding requirements based upon Iwi/Hapū/Whānau needs in terms of projects and initiatives developed at regional and local levels, providing expert help to aid and monitor those projects in order to ensure viability and success.
- Provides the mechanisms by which funding may flow smoothly down to the applicants and project providers to ensure maximum output for input provided.
- Outlines the stages by which smooth transition may be effected from one stage to the next as the predetermined goals for those stages are achieved.
- Projects the time-span required for the completion of each stage and forecasts the total time-span by which the ultimate goals may be achieved.

We propose to divide the Organisational Structure into three sections – A, B and C.

Section A will deal with the role, functions and responsibilities of Government system.
Section B with those of Māori Affairs
Section C with those of Māoridom.
Section A will comprise Government, Minister of Māori Affairs and Kauhanga-nui Māori – Māori Policy Commission.
Section B will consist of Kāuru Taupuhi (Head Office) and Taupuhi Takiwā (District Offices).

Section C will comprise Kauhanganui-a-Iwi, Rūnanga-a-Iwi, Rūnanga Hapū, Whānau-ā-marae, Whānau-Matara.

Time Span: Three Years
Section A
Government and Ministerial functions are fixed by Statute.

KAUHANGANUI MĀORI (Māori Policy Commission)

- Te Kauhanganui Māori will be responsible to Government through the Minister, of developing general policy on behalf of Māoridom.
- They will glean and collate the policies developed at the local level by the Rūnanga-a-Iwi and Whānau groups for presentation to Government if these are adjudged to be of national significance to Māoridom.
- They will act as the interface and play an advocacy role with Government on behalf of Māoridom in matters of national significance, and advise the Minister on matters Māori.
- They will receive from Iwi Authorities the budget estimates of each region, the budget estimates of the Department of Māori Affairs for its operational costs, and present these to Government through the Minister.
- Block funding for Māori Regional Development will be dispersed directly to each Rūnanga-a-Iwi.
- Te Kauhanganui will, through Head Office, draw up a budget schema and define the categories of operations and other cost factors for which the Iwi Authorities may legitimately apply. This Schema will be reviewed annually to make provision for ongoing development of Māori initiatives and projects.
- The Kauhanganui will monitor Head Office operation and ensure that the policies, directives and services approved jointly by Government and the Kauhanganui Māori are implemented and delivered by the Department.

The Kauhanganui will identify issues which impact upon other Government agencies and departments, e.g. education, health, lands, justice, etc, with a view to developing alternate systems under Māori Mana.

Composition of Kauhanganui Members
- Twelve members
- Minister of Māori Affairs – ex officio
- Director-General of Māori Affairs – ex officio
    Ten Iwi Representatives - from Waka groupings; Te Tai Tokerau,

Tainui, Te Arawa, Mātaatua, Horouta, Takitimu, Tokomaru, Aotea, Kurahaupō, Ngāi Tahu.

The Iwi Representatives will be elected by the Rūnanga-a-Iwi of each waka grouping together in conference. Since within each waka grouping several Iwi groupings exist, representation will rotate amongst them on a basis to be decided by each waka grouping.

Meetings

The Chairman will be elected from the Iwi Representatives at each Annual General Meeting and he/she will hold office for a term of one year. The Kauhanganui will meet on a regular basis. They will hold an Annual General Meeting attended by the Chairman of each Rūnanga-a-Iwi and Kauhanganui-a-Iwi, at which the Kauhanganui-Māori will:

1	Present properly audited accounts;
2	Present budget estimates;
3	Present a Progress Report on its activities;
4	Present a forecast on future directions, policies and initiatives.

New Zealand Māori Council

On taking office, the Kauhanganui Māori will take over the activities and operations of the New Zealand Māori Council which will be phased out.

Section B
I. Kāuru Taupuhi (Head Office)

The adjective *taupuhi* defines the Department's new direction, roles and functions as being supportive and facilitative. Under the Authority of 'the Minister' and the 'Kauhanganui Māori' the Head Office will:

- Implement general policies as directed by the Minister and Kauhanganui Māori.
- Deliver the services to Māoridom delegated to it by the Minister and Kauhanganui Māori.
- Initiate training and other developmental programmes through the District offices (Taupuhi Takiwā) with an emphasis on 'People Development' in the areas of Management, Administration, Accounting, Communications, High-tech, etc and with a view to promoting the evolutionary process within Māoridom towards eventual self-determination.
- The Time-Span envisaged for the completion of this Stage I is three years.

149

II. Taupuhi Takiwā (District Offices)

- Will implement at the local level those policies and directives promulgated by Head Office;
- Ensure the best delivery of services to the Rūnanga-a-Iwi and the hapū/whānau groups;
- To prepare the Iwi Authorities (Rūnanga-a-Iwi) for their future roles and functions, the District offices will provide specialist help to guide, assist, advise and monitor Rūnanga-a-Iwi initiatives and projects; management, administration and accounting procedures;
- Provide assistance to the Kauhanganui-a-Iwi by way of funding and equipment to assist them in the transmission of cultural lore and other elements to the rising generations.

Comments

In the first phase of evolution, the staff expertise found in the District offices is indispensable to the smooth transition from Stage I to Stage II, in which the Rūnanga-a-Iwi will assume more and more of the functions of the District Office. It is therefore obvious that a major function will be in the training of personnel in the field of general management needed by iwi to achieve their goals of self-determination. That phase out date will be 3-4 years away. As general departmental policy, it is suggested that staff members where expedient, be relocated at those offices within the iwi regions to which they are affiliated by blood, to provide the various Rūnanga with a core group of skilled personnel when the second stage is implemented. At the Second Stage the District office and plant will be transferred to the local iwi Authority. Stage I allows for a familiarisation and orientation period of Rūnanga take-over.

Section C - Māori Authorities
Foreword

This section deals with Māori Authorities and their traditionally recognised roles and functions. They still operate to a greater or lesser degree within the different iwi regions. Assimilationist policies of the past imposed by the dominant Pākehā majority have eroded and undermined the mana of the recognised iwi authorities by:

a. Denying Māoridom generally, and recognised Māori Authorities, any real policy and decision-making powers;

b. Interposing its own selected and appointed Māori Authorities, so-called, as the interface between Government and Māoridom, (eg Māori Land Court, Māori Trustee, New Zealand Māori Council, Māori Trust Boards, Departmental Of-

ficials, etc), with whom they have made contractual arrangements and carried out other negotiations thus locking out
the traditionally recognised authorities.

c.   Setting up under the aegis of the Māori Affairs Department,
or by sponsorship, other Māori Groups accountable not to
Māoridom but to Government, e.g. Māori Wardens, Māori
Women's Welfare League, etc. This is not to denigrate their
work but to point up the whole question of authority and
accountability.

It is little wonder that Government having created such disorder and confusion is itself confused as to who the real Māori and Iwi Authorities may be. It
is therefore imperative that these be defined and distinguished before any
negotiations are entered into. The first step is to define who or what the
Māori Authorities are not. They are not sector organisations such as Māori
Women's Welfare League; pressure groups such as the Waitangi Action Group;
nor official groups set up under Government or the Department such as
Kōkiri Centres.

Legitimate Māori Authorities

Māori Authorities acceptable to Māoridom as a whole are those that fit Māori
categories of traditional leadership and those bodies appointed by the iwi to
execute their wishes and negotiate on their behalf. We must therefore distin-
guish between Traditional and Executive Leadership.

Traditional Leadership - Kauhanganui-a-Iwi

The Kauhanganui-ā-Iwi comprised in former times the traditional 'paepae' of
elders – the kaumātua whose mutually interdependent roles combined together to uphold the mana and mauri of the people. There were three recognised bases of mana, *mana atua*, *mana tupuna*, *mana whenua*. These were the
mana or authority of the gods, ancestors and territorial rights. Their membership of the Kauhanganui through these various sources made their participation in the councils of the people as theirs by right.

They were the *amorangi*, the *tohunga*, and leaders of the people. As
those who 'fronted up' and acted as the interface between the iwi/hapū and
the rest of Māoridom, to them was applied the proverb, 'Te Amorangi ki mua,
te hapai ō ki muri'. And to illustrate the interdependence between 'mua and
muri' – the proverb 'Ki te tika ā muri, ka tika ā mua' was applied. 'When the
rearguard is functioning efficiently, the vanguard will also function effectively'. There are now two fronts upon which the Iwi must operate, - the
Māori Front and the Pākehā Front. The Kauhanganui-ā-Iwi will operate on
the Māori Front, and the Rūnanga-ā-Iwi as the Executive Leadership will

operate on the Pākehā Front. The Kauhanganui members are drawn from the marae-based whānau leadership of kaumātua, hence; whānau isolation under this system is virtually impossible.

Functions and Role of Kauhanganui

1. To uphold the *mana*, *mauri* and *tapu* of the iwi/hapū/whānau.
2. To be the repository on behalf of all whānau groupings of the cultural taonga – the lore, traditions, history, whakapapa and other cultural elements of the people and transmit them to their children and *mokopuna*.
3. To develop *wānanga* and other teaching programmes on behalf of their people. (This is not an area in which the Māori Affairs Department should be engaged except in providing the funding, equipment and plant under the direction of the Māori Policy Commission to enable Te Kauhanganui-ā-Iwi to carry out their task)
4. To establish *kaupapa Māori* for the Iwi.
5. To promote and direct *Kaupapa Wairua* for the Iwi.
6. To monitor the policies of the Rūnanga-a-Iwi as to the benefits of such policies for the iwi on a long term basis.

Rūnanga-ā-Iwi (Tribal Trust Boards)

The Rūnanga-ā-Iwi is the Executive Leadership appointed or elected by the iwi to the Tribal Trust Board, on the basis of their competence and expertise in the fields of:

- *Economy* as analysts, controllers, managers in Resource Development, Marketing, Trade, Finance, Accountancy, High Tech, Communications, etc
- *Professionalism*, eg Education, Justice, Labour and Employment, Health, etc.
- *Cultural*, Tikanga and Kaupapa Māori
- *Tikanga Wairua*

Their term of office will be determined by the Iwi assembled at the first Annual General Meeting of the Rūnanga. Membership is open to all beneficiaries of voting age of both sexes.

Functions

They will be the interface between the iwi and Government and other Public Bodies, Corporations, Businesses, etc. As members of the Trust Board, they shall negotiate benefits and contractual agreements with the appropriate body or bodies on behalf of the iwi.

- They will not, however, usurp hapū/whānau rights of negotiation unless specifically directed by whānau/hapū or individuals on their own behalf.
- They will establish policies, develop programmes at the be-
hest of the iwi/hapū/ whānau and present and advocate these
to government through the Kauhanganui Māori.
- They will monitor the operations of the District Office, support and facilitate those operations to ensure the best delivery of services to the people when and where required.

Accountability
1. The Rūnanga-ā-Iwi (Trust Board) shall hold an Annual General Meeting
at which they shall present properly audited accounts, give a financial
report, an account of their stewardship, and present a forecast of future
directions, policies and projects to the beneficiaries.
2. They will draw up a general agenda which will include policy submissions, budget estimates, new initiatives and projects proposed by hapū/
whānau (not by individuals except through their whānau) groups and if
they are of national significance, present and advocate them at
'Kauhanganui Māori' (Māori Policy Commission) level.
3. They will present their own policies for the approval of the meeting.

In order to expedite matters and allow the Rūnanga to react quickly to the
demands of new and/or changing conditions and situations, the Rūnanga may
initiate such projects or policies if the Executive Committee of the Kauhanganui-
ā-Iwi endorses them. But if in the opinion of that Body such new policies are
contrary to the best interests of the beneficiaries they shall have the power of
veto. That veto shall apply only until, or if, the AGM overturns such a veto.

III.4 Comments
The Iwi Kauhanganui and Rūnanga provide the leadership on two fronts that
ensures the holistic approach advocated by Sir Apirana Ngata in his statement
which commences, 'E tipu e rea', identifying the three pronged approach of
the:

1. Politico-economic
2. Socio-cultural
3. Spiritual

The first is here provided for by the Rūnanga, and the second and third by
the Kauhanganui. This holistic approach provides consistency and unity of
approach across the board because of commonly held value systems, norms

and attitudes thereby avoiding social distortions and disorders. The restoration of traditional leadership together with the provision of an executive leadership will, more than any other factor, help heal the disorders endemic in Māori Society.

Because the Kauhanganui holds the real mana of the people and the AGM provides the forum for people consultation, the Rūnanga is accountable to the beneficiaries and the flax-roots are not isolated from the mainstream or neglected. This has in the past been a major grievance of the beneficiaries of most Trust Boards. Whilst accountability has under the Trust Board Act been accorded to Government, the trustees have never been accountable to the beneficiaries.

In living memory, my own Tai Tokerau Trust Board has never presented audited reports of its accounts or of its stewardship of iwi assets to the beneficiaries. To be a beneficiary one must enrol officially. To vote one must be on the official roll of the Trust Board. No account is taken of Māori protocol and of a person's natural right by birth. In that sense, the Trustees themselves denigrate *mana tupuna.*

Cultural values and self-identity are destroyed under a system that panders to Pākehā protocol and downgrades its own systems. Rangatiratanga is not dependant upon a piece of Pākehā paper, it is the natural heritage of every Māori through *mana atua, mana tupuna, mana whenua.* Nor can it be bought with money. Tuku Rangatiratanga by Government to Māoridom perpetuates a myth which many modern Māori have blindly accepted. Both the preamble and Article II of the Treaty of Waitangi in the Māori version guaranteed 'rangatiratanga'. The Māori signatories ceded 'Kāwanatanga' under Article I. That is the only power that Government can legitimately hand back.

Whānau Matara
The term 'matara' means detached, distant, scattered. A *whānau matara* refers to whānau members of an iwi or hapū that have migrated out of their own territories to other areas wherein they have no claims to mana whenua. This is a problem created by urban displacement or drift. Displacement was an organised relocation by Government through manpower, and Māori Affairs Department schemes to provide a labour force for the production and manufacturing sectors in Urbia. Drift was a voluntary relocation by those seeking jobs elsewhere. As a result of these combined forces many 'whānau matara' are now located in major urban areas far removed from their tribal roots. This poses a problem of servicing these groups. Nearly all of them have formed hapū and/or whānau groupings. Many have established marae or independent headquarters with hapū or whānau committees. Others circulate from house to house holding whānau meetings. They band together to

promote certain aims and objectives. Those aims and objectives generally held in common by all these groups are:

1.   To form a support group to promote the welfare of members of the hapū/whānau
2.   To preserve their identity by meeting regularly in fellowship together, or for the purpose of transmitting the lore and history of their iwi and hapū
3.   To develop initiatives and projects for the benefit of their members
4.   To keep open lines of communication with their 'homebase'. In this regard, they draw upon the resources of their home bases, and, in turn, provide funding and other resources of the home base.

Thus the links between the urban and the 'home' whānau are maintained.

Alternatives
There are several alternatives for servicing Māoridom in Urbia:

a.   Divide the urban area into geographic regions and service those Māori resident in those areas from a district office.
b.   Establish a structure which will enable the hapū/whānau in urbia to be serviced wholly by the Rūnanga of their particular iwi in the home base.
c.   Form an urban 'waka' grouping based upon those principles of membership of the 'Kauhanganui Māori' (Māori Policy Commission); and under that umbrella, form the appropriate iwi divisions to correspond with the Rūnanga-ā-Iwi divisions within the established 'home' territories.

Preferences
1.   The third option is preferred. It corresponds with Option Two in fulfilling the urban whānau objectives of maintaining the links with the home base.
2.   It prevents the proliferation of pseudo-Māori authorities, and established Urban Māori Authorities whose legitimacy is derived from their iwi foundations.
3.   In matters of general policy affecting them in their urban situation, their Rūnanga at 'home' can be their advocates to the Māori Policy Commission.
4.   In matters of servicing, the District office can negotiate with

the various 'Waka Rūnanga' established in the urban area.

5. The District office could form an advisory Kauhanganui of Elders to support the office in matters of general cultural initiatives, and be the group to organise and resource cultural teaching programmes available to all the iwi or particular hapū/whānau groups.

6. A 'waka grouping' system would conform with those structures already proposed under the 'Te Ara Hou' structure for the Department of Māori Affairs and ensure uniformity and consistency of systems throughout Māoridom.

7. An 'ad hoc' Rūnanga Māori could be formed in Urbia consisting of members representing the various 'waka' to share ideas, plans overall strategy, and support each other in particular or common projects.

8. They may also work together to set up Māori Health, Education and other boards or agencies to service Māori needs in Urbia

9. This combined 'Waka Rūnanga' could, with tangata whenua, lay down the parameters of *Mauri-tangata* and *mauri manaaki* to govern the relationships between the Tangata Whenua and Whānau Matara.

The possibilities and permutations for different methods of establishing working relations and developing strategy are infinite and exciting.

Stages of Transition
Stage One

- Consultation process with Māoridom, setting up of 'Rūnanga-ā-Iwi (Trust Boards) or Interim Boards where required, to be completed by 1 April 1988.
- Kauhanganui Māori, Māori Policy Commission to be established by 1 April 1988.
- Head Office to draw up training programmes, brief staff, set up training mechanisms and implement those programmes through District offices with a view to developing those skills in general management needed to prepare the Rūnanga-a-Iwi for eventual take-over. Implementation at Rūnanga level by mid-April.
- Head Office to prepare budget estimates for 1988-89 taking into account not only its operational cost overall but the projected needs of the Regions serviced by District offices.

- Depending upon the quality of training offered, the familiarisation process needed to prepare the various Rūnanga to assume those operations carried out by District offices; and to shoulder the responsibilities required of them, the date for completion of Stage One will be determined. The time-span envisaged is three years.

Goals

The goal to be achieved before transition to Stage Two is decided are:

1. The thorough familiarisation of the Māori Policy Commission with the scope and extent of Departmental operations and responsibilities.
2. To train the Rūnanga to that stage of efficiency in management skills that will enable them to assume the functions and rates of the District office.

Endnotes

[1] Maimaru (sometimes Mahimaru) is a marae located at Awanui, outside of Kaitaia.

[2] A version of this *pepeha*, together with a translation can be found on page 84.

HUI PROTOCOLS
NGĀ TIKANGA WHAKAHAERE

Introduction

The protocols for the hui are summarised and implicit in this ancient *karanga* used by our tupuna to welcome guests to a hui for the purpose of dealing with social and political issues impacting upon waka and iwi.

Nau mai taku manu[1] , piki mai taku manu.
He manu aha ka tau?
Kūaka mārangaranga ki te tāhuna,
Korimako pae ki te kōtātara.
Pīwaiwaka i kutia ai te mate[2] ,
Kōtuku rerenga tahi.

Nau mai i runga i te kōmuri aroha, i te ata hāpara,
I te kōrehutanga o te tai awatea,
I te kakarauritanga o te maru ahiahi,
I te Pōkerekeretanga i parangia ai Te Ao-tū-roa.

I ahu mai koe, e taku manu
I te rapunga, i te kimihanga, i te hahautanga.
Ki manu-o-uta, ki manu-o-tai.

Tūria te marae e tāmara mā,
Whaikōrero koe ki te pāuauatanga,
I puta ai tō ihu ki Rangiātea,

I mau ai Te Puni Wāhine, Te Tira Taitama
Te Kāhui Tara, Te Teretere Pūmahara.
E mara mā, ko ngā haere kia haeretia,
Ko ngā kōrero kia kōrerotia.
He kōrero hoki te kai a te rangatira.
Heoi anō rā.

Welcome to our honoured guests!
Wing your way hither, alight in our midst!
How may we fittingly portray you?
As a flock of godwits alighting on a sandspit?
Or a chorus of bellbirds assembled to sing?
Or the waggish fantail who unwittingly awoke death?
Or a white heron of solitary flight?

Welcome to those borne hither on the breeze of love,
Winging your way in the pearly dawnlight,
At the zenith of the noonday sun,
In the descending gloom of eventide,
In the dark night of a slumbering world.

Already, you have searched, explored, debated,
With birds from inland and from the shore.
Now take your stand on the marae.
Share your concerns about the state of affairs.
Let your wisdom lead us into the light.
Let it be as a mantle over the assembly of women,
The band of young people,
Over the conclave of chiefs and the council of seers.

To you who have elected to come,
Speak your minds, voice your concerns.
Wise speech is the food of chiefs.
And so I rest my case.

Guidelines

Guidelines for the Tai Tokerau hui have evolved over the past year and the format established by previous hui has been arrived at by consensus. Because of the breakdown of our cultural values and social structures, some adaptations and even compromises have been introduced to allow for a blending of the traditional and modern to meet present day demands.

159

Traditional rule was exercised by the elders/chiefs/tohunga, but the power they then held was tempered by kinship bonds and the need to validate leadership by wise and generous rule. Because of Government policy to appoint Māori leaders under their systems of protocols and laws, those appointed do not necessarily speak for their iwi or Māoridom. Under such a system, conflict of interest often arises.

Traditional consensus decision-making was the method of operation for the achievement of social and political goals. This principle must be adhered to if the *integrity* of the hui is to be maintained.

Since some organisations, for example Trust Boards, are accountable to Government rather than to their people, conflict of interest is bound to arise and lobby groups can hijack a hui – or a person, *rūnanga* or group can introduce hidden agendas to elicit the support of the hui.

Code of Ethics

The essential issue is the integrity of the hui. People speak for themselves upon their own *mana* not on behalf of their rūnanga, trust board or organisation. Their brief is to speak on issues impacting on the whole of Te Tai Tokerau, to the end that Te Tai Tokerau might define as its stance on issues such as *wāhi tapu,* conservation, fisheries, air waves, rates, resource management and so on.

They shall address *issues* not personalities. If names of people are mentioned, it must be in relation to the issue. If criticism is expressed, let it be constructive. Simply express the facts, not in anger, but in love and for the good of the Tai Tokerau people. Anger results in clash of personalities and the real issues are forgotten.

Freedom of speech on the marae and in the forum of the Te Tai Tokerau hui is qualified. The topics before the Te Tai Tokerau hui are Te Tai Tokerau issues. In this regard, the decision of the Chairman must be respected to ensure the rights and dignity – *te mana me te tapu* – of each one present. Local issues are dealt with at the rūnanga level.

In regard to the consensus principle, the hui has always adopted the tradition of reaching agreement on all issues. Nothing is ever put to the vote. In accord with tradition, this has worked well and people have gone away satisfied. In conclusion, let us build together in the spirit of unity and the bonds of love, for your labour is not in vain in the Lord. Kia ora mai. Kia piki hoki tō ora, te kaha, me te rangimārie o Te Atua ki a koutou.

Endnotes

[1] Manu = (lit.) bird, used as metaphor for *manu-hiri* or guests, visitors.

[2] I kutia ai te mate = refers to Māui's death when the *pīwaiwaka,* or fantail, awoke Hinenui-i-te-pō and crushed Māui between her legs.

—————— FISHERIES COMMISSON HUI ——————
16 February 1993

Introduction

The Sealords Deal is now a *fait accompli* and there is no real point in traversing old ground, nor being judgemental about the rights and wrongs of the matter. The major challenge is to address and resolve the issues which have arisen regarding distribution and allocation of assets.

The reality is that the Sealords Deal is now part of the general body of Government legislation and the Crown's concern would focus upon durability. There is a tremendous amount of uncertainty and disorientation amongst our people. Polarisation is increasing by the minute and has flared up into open opposition between certain parties and the rift is widening. Our people 'on the ground', the 'flax roots' are becoming victims in a war of attrition which is escalating between certain parties and in which our people are being caught up.

The major element that threatens the durability of the Crown settlement is **uncertainty.** If this process leaves our people in a state of uncertainty they will continue to oppose the process. There is also a sense of grievance amongst our people about the signing away of their Treaty rights without their mandate. There are certain perceptions within Māoridom that drives that uncertainty:

· Fears that the Commission will end up contending with each other

and in the end creating phenomenal winners and abject losers
- A sense of grievance amongst the majority of people that the negotiators without their mandate signed away certain of their Treaty rights thus denigrating their *mana* and *rangatiratanga*

The challenge that faces this hui is to ensure that the process yields choices and if those choices are not forthcoming, then they will work negatively towards destroying the durability of the fisheries deal. The second challenge is to minimise our peoples' sense of grievance and put in place incentives that will make people work together toward common goals.

The Time Frame

This brings me to the most crucial point of all and it affect government timeframes. Underlying the whole basis of consultation and that of (tikanga) ways of doing things, there is a basic conflict between tikanga Pākehā which driving the present process and tikanga Māori which is being pushed to one side. And if we think we are going to address and resolve the issues which face us in one day, then we've got to think again. This matter will not be settled today, nor should we try to do so. To hurry the process and force people to come to decisions without allowing time for informed discussion and mature reflection will create a greater mess than what we are confronted with at the moment.

We must allow tikanga Māori its place in the process if we hope to achieve positive and satisfactory outcomes. Tikanga Māori is summed up in the following *ohaaki*:

Tūria te marae e tāmara mā,
Whaikōrero koe ki te pāuauatanga,
Kia puta ai te ihu ki Rangiātea.
E mara mā,
Ko ngā haere kia haerea
Ko ngā marae kia tūria.
Ko ngā kōrero kia kōrerotia
He kōrero hoki te kai a te rangatira.

Tikanga Māori ensures that matters will not be rushed. *Kaua e kaihorotia, kei rāoa!*

- that they will be deal with prudently and with patience
- that they will work towards achieving justice and fairness
- they there must be no coercion

- that the tribes must continue consultation until consensus is achieved

Role of Government

This is the bit that hurts. The role of Government, as I see it, must be to facilitate the consultation process within Māoridom. Nothing more, nothing less. They must be prepared to change the legislation regarding the appointment of the members of the Commission by requiring the endorsement of the Minister of Māori Affairs. This is not to denigrate the Office of the Minister but to allow for tikanga Māori to operate.

Our people perceive Government as perpetual meddlers and manipulators. Government must be see as having nothing to do with the appointment of, influencing the appointments or requiring the approval or endorsement of Government to accept the peoples' choices. The process of selection is an iwi function – they choose, they appoint, they approve their representatives.

Hui Māori

To rush matters can only create greater grievances and dissatisfaction and opposition. I then would press for a follow up hui at an appropriate Māori venue such as Ngāruawāhia Marae to allow Māoridom to achieve consensus. If it takes a whole weekend to arrive at consensus it will have been time well spent and we won't have to repent at leisure over mistakes that could have been avoided. This will be a grand opportunity for both Government and iwi to work together in partnership under a non-taxable *koha* system to finance the cost of such a hui.

Pan-tribal Dimension

I now draw your attention to the pan-tribal dimension. We are here as tribal representatives and are concerned that the tribal interest should in no way be compromised. That is part of my concern, but my primary concern arises for two reasons. Under the Sealords deal, the settlement impacted upon all of Māoridom. Whether they agreed to the conditions or not, it was decreed that to settle the deal all Māori will lose certain Treaty rights and their protection under the 1989 Fisheries Act.

The Māori Fisheries Commission had recommended the principle of *mana moana* as the criterion upon which allocation and distribution of assets and quota should be made. Since the Sealords deal, the ground rules have changed and Māoridom is now polarised – some supporting the Mana Moana principle and other the pan-tribal population criterion on the basis that the settlement was pan-tribal.

163

I want to remind the tribes that there are other Māori *kaupapa* and tikanga which are also relevant to the situation. And a Māori Hui is the place to examine such kaupapa and tikanga and seek ways through the difficulties. The kaupapa I refer to is *manaaki* and the tikanga is *tuku rangatira.* In the pre-European contact period the coastal tribes made provision for the inland tribes to:

- have access to the sea
- provide *papakāinga* sites which the inland tribes occupy whilst fishing, gathering mātaitai and other provisions for their tribes
- provided *taiapure* (reservations) and *tauranga ika* fishing reefs and grounds for sole use of their *tuawhenua* tribes

The gift by Ngāti Maru of Kennedy Bay to Ngāti Porou is a magnificent example of tuku rangatira under the principle or kaupapa of *mauri manaaki.*

In the case of Muriwhenua, our decision to heed the plea of Ngāi Tahu to allow for a pan-tribal process to be introduced as the basis for negotiation rather than for the Muriwhenua tribes to negotiate with the Government at their tribal level and bind the rest of the tribes to precedents set by them. They asked us to row the canoe together.

Muriwhenua agreed and, through the New Zealand Māori Council, opened the doors for pan-tribal participation. This is another example of tuku rangatira, and a precedent by which the tribes can work together to promote the well being of all Māori.

Whāwhāngia, whiriwhiria, whakatauria te kōrero i runga i te whakaaro kotahi, he mea paihere nā te rangimārie.

Appendices

APPENDIX ONE
A Sermon by Rev. Takiwairua Marsden
delivered at the *tangi* for Rev. Māori Marsden
Te Patukōraha Marae, Kaitaia, 1993

I want to read two passages that I really want to speak to, in regards to Māori, and so an Old Testament lesson which describes God's call to Jeremiah to be a prophet goes like this, and Jeremiah here is speaking and he said "The lord said to me I chose you before I gave you life and before you were born, I selected you to be a prophet to the nation. I answered, "Sovereign Lord I don't know how to speak, I am too young", but the Lord said to me "Do not say that you are too young but go to the people I send you to and tell them everything I command you to say. Do everything I command you to say, do not be afraid of them, I will be with you to protect you, I the Lord have spoken". Then the Lord stretched out his hand touched my lips and said to me, "Listen I am giving you the words you must speak. Today I give you authority over nations and kingdoms to uproot and to pull down, to destroy and to overthrow, to build and to plant. The Lord said, the Lord asked me "Jeremiah what to do you see?" I answered "A branch of an almond tree". "You are right", the Lord said, "And I am watching to see that my words come true". Then the Lord spoke to me again, "What else do you see?" he asked, I answered "I see a pot boiling in the north and it is about to be tipped over this way."

He said to me "Destruction will boil over the north on all who live in this land... .and I am calling all the nations in the north to come, their kings will set up their thrones at the gates of Jerusalem and round its wall and also round the other cities of Judah. I will punish my people because they have sinned and the north is not exempt from that. They have abandoned me, have offered sacrifices to other gods and have made idols and worshipped them. Get ready Jeremiah. Go and tell them everything I command you to say, do not be afraid of them now or I will make you even more afraid when you are with them. Listen Jeremiah, everyone in this land, the kings of Judah, the officials, the priests and the people, the bigwigs, will be against you, but today I am giving you the strength to resist them. You will be like a fortified city, an iron pillar and a bronze wall. They will not defeat you for I will be with you to protect you. I the Lord have spoken."

And a short reading from the Gospels which simply says this and I quote:

Jesus said to some Jews who had come to believe in him, "If you remain in my word you are truly my disciples, my followers. You will know the truth and the truth will make you free."

Māori would say that the most explosive event of the decade between 1920 and 1930 happened in 1924, on the 10th of August in fact. That was the day Māori was born. Māori might even concede though, what I already know, that if there was an event that eclipsed the 1924 phenomenon, it actually happened in 1926, the 18th of September, to tell the truth, when I was born. We were born in a *wharetini.* A *wharetini* might be compared to a *kuratini* but you'd be wrong, because the *wharetini* I'm talking about is a shack that was built entirely of corrugated iron. In fact it had no window but there was one loose sheet of iron that ran across the back wall of that tin shack and we propped it up with the bedsteads when we took it down at night and during the day we took the bedsteads away and we let in the glorious light of the day and a bit of fresh air and, man, did we need both.

And one of the other interesting things about that home was that we were in constant touch with Papatuanuku. I said to Māori the other day, "Hey bro, do you know why you're sick? You've given too much of yourself to your Lord and to your people and you never gave enough of yourself to yourself and to your family." And he said "You're spot on bro." And I also said to him "Māori I take time out to give quality time to all of the things that I am responsible to. I take two days out at least a week to be at home, to do a bit of gardening, to patch up the leaks that I should have patched up the year before, but also that I might be near the ground of my being."

And Māori said "Yeah that's my problem all right", he said "I have never taken my shoes off long enough to touch the ground". He'd never taken his shoes off long enough to touch the ground, and so that he should have known better because we had constant touch with Papatuanuku. And

Papatuanuku was the bare, mud flood in our house, and it was swept as dry and as firm as concrete and it wasn't swept with a broom from New World. It was swept with a broom from the bush just behind our house where we went and got the *puaka* and tied it with a flax and my mother swept the floor out with that and the *puaka* is the brush of the teatree. There was plenty of that sort of resource at that time.

And then one of the other things that we were very privileged to have was a father who was nearly as clever as his sons. He was an avid reader, my father was, he'd read all night and he'd chant those *pao* all night and those *whakapapa* all night and how could you miss, how could Māori miss picking them up, we all slept in the one room. But he was an avid reader and you already know from what I've said of the financial exuberance of that place. It was non-existent, and my father couldn't afford books so we used to be able to bring books home from school and so my father would read all those books all the time when we brought them home from school. He particularly liked 'Hyawatha'.

And so at intervals of three months he would say to me, "Will you bring 'Hyawatha' back?" But it was indeed, really, a teaching that he gave to us where we all became very avid readers. There wasn't very much else to do anyway. But that was a blessing because Māori became a very avid reader, so avid indeed that sometimes he forgot to eat and he was also very able to get to the depths of reading in order to plumb the depths of knowledge. But one of the other things about Māori and I noticed that in his bookcase (there are some of these books I'm going to refer to) that Māori always liked cowboy books and a lot of our generation might have and so that we had sayings like 'that critter is as ornery and as cantankerous as a tick in a longhorn's ear'. That's where Māori got his knowledge from.

So folks, lets explode a few myths, a few myths that have been even floating around here during the last two or three days. But you understand from that though, that we lived in very severe material poverty and it was not just a material poverty that spoke about the material things that we were not able to get but that sometimes the trousers that we wore were so worn out in the rear part of our anatomy that except for the grace of having lining in those trousers in those days, which we do not have nowadays, because you can't sell them as fast if you have lining in them, except for that, we might have been guilty of showing parts of our body that we shouldn't have been showing. But that was an example of the sort of poverty materially that we lived in. It was also an example though, of the faith that we were taught during that time. In the morning, *pātōtō, ka karakia mātou, tātou katoa rā i aua wā ako ana aianei. I ngā ahiahi, pātōtō, kua karakia ana, ae, engari ehara i te mea he minita tō mātou papa, e hia te roa e karakia ana, ka mutu, me rongo te tangata ka tika. Ae, i rongo mātou.*

And so we never had much money. I would be very surprised if at any one time Māori had as much as the exorbitant sum of say seven or eight thousand in his bank at one time. If he did have, firstly it would have been accidental. Secondly, it would not have been his and thirdly, he would have spent it all the next day. But you see there is also a deeper meaning in that because if you possess money accidentally you don't possess it intentionally and if you possess money intentionally and perhaps Māori did really get down to that sort of thinking, I'm sure he did, if you possess money intentionally, you *pao* some more from here and you *pao* some more on over here and you *pao* some more on from there and you will *pao* that money on and that money will have some strings attached, and people start to pull the strings that are attached. This translates into people who start to put their thumb on you and press you down.

Māori, folks, was a free man because he didn't have any money... One of the effects of having money and having the thumb over you is that you can become fairly naturally and I suppose even rather easily, corrupt. I don't know if he was free of that but I would certainly hope he was, in fact, I think that his life would testify to that. And because of all of those things, he was a free man and our Lord Jesus Christ said to some Jews who had come to believe in him "If you remain in my word, you are truly my disciples, my followers and you will know the truth and the truth will make you free." What did Jesus mean by "If you remain in my word?"

He meant that we are to pay entire attention to the word that he has written, to the word that he speaks to us day by day and to remain in his word is to try to penetrate the depth of our Lord's mind and we do that by study, we do that by reading and there are books like the Bible that we go back to and back to and back to and there will be new insights for us because we live in different times, because the insights that were not available to us at a point in the past will be revealed, as is the process of revelation because we have come to a new place where there is a new deposit of revelation. And we go back to those sort of books because there is always revelation there for us. Mills and Boons are not those sort of books.

And that was what Christ was saying when he said "If you remain in my word you will know the truth and the truth will set you free" and the truth sets you free in three very important ways. The truth sets you free because as you remain in Christ's word, you remain in fact a Christ person yourself, and not only do you remain a Christ person but forever you will walk with Christ. You will never walk alone and so there is no fear because you always have your Lord to walk with.

Secondly, it releases you from the fear of people who are in high places, people we bow and mollycoddle, people in high places. We do that because we are frightened of them and we do that too sometimes because we have ulterior motives in trying to get alongside the power. But in order to be able to be free, if you are a person of Christ, nobody but nobody should frighten you, for each and every one of us has been made in the image of God and each and every one of us in the economy of God is exactly as precious and as valuable to God as the next person, and when we understand, hey folks you don't have to be frightened, you are set free. There is another person that we need to be set free from and that is old Mr Ego and we need to be set free from ego because I have seen quite a bit of it around here over these last few days. Some of it was accidental but some of it was, unfortunately, not only intentionally but habitual, and people, what I'm saying is that we've got to be people like what our Lord describes, as the prophets who come forward because the Lord says to them "Be determined and be courageous."

The prophet is always called with that instruction from our Lord, not only an instruction but a downright command, "Be determined and be courageous", *mātou ngā Marsden he mātenga paukena*, we the Marsdens are pumpkinheads, and, pumpkinheads, they are stubborn people and man you can say that about Māori can't you. And in fact you can take stubbornness to its extreme and when you do that you become oppressive and man I've felt Māori's oppression, I'm sure you fellows who laugh have also felt it. And that's a determination that is being taken to the extreme if it occurs. But there is also the determination that is the determination for Christ our Lord.

The determination who knows the balance, who switches off when that determination becomes oppressive. And it is these sorts of qualities that make people like Māori, but Māori as I have explained to you has his chinks in his armour, so folks, what I've also heard here during this week is people worshipping Māori> Māori is not to be worshipped. Māori is to be accorded the dignity of being a person that was used by God in a very wonderful way but ultimately the power and glory and the majesty belongs to God himself.

Our vision therefore is to say "Hey Māori, thank you, you're not a bad guy. Thank you for all you've given to us but Māori, we will mourn your passing from us physically but we will go on and learn the same things that you learnt." No, not all the same things because there are some things that you learn as a part of your history and so we learn things in our history and in that time when we are growing up, but nobody else can pick up later on and that's a part that Māori knew so well. He was a man of 'te ao kōhatu' and he could bring forward from 'te ao kōhatu' some very wonderful insights that we in a struggling society right here and now as Māori people say to this country of ours, that Aotearoa-New Zealand belongs to all of us, but that if New Zealand goes down the gurgler because of the people in high places, folks, let us hold fast to Aotearoa that we as Māori people may be the sort of people that holds on to things that are valuable. But let us not either be still trying to hold on to those valuable things by the oppression of others, for if people are to be free, if I am to be free, then I have to respect the freedom of others. And so that the vision that is ahead of us doesn't reside in Māori. It's nothing new, what's happening now is nothing new. There's nothing new in all the world. What Māori's doing, the vision that Māori had is just simply contained in the grand commission of our Lord and our Lord says "all authority in heaven and earth has been given to me, go therefore and make disciples of all nations, teaching them all that I have commanded you, baptising them in the name of the Father and of the Son and of the Holy Spirit." And "hey" he says to us "though I am with you always even to the close of the age." And the vision for us is the mission that our Lord Jesus Christ left to us in the grand commission that he gave to his disciples and handed down through every generation. Go for it!

_____ APPENDIX TWO _____
Miscellaneous Definitions and Statements

Appendix Two contains a sample of statements and definitions of various concepts by Rev. Māori Marsden as they appear in the main text of this book. These concepts appear in Part One and primarily concern aspects of the traditional Māori worldview.

Ihi
...a 'vital force or personal magnetism which, radiating from a person, elicits in the beholder a response of awe and respect.'... It is a psychic and not a spiritual force. Psychic force is an intrinsic quality in human beings, a personal essence which can be developed more highly in some than in others; spiritual force (mana) is a gift endued by the gods.p.4

Iriiri, rūmaki, uhi
Iriiri, rūmaki and _uhi_ are alternative names for the rite of baptism. Iriiri describes the purpose or function of the rite. It means literally, 'to place upon, to endow' and signifies that baptism was the rite of enduement with authority. Uhi (to sprinkle) and rūmaki (to dip into) describe the method. p.10

Kairarawa
A means to replenish mana was the rite of kairarawa or cannibalism. The word 'rarawa' in this context means with violence or with force. It is a term

used to denote the forces that underlie the whole range of divine powers implied in the terms mauri, ihi, tapu and mana. Kairarawa denoted the consumption of the life force and the psychic and spiritual forces of the enemy which replenished one's own powers. p.13

Kaitiakitanga

1...the gods placed guardian spirits over places or things to watch over the property dedicated to them. These guardian spirits (kaitiaki) manifested themselves by appearing in the form (ariā) of animals, birds or other natural objects as a warning against transgression, or to effect punishment for breach of tapu. p.6

2...Other demonic spirits were called maitū, but these were sometimes invoked as familiar spirits who became guardians for members of a whānau, and in this role were known as kaitiaki. Their counterparts in the natural world were taniwha. These dragon-like creatures dwelt in certain localities and could be independent and unattached from the local tribe. As such, they were devourers of men. But where they were attached to the local tribe, they acted as guardians and manifested themselves as animals, fish, birds or reptiles. Strictly speaking, these were not spirits but occult powers created by the psychic force of ancient tribal tohunga and by the mana of their creative word, given form and delegated as guardians for the tribe. p.19

Kaupapa

Kaupapa is derived from two words, *kau* and *papa*, in this context 'kau' means to appear for the first time, to come into view, to disclose: 'papa' means ground or foundations. Hence kaupapa means ground rules, first principles, general principles. p.66

Kawa

Kawa, to borrow theological terminology, is 'liturgical action'. It is applied to the way in which the progressive steps of a religious ritual is ordered. Strict rules were applied to the conduct of kawa and any mistake or contravention of the ritual or failure to complete the ritual was a transgression (hapa) and was taken as an ill-omen. p.47

Te Korekore

...Te Korekore is the realm between non-being and being: that is, the realm of potential being. This is the realm of primal, elemental energy or latent being. It is here that the seed-stuff of the universe and all created things gestate. It is the womb from which all things proceed...p.20

Mana

Mana means spritual authority and power as opposed to the purely psychic and natural for of ihi. In a theological sense, it may be translated as charisma… mana as authority means 'lawful permission delegated by the gods to their human agent to act on their behalf and in accordance with their revealed will'…mana…essentially means 'that which manifests the power of the gods.'…p.4

Mauri

Immanent within all creation is *mauri* - the life-force which generates, regenerates and upholds creation. It is the bonding element that knits all the diverse elements within the Universal 'Procession' giving creation its unity in diversity. It is the bonding element that holds the fabric of the universe together. p.44

Pure

To counteract the effects of tapu, the Māori employed what they termed 'pure' rites (purification rites). They were designed to cleanse from tapu, neutralise tapu, or to propitiate the gods… Popular belief held that by cooking, the mauri of the plant was released and thereby made common (noa) or neutralised, a state of things abhorrent to the gods, thus ensuring their departure. As tapu could be transmitted by contact, so could its opposite profane state be transmitted by contact with objects made noa (neutral, common, profane, sterile). p.7

Rāhui

In order to conserve the resources and ensure their replenishment and sustenance, the Māori introduced the tikanga or custom of *rāhui.* Rāhui was a prohibition or ban instituted to protect resources…p.69

Tapu

It has both religious and legal connotations. A person, place or thing is dedicated to a deity and by that act it is set aside or reserved for the sole use of the deity. The person or object is thus removed from the sphere of the profane and put into the sphere of the sacred. It is untouchable, no longer to be put to common use. It is this untouchable quality that is the main element in the concept of tapu. In other words, the object is sacred and any profane use is sacrilege, breaking of the law of tapu. p.5

Te Ao Mārama

Te Ao Mārama is the realm of being…p.21

Te Ao Tua-ātea
Te Ao Tua-ātea is the world beyond space and time...p.61

Te Korekore, Te Pō, Te Ao Mārama
Te Korekore is the realm of potential being, Te Pō is the realm of becoming and Te Ao Mārama is the realm of being. p.21

Te Pō
Te Pō is the realm of becoming…p.21

Tikanga
Tikanga means method, plan, reason, custom, the right way of doing things. p.66

Tohi
A dedicatory act placed a person or thing under tapu. The consecratory act was the means by which the person or thing was endued with mana. Earlier, we saw that whilst persons were filled with the spirit of the gods themselves to endue them with power, places and things were not filled or possessed, but brought under the patronage of the gods who consigned guardian spirits to oversee the object or place. The consecration of a person was accompanied by a sacramental act and these acts were called 'tohi'. This word means literally 'to endue'. p.10

Tohi Whakahā
Tohi whakahā, or *tohi mauri*, is the enduement of mauri (life principle) by infusion (whakahā) of the breath (manawa). It was used on two main occasions: after neutralisation of a person's mana and vitality through the use of cooked food (umu pure); or at the initiation of a novice into the order of tohunga. In the former case, after a person had transgressed the tapu of the gods he went through the 'pure whakanoa' in which cooked food was placed on his head and the spirits causing his sickness were exorcised. This not only neutralised the mana and tapu of the opposing gods, but also the mana and tapu of his own tutelary gods, as well as debilitating his vital force. Sickness and death resulted from the depletion of the natural vital force through the agency of the gods or evil spirits, and this mauri ora had to be replaced through the tohi mauri. pp.11,12

Tohunga
The word *tohunga* is often translated as 'expert' (for example *tohunga-tā-moko* is rendered in English as 'expert carver'). Such use is wrong and stems from the mistaken idea that because the Māori used this term in association

175

with recognised experts in a particular field the word must mean expert. The word tohunga is derived from the stem 'tohu' which as a verb means a sign or manifestation. Tohunga is the gerundive of tohu and means a 'chosen one' or 'appointed one'. The tohunga was a person chosen or appointed by the gods to be their representative and the agent by which they manifested their operations in the natural world by signs of power (tohu mana). p.14

Te Tuha

Te tuha was the tohi of the 'sacred spittle' employed by the tohunga taura (as distinct from the tohunga ahurewa), to impart mana. The taura were the tohunga of the dark powers and in order to impart their mana to their disciples, they spat upon the disciple's head and invoked the spirits of the dark powers to possess the disciple and empower him with the dark arts of mākutu and whaiwhaiā - the casting of spells to bring sickness and death on their enemies...p.12

Te Whakapā

Te whakapā was a *tohi* employed by a father before his death to impart the family mana to his eldest son. p.12

Tua-ātea

Tua-ātea, the transcendent eternal world of the spirit, is ultimate reality. p.62

Wehi

Wehi may be translated simply as awe or fear in the presence of the ihi of a person, or of the mana and tapu of the gods. It is the emotion of fear generated by anxiety or apprehension in case one gives offence to the gods, or a response of awe at a manifestation of divine power (mana). p.7

The 'Centre'

1. All things, no matter how specialised must be connected to a centre. This centre is constituted of our most basic convictions - ideas that transcend the world of facts. This does not mean that they are purely subjective or relative, or even mere convention. But they must approximate reality whether in the world of sense perception or the real world behind that. Such ideas without this approximation inevitably lead to disaster. p.59

2. The centre is where he must create for himself an orderly system of ideas about himself and the world in order to regulate the direction of his life. If he has faced up to the ultimate questions posed by life, his own centre no longer

remains in a vacuum which continues to ingest any new idea that seeps into it. p.59

Knowledge
Knowledge is a thing of the head, an accumulation of facts. p.59

Myth and Legend
Myth and legend are an integral part of the corpus of fundamental knowledge held by the philosophers and seers of the Māori and indeed of the Polynesian peoples of the Pacific from ancient times... Myth and legend in the Māori cultural context are neither fables embodying primitive faith in the supernatural, nor marvellous fireside stories of ancient times. They were deliberate constructs employed by the ancient seers and sages to encapsulate and condense into easily assimilable forms their view of the World, of ultimate reality and the relationship between the Creator, the universe and man. pp.55,56

Sacrament
It is not generally realised that prior to the advent of Christianity, the Māori possessed a sacramental system which included sacraments parallel to those of the Christian church. This probably explains why Christianity was so readily accepted by the Māori and further explains his strong allegiance to the sacramental churches. Because of the parallel between the systems, we can make comparisons between them to help us understand the principles underlying both. According to the Augustinian definition of Western Christendom, a sacrament is 'an outward visible sign setting forth and pledging an inward spiritual grace'. To the Māori, a sacrament is simply 'the means by which mana (charisma, grace, spiritual power) is transmitted to humans'. The means used could be a specific element (water) from the created order; or another person by tactile transmission. The personal agent instrumental in this act must himself have been previously endued with the spirit of the gods since he can only impart what he himself already is. p.11

Wisdom
Wisdom is a thing of the heart. It has its own thought processes. It is there that knowledge is integrated for this is the centre of one's being. p.59

Worldview
Cultures pattern perceptions of reality into conceptualisations of what they perceive reality to be; of what is to be regarded as actual, probable, possible or impossible. These conceptualisations form what is termed the 'world view' of a culture. The World view is the central systematisation of conceptions of reality to which members of its culture assent and from which stems their

value system. The world view lies at the very heart of the culture, touching, interacting with and strongly influencing every aspect of the culture. p.56

The Māori Worldview

1. ...the created universe is divided into Te Pō and Te Rangi, which in themselves are divided into twelve planes. In between floats the earth sphere or sphere of day (Te Ao Mārama). The Pō and Rangi are in turn encompassed by the realm of Te Korekore... the Māori does not, and never has accepted the mechanistic view of the universe which regards it as a closed system into which nothing can impinge from without. The Māori conceives of it as at least a two-world system in which the material proceeds from the spiritual, and the spiritual (which is the higher order) interpenetrates the material physical world of Te Ao Mārama.

We may also conclude from the concepts of mana and tapu, and the nature of the creative acts of Io and his regents, that while the Māori thought of the physical sphere as subject to natural laws, these could be affected, modified and even changed by the application of the higher laws of the spiritual order.

In some senses, I suspect the Māori had a three-world view, of potential being symbolised by Te Korekore, the world of becoming portrayed by Te Pō, and the world of being, Te Ao Mārama...pp.19,20

2. Two conclusions emerge...the idea of continuous creation and the idea of a dynamic universe. These ideas are inclusive. The universe is not static but is a stream of processes and events. This concept also includes the idea that history is not cyclical but lineal - it is an on-going process. But the Māori did not develop the idea of a goal of history...

Further, since the universe is dynamic and the earth is not simply *Papa* (rock foundation) but Papa-tua-nuku (rock foundation beyond expanse, the infinite), the universe itself is a process or event within the cosmic process by which Io orders creation. The ultimate reality, therefore, is Io, and the expression of this reality is the cosmic process in which all things are immersed and find their reality. So the temporal is subordinate to the eternal, the material to the spiritual, for the situation below is ordered by an ideal determination from above by Io as origin of the cosmic process.pp.21,22

3. The idea of manipulating environment is based on the Māori view that there are three orders of reality, the physical or natural, the psychic and the spiritual. Whilst the natural realm is normally subject to physical laws, these can be affected, modified and even changed by the application of the higher laws of the psychic and spiritual. p.5

4. ...Like the New Physicists, the Māori perceived the universe as a 'process'.

But they went beyond the New Physicists idea of the Real world as simply 'pure energy' to postulate a world comprised of a series of interconnected realms separated by aeons of time from which there eventually emerged the Natural World. This cosmic process is unified and bound together by spirit. p.31

Philosophy

Philosophy…is the reach of thought beyond the foreground of life situations, to understand all time and existence, and that effort itself. It pursues answers to the three fundamental questions: What is the nature of reality, the nature of right and wrong and the grounds of valid belief? These are called respectively: metaphysics, ethics and epistemology. p.27

The 'Educated Person'

1. A truly educated person is not one who knows a little about everything, or everything about something but one who is truly in touch with his centre and has no doubts about his basic convictions. If he has faced up to the ultimate questions posed by life, his centre no longer remains in a vacuum which ingests everything that seeps into it. Those ideas are likely to lead to a denial of the meaning and purpose of life which in the end leads to total despair and meaningless. Fortunately, the heart is often wiser than the head. So he is saved from despair but lands in confusion. Only by fronting up to the questions of his fundamental conviction will he create order out of disorder. p.28

2. A truly educated person is not one who knows a bit about everything, or everything about something, but one who is truly in touch with his centre. He will be in no doubt about his convictions, about his view on the meaning and purpose of life, and his own life will show a sureness of touch that stems from inner clarity. This is true wisdom. p.59

The Route to Māoritanga

The route to Māoritanga through abstract interpretation is a dead end. The way can only lie through a passionate, subjective approach. That is more likely to lead to a goal. Abstract rational thought and empirical methods cannot grasp the concrete act of existing which is fragmentary, paradoxical and incomplete. The only way lies through a passionate, inward subjective approach. p.2

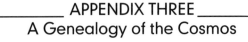

APPENDIX THREE
A Genealogy of the Cosmos

The *whakapapa* or genealogy that follows is an abridged version of 'creation' whakapapa that Māori makes reference to on many occasions throughout his writings. It serves as a backdrop to his thinking and understanding this whakapapa table is vital to understanding Māori's interpretations and views. The version reproduced here is a composite of whakapapa that Māori recited at his final seminar at Te Wānanga-o-Raukawa in 1993 and of material contained within his writings. It is abridged as the many names for Io, the various Kore, Kōwhao, Anu and Pō are not included. The translations are by Māori himself.

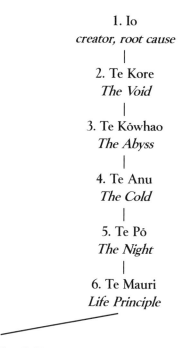

1. Io
creator, root cause
|
2. Te Kore
The Void
|
3. Te Kōwhao
The Abyss
|
4. Te Anu
The Cold
|
5. Te Pō
The Night
|
6. Te Mauri
Life Principle

7. Te Pū, 8. Te Weu, 9. Te More, 10. Te Aka, 11. Te Rea
7. Shoot, 8. Taproot, 9. Laterals, 10. Rhizome, 11. Hairroot

12. Te Rapunga, 13. Te Whāinga. 14. Te Kukune, 15. Te Pupuke, 16. Te Hihiri
12. Seeking, 13. Pursuit, 14. Extension, 15. Expansion, 16. Energy

17. Te Mahara, 18. Te Hinengaro, 19. Te Whakaaro, 20. Te Whē, 21. Te Wānanga
17. Primordial Memory, 18. Deep Mind, 19. Sub-conscious Wisdom, 20. Seed-word,
21. Consciousness Achieved Wisdom

22. Te Hauora, 23. Te Ātāmai, 24 Te Āhua, 25. Wā, 26. Ātea
22. Breath of Life, 23. Shape, 24. Form, 25. Time, 26. Space

27. Ranginui/Papatuanuku
27.Heaven-Earth (The Natural World)

Index